W9-AAN-529

Abel's Outback

BOOKS BY ALLEN ABEL

But I Loved It Plenty Well (1983)
Scaring Myself Again (1992)
Flatbush Odyssey (1995)

Abel's Outback

Explorations and Misadventures
on Six Continents, 1990–2000

ALLEN ABEL

Copyright © 2001 by Allen Abel

All rights reserved. The use of any part of this publication reproduced, transmitted in any form or by any means, electronic, mechanical, photocopying, recording, or otherwise, or stored in a retrieval system, without the prior written consent of the publisher – or, in case of photocopying or other reprographic copying, a licence from the Canadian Copyright Licensing Agency – is an infringement of the copyright law.

National Library of Canada cataloguing in publication data

Abel, Allen J., 1950–
    Abel's Outback : explorations and misadventures on six continents, 1990–2000

ISBN 0-7710-0706-X

1. Abel, Allen J., 1950–   -Journeys.   2. Voyages and travels.   I. Title.

G465.A23 2001   910.4   C00-933176-X

We acknowledge the financial support of the Government of Canada through the Book Publishing Industry Development Program for our publishing activities. We further acknowledge the support of the Canada Council for the Arts and the Ontario Arts Council for our publishing program.

Text design by Sari Naworynski
Typeset in Minion by M&S, Toronto
Printed and bound in Canada

McClelland & Stewart Ltd.
The Canadian Publishers
481 University Avenue
Toronto, Ontario
M5G 2E9
www.mcclelland.com

1 2 3 4 5   05 04 03 02 01

Contents

Preface

———————— • ————————

"I tramp a perpetual journey," Walt Whitman wrote, but the reporter gets to overturn poetry: we journey as perpetual tramps.

In a mud-daubed hovel on the sands of Africa, we are welcomed, and seated for the dance. In the tinsel of an Arctic sunset, men bid us join them in whispered prayer. In the folds of the Pyrenees, we are bedded in a cloister of piety and stone that knew the first millennium of Christ.

Tables are set for us in languages we do not speak, spread with foods we do not cater, served in homes we habit for an hour, or a day.

Like hoboes, we feast on tears and histories, until, sated, we travel on.

What follows are the menus of those accidental banquets, a bill of fare of strangers' lives that I have been privileged to enter, and pained to leave.

My gracious hosts asked me for no payment. Fairness is the price of the vagrant's meal.

Writing is not a career for which I had training or desire or blood. As a boy, my unformed Brooklyn head was littered with song lyrics, subway maps, baseball statistics, and dialogue from the *Adventures of Superman*. And so it has remained.

Local police chief (stunned): "But, Monsieur Kent, how did you get to Cap-Haïtien so fast?"

Clark Kent (winking): "I . . . *flew*."

Squatting silently in front of the television, transfixed by Sputnik and Sergeant Bilko, I absorbed the reporter's skills: shut up, look close, listen hard.

Ten years later, I was an unmannered sports reporter for a great metropolitan newspaper, or, in my case, the Troy *Record*. (I was a fired bowling-shoe salesman looking for a job. Any job.) In 1972, the first newspaper column I ever wrote won a New York State Associated Press award. The next October, when the *Record* paid my way to the World Series, I thought that all my life's ambitions had been fulfilled.

That was four thousand stories ago.

What a gift it has been to see the world in two centuries, and to cross the bridge between them.

As midnight struck to begin 2000 in Times Square in my old hometown, I gave my sister a typically passionate Abel peck, and then I began to cry.

We were standing on the corner of Broadway and 47th Street and people were screaming and leaping around us and fireworks were exploding and confetti was falling and I was blubbering, "I made it! I made it! All the Third World drivers and the planes couldn't kill me. I made it!"

"You've got ten minutes to file your story," my sister said. So I stopped crying and ran for a phone.

I am grateful to all the editors from Troy to Toronto who sent me off, trading faith and expenses for anecdotes and quips. To my publisher, for deeming these stories worth reading again. To my producers at CBC Sports, whose confidence in me as a host of Olympic travelogues has given me the greatest joys of my working life.

To my father, who came to China and Europe and across America with me; to my sister, a generous and caring teacher. And to my mother, who waited 50 years on Flatbush Avenue for me to come home.

To everyone who went along. And to Walt Whitman of Brooklyn, who understood:

Not I, not any one else can travel that road for you,
You must travel it for yourself . . .

For after we start, we never lie by again.

AUSTRALIA

Previous page: Sandfire Roadhouse,
Western Australia (Yette Vandendam)

There's a gash across Australia called the Great Central Road. It's one wide lane of pure red sand, a thousand miles from Kalgoorlie in the southwest of the continent to Ayers Rock in the middle, and deserted beyond description.

You pass an average of two cars a day out there, but that is hardly newsworthy. There are stock routes in the state of Western Australia that sometimes do not see a vehicle a year.

Every two or three hundred miles along the Great Central, there's a roadhouse – a cinder-block fortress with iron bars across the windows and steel cages round the petrol pumps. Inside, it looks like a 7-Eleven, but its wares spell survival, not convenience. Near each store is a community of a few dozen dilapidated Aboriginal dwellings, the domain of a beggared people locked down in the land of their fathers' Dreaming.

Five of us crossed here in 1999 in a big Land Cruiser – my CBC crew and a young driver from Perth who plied this lifeless scar four times each month and exulted in the desolation. We spread our swags out on the dirt, whispered our brave goodnights, and slept with hoods drawn tight to keep the scorpions from marching through our ears. In the morning, I heard not a single bird singing.

That was when I began to comprehend Australia: the insularity, the emptiness, the mateship. Here were nearly 20 million people, I thought, with the Great Central Road behind them, and nothing before them but the ocean.

In 2000, I vowed, I would return to Australia the proper way – by sea.

To Australia by Sea (1)

———————— • ————————

When all men flinched, then – he felt sure – he alone would know how to deal with the spurious menace of wind and seas . . . he exulted with fresh certitude in his avidity for adventure, and in a sense of many-sided courage.

— Joseph Conrad, *Lord Jim*

A thousand miles east of Australia, on a ship of freight and fools, we are tossing like a child's bathtub toy on the brim of a sea gone mad.

A Force 9 gale is blowing from Antarctica, flogging the Tasman Sea with gusts of 50 knots and more. There are 40-foot waves defying our moaning engine, and a 30-foot swell that, as the vessel dips and soars, sends crockery crashing, suitcases flying, and an elderly traveller named Jim clean off his chair, down into the lap of a lady named Margaret.

Welcome aboard the MV *America Star*, a 24,000-ton container carrier of the Blue Star Line, bound for Sydney and the Games of the XXVII Olympiad, unless she heaves to, keels over, or breaks

4

into pieces en route. As the late-winter tempest assails her, she is 30 days out of Savannah, Georgia, with an English captain, an Australian chief engineer, 25 Filipino deckhands, and nine paying passengers, the last of whom came aboard in New Zealand just three days earlier, expecting a quick and quixotic last lap to Oz, a holiday, a lark. Forty-eight hours of pandemonium cure me of that dream.

At the worst of it, I lie sleepless for two days and two nights, stunned that a 713-foot freighter could flip and flop so cruelly, barely able to stumble down to the dining lounge for dry toast and tea, clutching the sides of my bed to keep from being flung to the floor of my cabin. At the crest of each surge, the 30-year-old ship teeters, dives, then slams its battered bottom in the trough below, shuddering and thudding as it climbs back up the water-mountain like The Little Engine That Could.

Every time the *America Star* plunges sideways, the coat hangers in my closet ring out like the bells of Notre Dame. A grapefruit rolls from end to end in my stateroom; the toilet gurgles like a drowning cow.

I envision myself laid out on the poop deck and Groucho Marx standing over me, feeling for my pulse and saying, "Either this man is dead or my watch has stopped."

Trapped in the bunk, I try to concentrate on anything but the pitching of the ship: baseball lineups from the 1960s; the nations of the world in alphabetical order; lyrics to old Nashville songs. It doesn't work. Like Conrad's Jim (of whom I had been reading, tucked in my little cot, brimming with jaunty nautical spirit, just after departure from Auckland, back when the wind was still), I believe:

> as any other man would have done in his place, that the ship would go down at any moment; the bulging, rust-eaten plates that kept back the ocean, fatally must give way, all at once like an undermining dam, and let in a sudden and overwhelming flood.

Below our keel is a chasm that, at its maximum, is 17,000 feet deep. Whatever is lurking down there – great white sharks, coelacanths, plesiosaurs, giant squid – had better be hungry. They'll get me, I figure, and the old folks in Cabins 3, 4 and 5, the Tagalog-speaking crewmen, all those fish fingers and pot pies and Sara Lee cakes in the galley freezer, plus the tankers on "A" deck that are filled with thousands of gallons of Jamaica rum.

Day and night, the gale blows, a dry wind bearing neither rain nor snow. Captain Michael Power, 32 years at sea, tries to run around the worst of it – steering us first toward the South Pole, then Tasmania, even back, for a time, toward New Zealand. With the gale bellowing against us, and the ship's antique diesel engine churning out only 13,000 horsepower, burning 40 tons of diesel fuel each day at US$100 per ton, we have slowed from our top speed of 17 knots to a humble seven. At home in summertime Canada, I rollerblade faster than that.

Our master is a gentle, soft-spoken man – a Captain Shy-liner – hardly cut in the mould of a swaggering Bligh or Long John Silver. His first concern, he tells his passengers, is as it must be – for the integrity of the freighter itself, and the safe delivery of its cargo of steel plates, industrial chemicals, farm machinery, treated lumber, and booze. All we wayfarers can do is hold on and hope.

To the Blue Star Line, we are an afterthought, a nod to the custom of accepting a few passengers aboard a cargo vessel – a tradition that is dying out around the world, as mega-ships and car-carriers three times the size and power of our squat, grey *America Star* steam into an age where profit drowns romance. And romance there would be, were the Tasman tranquil and would the frightful lurching cease. Rising off our starboard beam is a full spring moon, and behind our lonely vessel, an albatross follows, never resting, for three full nights and days.

I stand in the companionway and watch her wheeling and dipping, indifferent to the fears of men. Like us, she is a wanderer, caught between the Tasmanian Devil and the magnificent deep blue sea.

There was a time, of course, when all who ventured to the Southern Continent gallantly braved – or were condemned to suffer – these raging waters. Sailing to Australia, I am deeply conscious that I am in the literal wake of 168,000 British prisoners – and 149 Canadian insurgents of the Mackenzie and Papineau uprisings of 1837 and '38, whose descendants, proud of their defiant ancestors, I hope to meet in New South Wales.

These were the sea lanes where, chained to the underdecks, awash in filth and pestilence, men and women endured the unendurable, only to come ashore and labour as slaves. Now the city they were forced to construct – and, later, liberated, to inherit and own – would be harbouring the world's eminent sportsmen.

One of those captured rebels from Upper Canada was a man named Benjamin Wait, a farmer from the Niagara peninsula. Sentenced to death for treason in 1839, he was reprieved from the gallows 30 minutes before the trap was to drop beneath him, and sentenced to transportation to Australia for life. Surviving a 22-week voyage, shackled to the timbers of the hulk that carried him to the extremity of the known Earth – a voyage that seemed interplanetary in its immensity and finality – he wrote:

When every noise was hushed save the lashing of the waves against the ship's sides, the creaking of the helm, the occasional tread of the crew on deck, or the heavy breathings of the human beings around me, has my heart experienced every vicissitude of human misery and passion – sorrow and grief, gloom and despondency, anger and the extreme of despair endured to an extent seldom felt by man. . . .

My early hopes; the gay dreams of youth, and the associations of riper years were blasted – gone – for ever!! I saw my

poor family, feeble, and destitute, and lonely, and in grief. . . .
The future exhibited a path of sorrow, suffering and danger; a
life of toil and slavery and a bed of thorns; while a review of
the past pierced my soul with a thousand agonies . . .

Surely if there are places in human abodes deserving the
title of Hell, one is a transport ship, crowded with felons,
culled from England's most abandoned criminals. . . . Though
amid the tumult of hundreds of beings, scarce human, I
suffered it not to disturb me. I felt not of their species, and
gave no ear to their confusion.

What, I wonder, would the prisoners of Olde England think of
this, then – their Hell, their Australia, given to pleasure, to luxury,
to sport?

I was looking for a novel way to travel to the Olympics, but I didn't
expect the novel to be *Moby-Dick*. Yet here I am on Day 2 of the
windstorm, staggering astern, bent horizontal, bucking the gale,
climbing up the stairway from "D" deck to the bridge, determined
to announce to our captain, as Starbuck to the deranged Ahab:

God is against thee, old man, forbear! 'tis an ill voyage! ill
begun, ill continued; let me square the yards while we may, old
man, and make a fair wind of it homeward, to go on a better
voyage than this.

However, when I burst onto the scene, the old man – actually,
he is younger than I am – is below, enjoying his lunch, and the
MV *America Star* is in the hands of her third officer, a Filipino
named Apollonion Hemedez. "It is worse than we expected," he
says with a smile, the grandest understatement on the Seven Seas.

He shows me the weather charts, faxed via satellite from some
Mission Control on some stationary continent. The isobars

between New Zealand and Australia are jammed together like stripes on an anorexic zebra.

Everywhere else on Earth, it seems, is calm and clear today.

"On our last voyage," Third Officer Hemedez says, trying to calm me down, "two days before we reached Auckland, we lost the starboard gangway, some of the containers were knocked over, and two portholes were smashed in by the waves and the cabins flooded."

He points to an indicator on the wall that measured the maximum list during that tumultuous crossing at 42 degrees from the vertical. A few more inches, he giggles, and over she goes. Compared to that thrill-ride, we today are merely drifting with the tides. This is only Force 9 on a scale of 12, and 12 is a hurricane.

Officer Hemedez works two watches on the bridge each day – 8 a.m. to noon, and 8 p.m. to midnight. He doesn't have to wrestle a great wooden wheel or man the tiller; the ship is steered by auto-pilot and a satellite geo-positioning system that tracks its latitude and longitude down to one one-thousandth of a degree.

"Every day. Same thing. Nine months," he says. "This is a bad job."

He is the son of a sugar-cane farmer from the island of Luzon, and he had never been on a ship in his life before he decided to make the sea his vocation and enrolled in a course for baby Ahabs. He says, "I thought it was the best way out of our life of poverty in the Philippines," and this may have been true, but the cost of his choice has made him sad and rueful.

At home are a wife and a three-year-old son that the father has seen only three times. On the Blue Star Line, a Filipino ships out for nearly a year without a visit home, telephones – if he can afford it – from a seamen's hostel in Melbourne or Manzanillo or Philadelphia, husbands his wages, longs for his wife, and takes his pleasures rarely and dearly.

"It is a long time, very lonely," Apollonion Hemedez says. "Sometimes in port, Filipina girls come aboard, we have dancing and drinking."

"And the crewmen sleep with them?" I wonder.

"Not I, but the others," he replies. "It is natural for a man. Even Clinton."

The third officer admits that he and Captain Power do not always agree on how to manage the *America Star*, although the way the ship is rollicking, it is impossible for any two people to stand still long enough to see eye to eye about anything.

"Sometimes I don't like his system," Mr. Hemedez says.

"But he's the Master," I remind him. "He can command you to walk the plank."

"We are 25 Filipinos on this ship," says the third officer. "We push him."

The sea that threatens to swallow us is named for the 17th-century Dutch explorer Abel Tasman. I doubt that anyone is going to call me Tasman Abel.

This region, Tasman reported back to Amsterdam, was

> accursed in the sight of the mariner, when the winds roared and raged; where waves foamed and lashed and where DUNDER AND BLIXUM growled and flashed incessantly, a land of storm, fire and tempest, a coast rife with death, horror and shipwreck.

It is nice to see that nothing has changed.

Back in my bunk, lying sleepless through the second night of the gale, there is so much acid in my stomach that – like some of the 900 cargo containers in the holds and out on "A" Deck – I should be made to wear a sign that says "Warning – Hazardous Materials." A white-jacketed steward named Jerry places a thick white coil on the floor of my compartment. A tag attached to it is marked: ESCAPE ROPE.

I would focus on the horizon, but the view from the porthole is blocked with a container sealed in Hamburg and filled with – what? – Hummel figurines, tinned sausages, a Mercedes-Benz limousine for Juan-Antonio Samaranch, or CDs of the Beatles, circa 1961, singing "Sie lieb' dich, ja, ja, ja"?

Outside, a blinding-bright moon plays hide-and-seek with the bubbling, scudding clouds. Salt-foam scours the windows, and the spray cascades in great white fountains higher than the fore-mast. Gusts shred the plastic wrappings from the bales of lumber out on deck.

The waves hurl us at their pleasure, toss us, govern our night, as they have the nights of all the mariners of all the nations since Abel Tasman; since Benjamin Wait; since the first brave and hungry men took to the sea. In 30 years of constant travelling, I have rarely felt so tiny; or, perhaps, so free.

I pick up *Lord Jim*:

. . . there was a fierce purpose in the gale, a furious earnest-ness in the screech of the wind, in the brutal tumult of earth and sky, that seemed directed at him, and made him hold his breath in awe.

Now I am living the same moment, on the same water.

Exultant and terrified, afraid and euphoric, I close my eyes, search for sleep. And there's Groucho again, in his swallow-tail coat, looking down at my prostrate body and declaring, "What this man needs is a long ocean voyage!"

– *National Post*

To Australia by Sea (2)

•

"It feels like there's a hole in the ocean," says Shorty Williams, a tall man from Alabama, as our cargo ship belly-flops into a canyon in the sea.

"The way the ship was banging and rolling last night," observes Shorty's wife, Cheryl, "I kept thinking we had hit something."

"We're in 17,000 feet of water," I say weakly. "It must have been a whale."

It is the third day of the infuriatingly imperfect storm that has been lacerating the Tasman Sea, and after 48 hours of prostration I finally have managed to join my fellow mariners at lunch. The tempest seems to be gradually abating; the gales that were whipping the waters off the Australian coast are down to a gentle Force 6.

At this pace, I reckon, the Pacific will be as calm as a millpond, four days after I disembark at Sydney.

For a landlubber whose previous idea of Neptunian adventure was a trip on the Toronto Island ferry, the passage from New Zealand to the Olympic land of Oz has been two parts nightmare and one part luxury cruise.

At the best moment – the first dawn after departure from Auckland, before the windstorm attacks – I wander out on deck into a haunting dreamscape. A huge ivory moon skims the brine as it sets, leaving its luminous footprints on an ocean as still and silent as Muskoka ice.

At the worst hour, I writhe sleepless and frightened at three o'clock in the morning as the MV *America Star* – a slow, rusting, 30-year-old container carrier, scheduled for the wrecking yard in 2003 – bucks and shakes and rumbles and plunges through waves so steep and solid that they feel like granite cliffs.

(To get a sense of the experience, imagine being padlocked with eight total strangers in a bed-and-breakfast in Vancouver in February, with one small window looking out on the pouring rain, and a medium-magnitude earthquake knocking you off balance, every 20 seconds, for a week.)

But all of that seems to be behind us as a Filipino steward in a starched white jacket passes along the narrow hallway outside my cabin, walloping the little four-note xylophone that announces yet another mealtime. Down in the passengers' cafeteria, his compatriots bring us minestrone soup, lamb kebabs, and banana pudding with custard sauce.

Soon, the coastline of New South Wales should come into sight. Every few seconds, I pivot around in my chair and eagerly search the northwest horizon, hoping to spy the Opera House, the Harbour Bridge, and Nicole Kidman.

But all I see is a sea that looks like a sink full of Aqua Velva, with a lather of Dream Whip on top.

Food always has been paramount in the minds of the men and women forced to sail these rampageous waters. In 1839, an American named Samuel Snow was ordered transported to Australia for taking part in a raid that was supposed to incite the citizens of Upper Canada to overthrow the colonial government and establish a republic. (It didn't, and 90 per cent of the men who were banished to the Antipodes for taking part in William Lyon Mackenzie's short-lived uprising were U.S. citizens.)

"I rightly remember," Snow wrote in his memoirs, "the orders given to the commissary in the distribution of our fodder was, FOUR UPON TWO, that is, four of us OUGHT to have what two of the marines DID have; but instead of these directions being strictly adhered to, I am sure that on many occasions, a whole BRIGADE UPON ONE, would have been nearer to the fact.

"Not that the gift of an English marine is better than ours, in discussing the important subject of PORK AND BEANS, but at this time their privileges were more exclusive."

And Benjamin Wait, a Niagara man deported for high treason, noted that "the first questions I heard asked by those who came on board with me, were, 'What do you get to eat?' and 'What is the quality?'"

The answer, on the convict ships, was – a thin paste of flour and water for breakfast, four ounces of salt beef and maybe a pint of pea soup for dinner, plus one hard biscuit to last the day and night. Six prisoners shared one cup, one spoon, one fork, one knife, and as many *E. coli* as their guts could reproduce. Scurvy killed 137 of the 240 men on Wait's prison ship, and those who survived had to fight for every morsel.

"When any one of them were near dying," wrote a pastor who accompanied one of these flotillas of the damned, "and had something given them as bread . . . the person next to him or others would catch the bread &c. out of his hand and, with an oath, say that he was going to die, and therefore it would be of no service to him."

"Pickpockets formed no small share of the cargo," Wait complained, "and they are truly the most expert and deceptive beings I ever met; they would take from under my very eye, the food I was eating, without my discovering the thief."

Aboard the *America Star*, victuals are in greater abundance, and are accompanied by a well-stocked bar. In mid-ocean, distant from customs officials and Australia's despised new GST, a bottle of Beefeater Gin is available from ship's stores for US$5.53.

A quart of Sprite, on the other hand, costs $7.20.

Hence the continuing popularity of freighter travel.

Each evening – there are eight of them between Auckland and Sydney – the paying clientele of the *America Star* assembles in the passenger lounge at exactly 5:30 for cocktails and an attempt to witness the mysterious "green flash."

This is not a comic-book hero, but a rare meteorological occurrence caused by the refraction of the Earth's atmosphere at the instant of sunset. As the disc drops below the horizon, a burst of lime-light sometimes is visible for half a second or less. (Even a blue flash, farther down the spectrum, has been recorded.) It is most often seen at sea, assuming flat water, clear skies, and a calm stomach, none of which is currently the situation.

"We saw the green flash last week," a woman named Cynthia informs me within seconds of my embarkation. "Be there tonight at 5:30."

"If I show up," I tell her, "the steward will say, 'I'm sorry, sir, I'll have to ask you to leave – we want to have Happy Hour.'"

Who are my fellow passengers? There are the Alabamans Cheryl and Shorty – a former mechanical engineer, truck driver, mortgage broker, Peace Corps volunteer, and rock climber – who have been aboard since mid-July and who intend to sail *all the way back to Philadelphia* without seeing an Olympic competition, an opera, or a kangaroo – a total of 73 days on the water.

There is Cynthia – who, it turns out, attended the same grammar and high schools in Brooklyn, N.Y., as I did, though she preceded me by 15 years – and her husband, who have spent at least $15,000 to purchase tickets for 36 Olympic events, including the Opening Ceremony, for which seats are priced at more than $1,000 each.

There are two widowers, each man hoping to sail away from his private grief. And there is a long-married couple of Sydneysiders

who evoke the famous description of the national character by
the Australian poet James McAuley: "The men are brave, con-
tentious, ignorant; The women very much as one expects."

This night, when I arrive in the lounge for the green flash – a
moment invested with the solemnity of the Annunciation –
a lively discourse is in progress on the subject of laundry. And
although I stare at the horizon with all my powers of concen-
tration, I fail to see the phenomenon, possibly because it is raining
like a scene from Somerset Maugham.

"Oh, well – maybe tomorrow," Shorty Williams says. "Hey! Did
you know you can actually take a tour of the engine room?"

In 1788, a Royal Marine named Ralph Clark wrote home from
Sydney to his wife, Betsey, of the pitiful voyage of the First Fleet of
convicts to Australia's fatal shore:

> what a Terrible night it was last of thunder lighting and Rain
> – dreamt of You my dear Sweet woman and that I was in bed
> with you. . . .
>
>   in the course of my life I never Sleept worse my dear wife
> than I did last night – what with the hard cold ground Spiders
> ants and every vermin that you can think of was crauling over
> me I was glad when the morning came . . . went out with my
> Gun and Kild only one Parrot – they are the most beatifuless
> birds that I ever saw – when it is please god that I am to Return
> to you dear woman I will bring Some of them home for you.

Two hundred years later, the men who ply the Southern Ocean
are no less anguished, no less wrenched from the ones they love.
One evening, while the tourists gather for the hallowed flash, I
wander down to the officers' bar on the Promenade Deck. There,
I find a man named Domingo slouched over a Guinness and a
cigarette, saying, "I thought this would be a good life. I was wrong.
This is no life."

I had not expected such melancholy, yet it is the same tale I have heard from every member I've met of the Filipino crew – a young man, seeking an end to poverty, signing up for a career at sea, and regretting his choice even before the last terraced hills of his island slide from view.

Up on the bridge for the night watch, again the lament – First Officer Dion Pablo, father of children aged three, five, and eight, whose lives he has entered, then forsaken, like a ghost – a month at home, nine months away.

"Maybe this my last trip," he says, but he knows it isn't.

Even in the 21st century, Australia is no less far away. And the emotions still echo Lieutenant Ralph Clark:

Kist your dear Pictour as Usual on this day and read the lessons for the day . . . oh that if you was only here and our dear Boy I should not wish to come home if the place agreed with our health but without you I would not stay if it was the best place under the face of heaven . . . no that I would not my dear Beloved wife for without you I cannot live. . . .

I fall asleep just after dinner on the eighth evening, never having seen the green flash, knowing that we are only a few hours out from the container terminal at Botany Bay.

It was at this place that the first encounter between red-coated Royal Marines, shackled convicts, and unclad Aboriginals took place in 1788, presaging the doom of a Stone Age people, and the rise of a unique nation. I try to imagine the moment, so vivid and vital in the histories of this country that I have been reading in my stateroom, these past few rolling oceanic nights:

I gave two of them a glass of wine (one officer reported), which they no sooner tasted than they spit it out. . . . They wanted to know of what sex we were, which they explained by pointing where it was distinguishable, as they took us for women, not having our beards grown. I ordered one of the

people to undeceive them in this particular, when they made a
great shout of admiration. . . .

At 1:15 a.m., I am jolted awake, not by the delirious heaving of
the ship – I have become inured to the motion – but by a sudden
stillness. The engine has stopped. There are lights outside. The
anchor is down, the halyards fixed, and this is Sydney, Australia.

At midmorning, I say my goodbyes and shoulder my duffel and
bounce down the long, grey gangway to make landfall on a long
pier busy with roaring trucks and giant cranes and stacked a
hundred feet high with containers – the noise deafening, the sun
blinding, the ground still strangely seeming to heave and buckle
beneath my feet.

In the distance is the downtown skyline, soon to be the Emerald
City of ten thousand athletes and the thousands more of us who
come to cheer and honour and eulogize them, and to profit and
prey on their dreams.

"How ya goin', mate?" asks the taxi driver. It's the usual Aussie
greeting.

"By ship," I tell him, with Olympian ecstasy. "It's the only way
to go."

– *National Post*

Outback Postman

•

This is the Australia of the picture books: a molten sunrise spreading its arms above a rust-red Outback plain.

The freeway is a scratch of boulders and sand, a weedy, rutted, one-truck-narrow trail through the scrublands, 600 miles northwest of Olympic Sydney. We barrel along it at a 60 miles an hour, clanging over the cattle guards, honking at the brainless Herefords in the right-of-way, bucking and bouncing and rolling like a freighter in a Force 9 gale.

In our wake, we scatter swooping pairs of parrots in electric Day-Glo green and slow-flying, black-billed storks bringing babies to the blue-eyed wives of ranchers, and scores of squawking cockatoos wearing white for the last time before Labour Day.

Sometimes we are axle-deep in water, and sometimes we scare up a cloud of dust to choke the sun. We pass fields of the first yellow and purple spring wildflowers, oceans of waving green grasses, and scattered scraggly stands of gum and mulga.

Far, far to our west is the famous Ayers Rock, and between us, and beyond it, an empty desert, an Antarctic without ice or snow. The shire we are in is the size of Denmark. About four thousand people live in it, three thousand in a single town.

All along the way, we see three kinds of kangaroos, each in abundance – grey, red, and dead.

The Aussies call this the Woop-Woops, the Back of Beyond, the Never-Never. Most of them have never been Beyond the Black Stump, as they say. Yet they will tell you – over a dry Hunter Valley cabernet sauvignon in Sydney or Melbourne – that the red earth of the Outback is in their souls.

This morning, the red earth of the Outback is in my hair and in my teeth. We have been on the road since four-thirty, awake since three. My guide and companion – my "mate" in this home-land of mateship – is a man named Athol Milgate, a native son of this Martian landscape. He would rather you call him Bull.

For the past ten years, Bull Milgate has performed the postal and parcel delivery service to some of the most isolated sheep and cattle stations in New South Wales – where the nearest neighbours are hours away, the children attend school by radio, and the ambu-lance, God forbid, comes by air. Twice a week, he pounds his weary pickup along this 330-mile loop, calling at hardscrabble farms with fanciful names like Emaroo and Salt Lake and Ballycastle.

Out here this morning, for more than eight hours, we don't see another car.

Bull never meets many of his clients, flinging their newspapers and junk flyers and love letters into empty barrels at their farm-stead gates, long before they and the sun are up. Others lure him off his precious schedule and into their kitchens, trading a cup of black tea for a few moments of human contact, a blessing rarer than rain.

Bull is near 60 – wise, reliable and generous, with candy in his pockets for the kids. He was one of 14 children, and already is the grandfather of eight, the image of Outback manhood: a shortish, square-jawed bloke in a blue polo shirt, tight black short-shorts, white calf-high socks, and black boots with elastic at the anklebones, transporting a belly the size of a pickle barrel that boomerangs up and nearly whaps him in the chin with every bounce of the truck.

Today, there are sacks and stacks of mail stuffed all around us in the front of the pickup. The flatbed behind us holds, among the morning's other parcel post, 1,440 bottles of Toohey's New bound for the pub in the hamlet of Lough, a two-week supply of beer for a town of 55 people.

Two-and-a-half hours into our circuit, with Jupiter and Saturn urging us onward and Orion doing a headstand in the northeast, the sun finally agrees to join us. Its first rays catch Bull and me singing along to the faltering signal of an AM radio station playing Jim Reeves' old classic, "He'll Have to Go."

There's a big grey shape moving through the shadows. It's an emu, escaping down the roadway in that fat-lady way of hers with her big feathery bum flopping from side to side and her drumsticks lifted up high like a trotting horse.

The mailman stops singing and laughs.

"Silly," Bull Milgate says.

Emaroo (emu + kangaroo) Station is the home of the Ponder family: Waldo, Helen, their little daughters, Katie and Anna, and a fluffy dog named Sandy. They bought it 12 years ago and have stuck it out, come hell or the high water of 1990, when the Darling River overflowed and made their homestead an instant island, with water lapping at the top doorstep and not even Bull Milgate able to get through with the mails.

On this land, they raise about 8,000 of Australia's 110 million sheep. Compared to other station families in Western Australia and Queensland and the Northern Territory, they are cosmopolites, able to drive in less than two hours into the sizable town of Bourke for fresh vegetables and a gourmet dinner at the Returned Soldiers' League. Waldo's brother lives on an adjacent property, and he is connected to the Internet by satellite, and the Internet changes everything.

When Bull Milgate roars to a halt at the Ponders' front door, he brings a box of beer for Waldo, a bottle of Johnny Walker Red for

Helen, and a stranger from a city of four million people who wonders how anyone could survive in what, to a city dweller, seems a desolate isolation.

"What do you miss the most?" I ask Helen Ponder, who went to primary school by correspondence, then boarding school in Sydney, and who has been to Germany once. She has graciously asked us to tea and we are sitting at a table in the dining room, with four-year-old Katie on Helen's lap and four-month-old Anna on Katie's, and big Waldo cooing and clucking, deeply in love with his tiny millennium gift.

"I wish we were closer to a bitumenized road," Helen says. (She pronounces the Aussie word for pavement in the Aussie way, BITCH-umen.) "I love horses, and I wish I could take my horse in a trailer to better places to ride."

And that is all.

"Why do they call you Bull?" I wonder out loud, when we're back on the rutted track.

"I was really wild as a young man," he replies. "My brother and I used to work in the killing yard, slaughtering the cattle and sheep, and I was so tough and not afraid in there that he said I was as tough as a bull. And the name stuck."

We haul up at Shindy's Inn in the village of Louth on the wide, lazy Darling, and Bull tumbles out of the cab and commences pounding at the door. It's time to deliver the five dozen two-fours of New, which are weighing the pickup down and slowing our pace.

After a few minutes, it is clear that having the postman ring the proverbial twice is not going to get us anywhere, and so he goes back and wallops the door a few more times and, finally, lights come on. Somewhere in the distance, cattle are lowing and magpies are giving us a pre-dawn concerto of cackles and sarcastic caws.

A publican named John Alexander Duncan opens the front door and he is the geophysical twin of Bull Milgate, enormously bulbous and eminently hospitable, even at this awful hour.

I wander inside, blinking in the sudden fluorescents, and stare at the old photos of village cricket teams and race horses and bales of cotton on transport trucks, and the mounted, dust-covered head of a 70-kilogram codfish taken in the river behind the inn, and more pictures of poor little Louth under water in some recent or ancient flood.

There's a sign pasted to the beer cooler: You Are in Sheep Country EAT MUTTON YOU BASTARDS.

Outside in the chill, I meet the duo. Neither man has ever been off this little desert island of Australia.

"If you could go anywhere in the world," I ask, as we tag-team the boxes of beer inside the pub, "where would you go?"

"Never thought about that," Bull replies.

"Most people say Disneyland, or maybe Paris," I say, trying to give him a hint. "What about New York, New York?"

"Don't know," he says. "Yeah, I guess so. One of them places."

"Ever been to Sydney?" I ask.

"Oh, yeah," Bull says. "Been there a couple of times. Go down, see the cousins, get home."

We order a couple of meat pies for breakfast, and Bull produces an apple he's brought for me, and some bags of chips.

"Is this the real Outback?" I ask John Duncan, as we await our morning meal.

"You're in it now, mate, I reckon," he says. "You'll know when you get to the other side of it, when you fall into the sea."

– National Post

The 'roo Shooter

The politics of the professional kangaroo shooter are simple: bush and gore.

It is just after sunset in the sheep and scrub country Back o' Bourke, a half-hour's drive from the famous town where the Outback "officially" begins. I'm in a big four-wheel-drive cruiser with enough comfortable seats inside for five people, and enough galvanized racks out back for the corpses of a hundred 'roos.

The man at the wheel tonight, 42-year-old Peter Keane, serves by day as Bourke's postmaster. But several nights each week, he uses a $2,500, .223-calibre, bolt-action repeating rifle – and an impressively steady hand – to pick off this continent's signature animals with a single shot to the brain at a range of a hundred yards and more.

The previous night, he took down and gutted 86 in eight hours. In rural Australia, where red and grey kangaroos hop along in mobs as thick as fleas on a mongrel, anything fewer than 50 is a paltry night's work.

He believes he bestows the most humane dispatch any living creature can hope for: "Happy one minute, and then in a second, the world ends."

"It's better than being a sheep or a cow," Mr. Keane reasons.

"Herded into a yard, crowded together, dogs all over them, shoved up a ramp, crammed in a truck, locked for a few days in a pen, then shoved up another ramp, and a bolt to the brain. I think this is a much better way to die."

Keane and Abel make an odd brace of huntsmen. The former has been shooting and trapping professionally since he was 18. The latter never has fired a gun outside the CNE midway. I have been duly warned the enterprise will be bloody, and I pointedly have been served notice several other 'roo shooters have been badly burned by animal-rights activists pretending to be journalists.

"I've been pretending to be a journalist since 1972," I tell my Nimrod as we set out, "but I've got no axe to grind with what you do."

He is a dark-eyed and soft-spoken man, with a facial resemblance to the comedian Michael Palin, but much more serious, and with a hearing deficit after thousands of rifle blasts.

Mr. Keane left school at 13, bought his first four-by-four five years later, and set off on a walkabout that has taken him from Australia's Snowy Mountains to the tropics of the Top End, but never off this island. He managed a pet-food plant for 10 years, then moved to the Bourke P. O. with his wife, Helen, and their children, now aged 12, 11, 10, and 9. He does not know if his two boys will take up this trade, "but they'll learn about it for sure," he says.

Mr. Keane is one of about 30 licensed 'roo shooters in Bourke – there are thousands of others across the continent – willing to bushwhack through thickets of red tape for the opportunity to earn, at most, a few hundred dollars a night, after expenses. The regulations seem stringent; whether all shooters obey them is beyond my knowledge.

"You'd make more money driving the truck that takes them to the packing plant," I suggest to the marksman.

"Yeah, but that's not what I choose to do," he replies. "I'm doing what I want to do, and what I can do with the skills I have."

What these men – and a few women – do is not "hunting." There is no stalking, no science, no chase. They buy a permit to work a certain patch of land, then canvass it by truck night after night, scanning the brush with powerful searchlights, leaning out the driver's-side window to assassinate any buck or doe that looks large and healthy enough to be profitable.

Most will be used for pet food. A minority will go to supermarkets in Australia and abroad, where their chops, loins, saddles. and cutlets are priced about the same as veal. The leather can be tanned, and you can buy a purse made from a kangaroo scrotum for about $10 in many souvenir stores.

If the kill is female, and she is carrying a joey, the young animal will be beheaded with a knife or shears, shot point-blank, or clubbed, then left for the wedge-tailed eagles.

On this night, in less than two hours on a property Mr. Keane describes as particularly unproductive, we spotlight at least a hundred kangaroos, most of them too small to shoot. Their numbers, always prodigious, have been soaring in this region after three years of good rain. And even a casual traveller in the Outback can see the two species are not rare. On most stretches of highway, you pass at least five – and sometimes 50 – reds and greys in various states of decay and desiccation in less than five minutes.

From the cab of the truck, Mr. Keane fires one bullet each at six of the larger males and takes down five, right between the eyes. (In a healthy kangaroo community, does outnumber bucks five to one, but he lets all the females bounce free, possibly to spare me the subsequent infanticide.) Then he drops from the cab of the truck, drags the kill to the tailgate, hangs it upside-down by the ankle, and slits its throat to release the blood.

With a swift peritoneal incision and a wrenching manual twist, he extracts the steaming intestines, drops them to the ground with a sloshing thump, then proudly shows off a carcass that, at 20 cents per pound, cleanly dressed at the chiller, might gain him nine or ten bucks.

Back in Bourke, a shooter named Chris Morrison lets me leaf through the *New South Wales Code of Practice for the Humane Shooting of Kangaroos.*

It mandates:

When shooting a kangaroo the primary objective must be to achieve instantaneous loss of consciousness and rapid death without regaining consciousness.

And:

The pouch young of a killed female must also be killed immediately, by decapitation or a heavy blow to the skull to destroy the brain, or shooting.

To say Mr. Morrison merely enjoys rural life would be a disservice. He also raises and sells parakeets; he has taught his young son to ride bareback on a feral sow that he bottle-fed from piglethood; and he is attempting to cross-breed the sulphur-crested cockatoo with the rose-breasted Major Mitchell, an experiment whose gorgeous participants can be found in cages in his backyard, screaming loud enough to knock aircraft off course.

He outlines some of the technical regulations: a shooter must wash his hands with soap and water after every kill; the handle of his knife must be plastic, not wooden; his 'roo rack must be without any spot of rust; if his blade accidentally punctures the intestines during dressing, the animal must be abandoned; and so on. Each animal – including the discarded ones – must be registered and tagged, and even the metal frame from which they hang during transport requires a separate licensing fee.

To go out at all, a shooter has to secure the written endorsement of a landowner on a form labelled *Application to Take Protected Fauna*, and he must justify the killing of a specified number of reds and of greys by alleging:

  a) damage to fences

b) damage to crops

c) competition for pastures

d) competition for water.

Completing all this paperwork, and paying all the fees, allows Mr. Morrison to take home about $1,000 after missing three full nights of sleep on a holiday weekend. That's what he figures he would have cleared not long ago, had a kamikaze kangaroo not bounded into his front fender during the drive home, wiping out all the profits with one repair bill.

The organization called People for the Ethical Treatment of Animals claims on its Web site: "Ninety per cent of kangaroo killers are 'weekend' hunters, killing by the most expedient methods available: running kangaroos down in trucks, poisoning their water, beating them to death, even impaling them on stakes and meat hooks and skinning them alive. . . . Some were killed immediately, but some hunters purposely just wounded them – sometimes leaving them to suffer for hours or days so that their meat would remain fresh. . . ."

To confirm this allegation, one would have to be present at 90 per cent of the kills, but Joshua Gilroy, senior kangaroo management officer for the New South Wales National Parks and Wildlife Service, tells me he believes violations of the regulations are rare.

Mr. Gilroy says, "Our main fail-safe are the tags that the shooters have to buy. You can't sell a carcass without a tag. Each tag is numbered, and they can only be obtained from us."

The wildlife officer estimates there are at least 20 million kangaroos across Australia, possibly more than 30 million, making them more abundant than ever before. Nine hundred thousand will be legally taken in New South Wales this year.

"If no 'roos were shot at all, would it make a difference to the grazing of sheep or cattle?" I ask him.

"In times of plenty, such as we have at the moment," Mr. Gilroy answers, "it would make no difference at all."

Peter Keane stops the motor for a second, cuts the lights, and I assume he has spotted his next target, but he's actually looking up at the stars.

Some lights are moving laterally, just above the western horizon – it has to be a satellite, an airplane, or the midnight boat from Pluto.

"I've seen a lot of funny things in the sky that I don't tell anyone about," he says.

"Don't you get lonely?" I wonder.

"I'm a bit of a loner. I enjoy me own company. I like to be by myself."

"What do you think about, 'way out here in the middle of the night?"

"When you're working, you're just thinking, 'Where's the next 'roo?' But when the shooting's done, then you have lots of time.

"You solve all the problems of the world on your way home. And when you wake up, you still got 'em."

– National Post

Stalking the Wild Platypus

———————————— • ————————————

MOUNT ROYAL NATIONAL PARK, NEW SOUTH WALES

Torn and bleeding, down on all fours, soaked to the skin, clawing his way through the underbrush of an untamed hillside, the author is paying the price of yet another of his brilliant ideas: stalking the wild platypus.

It is nearly dusk, and a young, strong park ranger named Steve Cathcart and I have been at this for six-and-a-half hours. There is no trail. The terrain is booby-trapped with wild raspberry bushes whose barbs shred our hands and faces and clothing, and supple lianas that snare us around the neck like hangman's nooses.

We hike with our arms overhead like prisoners of war to avoid the razor-bushes, or do the Australian crawl on our hands and knees, clambering over rotten trunks and sinking into mudholes, whipping branches back into the face of whichever poor sap is following behind. But these travails are minor compared to the worst menace of all – a thick, spiny plant whose thorns are so clinging and repulsive that the Australians call it "lawyer vine."

At the bottom of the defile is a gurgling little river that should – in theory – teem with playful platypuses, perhaps the most bizarre of all Australian mammals. It takes us more than two hours to tumble down to it. Then we try to step-stone along the stream, slip on the rocks, and both of us fall in the water.

Number of platypuses seen by us in this river: none.

"I think they need deeper pools," the park ranger explains.

Now we have to climb back up.

Hour after hour, Stanley and Livingstone wend their painful way.

Progress is loathsome and laborious. No one but my guide hears my yelping and cursing as I lurch into the lawyer vines. We are the only two people in the park today.

As we crash through this purgatory of bungee cords and Velcro, Cathcart tries to keep my spirits up by reminding me to look out for stinging nettles, and he assures me – after three hours of uphill bushwhacking – that we are so far above the stream that the crest of the mountain, where our truck is parked, must be just minutes away.

I haven't heard the words "ridge," "brook," and "thorn" so many times since I stopped watching *The Bold and the Beautiful.*

And now, it seems, we're lost.

It is 5:30 and the sun has disappeared behind Mount Royal when my companion sprints ahead and out of sight, if it is possible to apply the term "sprint" to crawling.

When I catch up, I see that he finally has decided to consult his compass.

I flash a big, insincere grin and ask, "What now, Ranger Steve?"

The duck-billed platypus – nicknamed "Syd" – is one of three cartoon mascots of the Games of the XXVII Olympiad. I thought it would be fun to try to see each of them in its natural habitat. Meeting "Olly" the kookaburra – a fluffy white kingfisher with a thick, pointed bill – was easy. He woke me up one morning when I was staying at a waterside bed-and-breakfast, about two hours north of the Olympic city.

"Hoo hoo hoo hee hee hee hee hee hee hee ha ha ha ha hoo hoo!" Olly said. And I saw dozens of his cousins, perched on telephone wires, as I drove around New South Wales and Queensland.

As for "Millie" the echidna – a spiny hedgehog that sleeps underground all day – I was advised by a senior officer of the National Parks and Wildlife Service to "forget it and go to the zoo."

But the platypus was another story. With diligence, patience, and some hiking, I was told, it still was possible to find Syd in the wild in New South Wales, where he and his ancestors had been living since the Cretaceous period, about 110 million years ago. Mount Royal would be a good place to try. The park lies north of Sydney, not far from the Hawkesbury River, where the British first encountered the platypus 10 years after the foundation of their convict colony.

"The tail of this animal was thick, short, and very fat," wrote David Collins, Sydney's first judge-advocate and historian, in 1797, "but the most extraordinary circumstance observed in its structure was, its having, instead of the mouth of an animal, the upper and lower mandibles of a duck.

"By these it was enabled to supply itself with food, like that bird, in muddy places, or in the banks of the lakes, in which its webbed feet enabled it to swim, while on shore its long and sharp claws were employed in burrowing; nature thus providing for it in its double or amphibious character. These little animals had been frequently noticed rising to the surface of the water, and blowing like the turtle."

The more the British learned about the platypus, the more confused they became. They called it the "water-mole," or "paradox." Was it a reptile, a mammal, or something entirely separate? The first skins to be sent back to London were dismissed as fakes. (It was common at the time for swindlers to sew the tail of a large fish to the body of a monkey and tout it as a "mermaid.")

Charles Darwin saw a platypus – his host shot it – while visiting on HMS *Beagle* in 1836 and wrote that Australian wildlife was so different from the rest of the world a person might assume "Two distinct Creators must have been at work."

Aborigines reported the platypus laid eggs in its riverbank burrows but the British refused to believe them. Not until 1864, when a captive female laid two eggs in a cage, was that fact accepted by men of "science." We know now the platypus and the echidna are the world's only egg-laying, warm-blooded mammals.

An echidna sometimes is glimpsed trundling along a roadside after dark, or balled up for self-defence in someone's backyard with a dog yelping at it. Seeing one would be a matter of luck. But the platypus can be found, as Darwin noted, "diving and playing about the surface of the water," in clear streams all along Australia's eastern coast. It is not on the list of threatened animals.

Bashing down the hillside to look for one, sliced to ribbons by the brambles, the only endangered species is me.

"No wonder the Aborigines used fire to clear the undergrowth," says Ranger Steve. "Imagine walking around here naked?" We've finally emerged from the lawyer vine and wild raspberries, onto an old logging road. Half an hour later, we're back at the truck.

Glum and defeated, we start back toward town. But the route down from Mount Royal crosses another rivulet, and – just as the last daylight is dying – we decide to stop the vehicle on the bridge and give it one more try.

I'm just walking down when I see Steve Cathcart waving his arms like a wild man and giving me the thumbs-up.

And there it is – a dark brown shape, lolling on the surface of the watercourse, noodling its bill from side to side, scaring up insects and crayfish. We've found our platypus – 20 paces from the road.

It stumbles and tumbles over a spillway and swims right toward us. It is about 20 inches long, and we can see its four webbed feet and its tiny eyes – it closes them while feeding underwater – and its flat beaver-tail. We clasp hands and slap each other's back and giggle like schoolboys.

"Seek and ye shall find," I whisper.

"What goes around comes around," says Ranger Steve.

– National Post

Take Your Medicine Like a Man

———————————— • ————————————

We are under a tent in the Australian Outback, on a spring night in September with sand in the air. Coming at me is a hazel-eyed heavyweight with a choirboy curl across his brow and a thousand rounds behind him. I am an unranked amateur in the first boxing match of my life.

The ring is a canvas mat on a dirt floor with no ropes to enclose it. Three hundred ranchmen and roustabouts, most of them already legless, as the Aussies say, on Victoria Bitter and Emu Lager, line the perimeter, smelling blood and whooping. I have no mouth guard, no headgear, no protective cup. I have a burning stomach and an empty head.

My opponent, a tall, fleshy menace nicknamed the Friendly Mauler, is windmilling his arms and grinning. Forty-nine years and seven months after I entered this world, he is preparing to knock me out of it.

"Why do they call you the *Friendly* Mauler?" I had the sang-froid to ask him just before the fight.

"Because the harder you hit me, the friendlier I get," he replied with a diagonal smile.

The referee blows his whistle, we come to ring centre to touch gloves, and reality jabs me: I can hide behind my fat red mitts, but I can't run. Not now, with all these cowboys watching.

"Come at me like I'm your worst enemy in the world," the Mauler commands.

"But I don't have any enemies," I reply.

"If you just muck about, people will laugh," he replies. "I don't like that. It makes me mad. So hit me! I can take a punch."

The tent has been erected in a ghost town called Birdsville, whose population of a few straggling dozens swells to about 6,000 for one crazed weekend every year. The surrounding region is sparsely populated too, a swatch of desert the size of Indiana with about 300 permanent residents. We are a long, long way from the Sydney Opera House, the Great Barrier Reef, and Elle Macpherson. But this, the men all say, is the true Australia.

A century ago, before the British colonies of the southern continent were joined into a single dominion, Birdsville was a bustling customs post where livestock from Queensland was counted and taxed, then mustered toward the distant sea. Today, Birdsville is a convergence of yellow sand highways, an artesian well whose water comes rocketing out of the ground at 210°F, a gas station, and the only licensed pub for hundreds of miles.

In 1882, to relieve the isolation, a race meeting was begun. This has grown into a bacchanal of beer drinking, boxing, whip cracking, bull riding, and thoroughbred racing on an oval of dust – a combination of the Kentucky Derby, Munich's Oktoberfest, the Calgary Stampede, and *Lawrence of Arabia*. Half the throng descends in private planes and camps out under their wings. The rest drive 18 hours or more on rutted trails from Brisbane or Adelaide and sleep (if they sleep) in the dust. A few men have been known to pull up on camels. Many, when the weekend is over, do not remember having been here.

A brotherhood of boxers who take on all comers has been a fixture at the Birdsville meeting and at other outback carnivals for more than a century. Now this manly sideshow has taken on a melancholy air. Under the big top, as I face the Friendly Mauler, I am a flat-footed footnote to history: Fred Brophy's Boxing Troupe – of which the Mauler is the paragon, the Nureyev, the prima donna – is the last of its kind.

"The last one left not only in the world but in Australia," Brophy says with typical antipodal hubris.

Brophy, 47, is a Queenslander whose father managed a troupe like this, as did Brophy's grandfather, and so on, back four generations to the family's Dreamtime. Now Brophy and his wife, Sandi, and their three children and their mongrel roster of sluggers, rasslers, and kickboxers, young and aged, whites and Aboriginals, travel from town to town across the infinity of soil and spinifex that the Australians call the Never-Never, peppering stooges like me with uppercuts and big, long, looping hooks.

"I'm gonna keep on going till I die," said Brophy as he hauled an enormous bass drum to the front of his tent on the evening of the big fight. "I'm not doing it for the money. I'm doing it for Australia. There's no one left in the world doing this. The other people who had boxing tents, they found easier things to do."

He mounted a ladder to a rickety catwalk, stood in front of a huge painting of himself, and began to wallop the drum. "Challenging all comers, and there's no one barred!" Brophy bellowed above the din of thousands who had come back thirsty from the race course and were listing to starboard in the ankle-deep sand of Birdsville's only street. Admission to the show was $15 Australian (about US$10), but those who fought would get in free.

As the drumming intensified, the pugilists paraded from the tent in robes and trunks and singlets: the Friendly Mauler, White Lightning, the Cave Man, the Spider Man, Kid Valentine, Young Cassius, the Palm Island Tiger. Six of us civilians bravely answered the summons and scaled the trellis to pose beside them.

"Are you scared?" I asked the fellow next to me.

He was about one-third my age, with a stomach the size of a bushel of apples, and wore a dirty grey bathing suit. "I'm much too drunk to be scared," he said, smiling. As it turned out, he would be my partner on a tag team.

The Friendly Mauler is a father of five from central Queensland named Glynn Johnston. "Why do men volunteer to fight you?" I asked him, and he responded with a staccato catalog of reasons: "To prove themselves. Bit of an ego trip – typical male, bit of bonding, something to talk about with their mates, have a few beers and tell how they did it."

I'd covered so many boxing matches that I thought I could box, too. In my sports-writing days I was at ringside for the best of them – Ali-Frazier, Frazier-Foreman, Leonard-Hearns, Roberto Durán's "*No más*." Throw in a few hundred Olympic and club brawls, and my secondhand education was complete. What would it be like in the ring, I wondered, with the lights and the crowd and the fear?

Suddenly I am to find out. Brophy blows the whistle again to start the fight, and I am prancing with innocent confidence toward the Friendly Mauler, who sticks out his left and taps me on the crown as I get nearer.

Remembering the Mauler's command to make the bout appear ferocious, I bow low and come in headfirst, completely neglecting to protect myself, and pepper as many fast little body punches as I can muster before my arms turn to lead. This takes about ten seconds. Then I straighten and notice that the Mauler is winding up to throw a haymaker. "He's going to pop me in the nose," I say to myself as the punch approaches. His aim is perfect.

"That hurts!" I tell my brain – time has stopped ticking; a heartbeat lasts an hour – "I should fall down." So I roll over, scraping my knees on the canvas, and tag my bulbous partner, who rumbles forward with his mouth open like a gasping salmon, throws a few punches, takes a wallop to the gut, and goes down as if shot.

After two two-minute rounds – the big boy and me getting the worst of it from the Friendly Mauler and the Cave Man, a small, quick, toothless, grey-haired 40-year-old Aboriginal (though, of course, the pros are pulling their punches) – my partner and I are ready to say, "*No más*," but Brophy strides to our corner. "Yer doin' grite, just grite," he says, and persuades us to give it one more go.

Round 3 lasts a hundred years. Still leading with my chin and remembering the rather distressing adage *Kill the body and the head will die*, I burrow into the thicket of the Cave Man's elbows and ribs and try my flurry of stomach blows again. He is unimpressed and taps me apologetically in the face, and I go down once more, this time crawling to tag off with Tiny.

When it finally ends and I realize that I have survived with only some bruising around the breastbone and a slight wobble in my nose, I meet the Friendly Mauler again at the centre of the ring. He hugs me, tells me, "I didn't think you'd really get in there and fight," and compliments my lion's heart. Good old Fred Brophy calls it a draw.

Out in the night, strangers approach, beer-handed, with congratulations and awe. "Good on yer, good on yer," they say.

Music is playing from a tent somewhere. Under a tapestry of Southern stars, the boxer dances home.

– *Sports Illustrated*

Waltzing Matilda

·

It is their "Danny Boy," their "Gens du Pays," their "Hatikvah," their "Shenandoah." The battle hymn of an obstinate republic. Next Friday night, in a stadium 1,200 miles south of this dusty little Outback town, it will resound from the throats – and the hearts – of 100,000 patriots.

You will hear the strange words dozens of times before these Olympic Games are over: billabong, swagman, coolibah, jumbuck, tuckerbag. The squatter and his troopers; one, two, three. The self-destruction of a mutinous, desperate man: " 'You'll never catch me alive!' cried he."

"Waltzing Matilda."

This is the village where the anthem that encapsulates the soul of our Olympic host nation was written – by a playboy lawyer from Sydney – and set by a grazier's daughter to an old Scottish tune. It was 1895. The swagman was far from jolly, but his tale is true.

I've driven 16 hours over two sun-scorched prairie days to come here from New South Wales. My goal is partly touristic – tiny Winton (population: 1,200) recently opened a superb museum dedicated to the history and import of the song – and partly

40

sentimental. It is not possible to spend time in Australia without sensing the country's intense attachment to a dead poet's scribble on a yellowed page. And this is where it began.

"We must be the only nation on Earth that made a hero of a fictitious suicidal itinerant worker," reads a display in the Waltzing Matilda Centre. "Why did we do that?"

Guiding visitors around the exhibition is a man named Allen Stockham, a former rodeo champion, cattle drover, and sheep stealer. Like the hero of the song, Mr. Stockham, now 67, has spent many nights beneath the Southern Cross, wrapped in the thick canvas bedroll the Australians call a swag.

Weathered and wise, dressed all in denim, under a ten-gallon felt Akubra, he walks me through the displays and says, "You can hear it a thousand times, and it still means what it says – defiance. Those old bushmen, that was their attitude. When the Boer War came, and then the First World War, the military took it overseas. The troops sang it everywhere they went. It was the same idea – they were defyin' the Germans.

"It should be the national anthem, but the British colonials, they couldn't let us have a song about a bushranger as our national anthem. Most of the bloomin' Australians were bloomin' convicts anyway – they were defiant right from the start and they picked it right up. And we still are."

The hero of "Waltzing Matilda" is a migrant farm labourer ("swagman") who is cornered under a eucalyptus tree ("coolibah") beside a waterhole ("billabong") by a landowner ("squatter") and his hired policemen after stealing a sheep ("jumbuck," from the Aboriginal word "jimbuc") for his dinner ("tucker").

He escapes arrest – and certain hanging – by leaping into the billabong, where his ghost may be heard by all who pass by.

The actual story is more convoluted. For decades, swagmen had roamed the sheep stations of Queensland, shearing the fine merino wool in season, begging and starving without. They were, at first, a merry lot of hobos. In 1877, they formed a bogus brotherhood whose rules included:

1. No member to be older than 100.
2. Members who don't care about paying will be admitted free.
3. Members found working will be expelled.

But their jocularity soon dissipated. In 1894, the shearers, believing themselves to be cruelly exploited by the ranch owners, many of whom were absentee British millionaires, declared a strike that quickly turned violent.

On a station called Dagworth, a day's ride north of Winton, the strikers fired off their rifles and pistols, causing and suffering no casualties, then set fire to the barns, killing dozens of precious sheep.

One of the ringleaders of the uprising, a man named Samuel "French" Hoffmeister, was found by troopers the next day, beside a billabong off the Winton track, still in his swag, shot dead by his own hand.

About four months after this, a 30-year-old Sydneysider named Andrew Barton Paterson, who had adopted the nickname "Banjo" (after his favourite horse) because it sounded more authentically Outback-ish, came to Dagworth to romance one young lady and wound up falling for another.

Banjo Paterson had been raised in the ranchlands of New South Wales before being educated, and admitted to the bar, in the metropolis by the sea. He already was one of Australia's leading frontier poets, in the masculine style of Rudyard Kipling and Robert S. Service, having published such stirring stanzas as:

The man from Snowy River let the pony have his head,
And he swung his stockwhip round and gave a cheer,
And he raced him down the mountain like a torrent down its bed,
While the others stood and watched in very fear . . .

At Dagworth, where memories of the strike and Mr. Hoffmeister's death still were fresh and raw – and where two other swagmen had drowned in billabongs in 1891 – Mr. Paterson began to compose a poem. He ostensibly was in the district to court the daughter of a neighbouring squire, but found himself keeping company with a Miss Christina MacPherson.

Miss MacPherson, it happened, recently had been to the horse races in the colony of Victoria, where she heard, danced to, and memorized a Scottish melody called "Thou Bonnie Wood of Craigielea."

"Let's set your new poem to music!" she declared to Banjo Paterson, sitting down to her harmonium. Their song was performed at the North Gregory Hotel in Winton a few weeks later, was relayed from farm to farm and swagman to swagman, and went to war in South Africa and Europe. By the time of its centenary, it had been recorded by everyone from Chubby Checker to the Coldstream Guards.

It is not the national anthem, although a poll conducted during the Melbourne Olympics in 1956 revealed that nine out of ten Aussies wanted it to be. (In Helsinki in 1952, the Finns played it during a gold-medal ceremony, assuming that it was.)

That honour goes, instead, to "Advance Australia Fair," a reasonably rousing tune we are likely to hear far more often than "O Canada" on the podium at Homebush Bay. And the word "jolly" was not in Paterson's original manuscript, which begins with "Oh! there once was a Swagman camped in a Billabong . . .")

Australia fell in love with the song, but, alas, Miss MacPherson did not fall in love with Andrew Barton Paterson. She died, unmarried, in 1936.

Mr. Paterson became a war correspondent for the *Sydney Morning Herald*, published hundreds of other poems and essays on Outback life and lore, and maintained his legal practice. He sold the publishing rights for "Waltzing Matilda," along with what he called "a lot of old junk," to a firm in Sydney for £5.

He passed away on February 5, 1941, – Allen Stockham's eighth birthday.

"I'd have been on the strikers' side," the old cowpoke says. We're sitting quietly now, in the archives of the Waltzing Matilda Centre, which contain thousands of books and articles pertaining to Banjo Paterson, the shearers' strike, and the hallowed verse.

"Most of 'em carried their swags and that's all they had and they were gettin' it tough. They were prepared to fight for what they wanted – that's still the attitude of the bloomin' bushman, I guess.

"The shearers today, they have a set of union rules. But now, we have shearers coming in from New Zealand, and they work seven days a week over there and they try to do the same thing over here, whereas we don't shear on Sundays, see? There's still friction over these things."

His sympathies for the swagman are well grounded; he spent most of his life in the saddle on these unforgiving yellow plains. On cattle drives, he was responsible for feeding the cowboys – they call them "ringers" here – and that often meant "borrowing" the odd jumbuck.

"It was part of the business," he says with a wink. "You had to know how to do it and not get caught."

But years on the range take their toll, north of the Tropic of Capricorn – Queensland is the melanoma capital of the world. Mr. Stockham's arms are scar-spangled, where dozens of little cancers have been frozen and removed.

The broad-brimmed Akubra protected his face.

"Look how clear it is," he says, lifting his hat.

So, who was Matilda and where did she waltz?

According to the history books at the museum in Winton, she was a rolled-up soldier's greatcoat from the Prussian wars of the 19th century, the closest thing to a soft, warm woman, far from home, they could embrace. They gave the garment a woman's name – as B. B. King would call his guitar, in another century, "Lucille" – and danced her down the front lines to their graves.

By 1894, the expression "Waltzing Matilda," meaning to carry a coat or bedroll on the trail, imported by European immigrants, had caught on with the swagmen of Queensland, though they more commonly used the expression "humping the bluey" to refer to life on the road.

It was picked up by Banjo Paterson, set to music by Christina MacPherson, and melded with a real tale from Australia's wild West into a verse that equally thrilled the swells of Sydney and touched the hardened men who lived a life of toil, hunger, and solitude in a rolled-out swag.

"Who'll come a-waltzing Matilda with me?" the swagman asks, a century later. And a warm, dry wind from the grasslands of Australia bears the burden of his sorrow to the world.

– *National Post*

LATIN AMERICA

Previous page: Kayapó Children, Brazil (Harry Phillips)

In 1973, it was possible to fly on Pan American World Airways from New York City to Caracas, Venezuela, and spend a week at an ocean-side hotel for only $205. To my roommate, D —— – a man of breathtaking penury – and me, this was a bargain that could not be missed. (I was raking in $54 a week at the Troy Record at the time, and D ——, also holding a baccalaureate in physics, was working in a costume-jewellery factory.) So we went to South America.

Three things occurred during that holiday that should have given me ample cause never to set foot on the continent again:

• A young Canadian I had met at poolside (and would later marry) was walking to dinner when she was dragged down a culvert and robbed of her purse and passport. This led to her running screaming through Venezuelan Customs and landing in New York for her connecting flight. When she declared her nationality, she was asked by a U.S. immigration officer, in lieu of papers, "What's the name of the hockey team in Montreal?"

• I signed up for an optional tour of Angel Falls – the world's highest cataract – and already had vomited seven times on the southbound flight when the pilot announced that it was too foggy to see the landmark anyway. Then we landed on a gravel strip in the middle of the jungle and I watched all the oil come gushing out of the starboard propeller.

• Back home in Troy, I developed a case of trenchmouth, a tropical infection that turned my gums the colour of cheesecake. Treatment consisted of hourly gargling with hydrogen peroxide, and then having my oral cavity scraped of residue, inch by inch, with a scalpel.

Twenty-two years later, flying down to Ecuador to produce a great television film, I should have been prepared for disappointment.

Up a Lazy River

·

As the equatorial sun expires in South America on Boxing Day, I am cowering in a speedboat in the Amazon wilderness and the captain is navigating by lightning. Ahead of us lies a malarial maze of floating logs, invisible sand bars, vampire bats, electric eels, and underfed piranhas. Seated behind the pilot and me in our hurtling little Love Boat are a television crew and the great-great-granddaughter of Charles Darwin. It is raining biblically.

We are bound for the pristine headwaters of the world's longest river, where howler monkeys haunt the trees and landlocked dolphins splash. Miss Sarah Darwin, thirty-one, a botanical illustrator from London, England, is to be the host of our documentary, *Darwin Returns*. After Amazonia, we plan to take her to the Galápagos Islands, whose unique life forms prompted her ancestor to form the theory of the transmutation of the species.

We have been on the water for six hours, roaring toward a jungle lodge near the junction of Ecuador, Colombia, and Perú. Our voyage has taken us deep into the tropical fastness, past the thatch-and-bamboo villages of the Cofán and Quichua peoples, down the broth-brown Río Aguarico. In the cecropia and kapok trees we have spied macaws, toucans, kingfishers. Now it is dark.

The captain is unconcerned. He is hunched forward, right hand on the throttle, left hand on the wheel, staring ahead into the blackness and the intermittent flashes of light.

"*Amigo*," I ask, for I am serving as translator on this cruise, "why not use the windshield wiper?"

The captain reaches below the instrument panel and holds up a pigtail of copper wires that dangle, disconnected, from his hand. "*No batería*," he smiles.

Then the motor dies.

It's our seventh breakdown. Gingerly, the barefoot motorman balances on the gunwale and tiptoes astern. He unknots a plastic grocery bag caught in the propeller and then, yanking the starter cord 12 or 14 times before the engine finally turns over, he barks at me to urge the throttle as *adelante* as possible, to prevent it from stalling again.

"Faster!" shout the executive producer, the cameraman, the sound recordist, and Charles Darwin's great-great-granddaughter in unison.

I shove the red handle as far as it will go. Now we are rocketing in circles. The captain is teetering on the starboard rail like one of the Flying Wallendas. The boat is listing like the *Edmund Fitzgerald*. And it's impossible to see whether I am steering us toward safe, deep water or straight toward the shore and certain death. Maurice, our French-Canadian cameraman and the survivor of a hundred war zones, chooses this moment to announce that he has never learned to swim. But within an instant, our helmsman has regained his seat and we are racing again through the Amazon gloom without even a light bulb on the bow to guide us.

"I have done a lot of stupid things in my life," Maurice screams into my ear above the hellish noise of the outboard. "But this is the stupidest."

"I am no longer afraid," I reply with uncharacteristic sang-froid. "I have had a wonderful career. I am at peace."

"We are in the hands of Allah now," the Catholic tells the Jew.

The next morning at breakfast I am about to take my first spoon-ful of muesli when Bill, the sound recordist, yelps, "Count the legs on the raisins!"

The cast and crew of *Darwin Returns*, as well as a vacationing middle-class Ecuadorian family – Dad, Mom, two sons – are in the care of a Quito travel agency specializing in deluxe Amazonian adventures, accommodating its clients in jungle bungalows, each furnished with a bed, a chair, a table, a candle, and spiders the size of cats. Here at Aguarico Camp, we have cold showers, square meals, chilled beer, and, so far, no story. This, we believe, is about to change, as we take Miss Darwin by motorcanoe even farther into the rainforest toward another camp, Imuya – "lake of the red howler monkeys." Today should be a feast of sounds and images.

We are fully prepared for wilderness travel. Miss Darwin has a slouch hat and sketch pad. Maurice wraps a protective rain cover-ing around his rented $100,000 digital camera. Bill wears a safari vest with more pockets than a billiard table. I carry two high-protein Power Bars in case we miss lunch. And Harry, the executive producer of this expedition, has outfitted himself with long under-wear, Gore-Tex socks, nylon rain pants, waterproof boots, a crew-neck pullover in the ninety-five-degree heat, and a jaunty little cap that makes him appear ready to tee off in the 1951 Masters.

We shove off into the milky stream.

An hour into the excursion, we have left behind all evidence of human habitation. The banks of this river – the black, winding Lagarto Cocha – are draped with soaring palms and wild mangoes. Our guide, Mónica, a vivacious young student from Quito, spots egrets and falcons and a troop of long-tailed saki monkeys with thick black fur.

It was in a landscape much like this, on the opposite edge of the continent, that the young Charles Darwin disembarked from the *Beagle* in February 1832. He was 23.

Delight itself, is a weak term to express the feelings of a naturalist who, for the first time, has wandered by himself in a Brazilian forest. . . . To a person fond of natural history, such a day as this brings with it a deeper pleasure than he can ever hope to experience again.

Sixteen decades later, we are up a lazy river with his great-great-granddaughter, revelling in the connection. ("Imagine if I were a Pasteur or a Curie!" Maurice sighs.) This is not Sarah Darwin's first trip to the tropics – she once spent several months in Australia's Northern Territory, sketching the native flora. But it is beginning to dawn on us that we may be a lot more excited about travelling *with* a Darwin than Miss Darwin is about *being* one.

For the past half-century, this section of the Lagarto Cocha has formed the de facto boundary between tiny Ecuador and big, bold Perú, the result of a land grab by the Peruvians during the Second World War while nobody was looking. Every few years, the two countries go to war over a swath of forest that might turn out to be rich in minerals and oil. In January 1995, the shooting started again. Not many men were killed; perhaps thirty on both sides.

As usual, nothing was settled. But, this being Latin America, the two countries have erected military installations all along the disputed frontier. It is a scene from another century – bamboo battlements and palisades linking turrets, as if built to a blueprint by the Wicked Witch of the West. But this sun-bleached Frontierland is no joke – as we steam nearer to an Ecuadorian camp, a platoon of young soldiers scurries to battle stations, carrying real guns.

"Don't shoot – we're journalists!" I holler as we advance into rifle range.

But by this time it is clear that the entire *destacamento* has turned out not to annihilate a boatload of gringos but to celebrate because we've brought women.

We are standing at the gates of the Ecuadorian fort, just below a placard that vows *We Will Fulfil Our Duty to Keep Firing and Resist Death, Day after Day.* From here it is just possible to read the slogan whitewashed on the barricades across the river: *Viva Perú, a Country with Balls.*

The commander of the fortress is a sergeant in designer sunglasses named Angel Guerra. (The surname, translated, means "war.") He and Miss Darwin are enjoying a philosophical discourse while a crescent of sex-starved recruits arcs around them, ogling. Maurice is scrambling to film the scene and our guide, whom we have nicknamed Mónica Amazónica, is fighting off the entire Lagarto Cocha Detachment with one hand and simultaneously translating irregular verbs with the other.

"Whose side are you on, God's or Darwin's?" the commandant asks Sarah. "Or do you believe, as Hawking says, that 'Where physics ends, God begins'?"

"Huh?" Sarah replies.

Sergeant War then launches into a lengthy expostulation on the history of the conflict with the dastardly Peruvians. It is true, he admits, that the men of this particular fortress have engaged the enemy only in volleyball. (Last year's deadly skirmishes were fought much farther south.) But history is history, and everyone here has pledged to fight to the death to get their territory back. The situation, he says, is "tense."

His oration concluded, I hit upon the capital idea of asking if we might take a side trip over to the Peruvian bank without being torpedoed. The middle-class Ecuadorian family looks at me with dumb horror.

"Think of it!" I enthuse, trying to win them over. "An international cruise! Have your passports ready!"

"Change money?" a soldier asks me, in English.

Sergeant Guerra is even less gladdened by the proposal. He says he will have to radio his commanding officer for authorization. He is about to place the call when an aide-de-camp reminds him that the Lagarto Cocha Detachment doesn't have any electricity.

The next thing we know we are all sitting in our canoe again, approaching the Peruvian camp. Several Ecuadorian soldiers wave their arms and whistle, trying to get the enemy's attention. I am being eaten alive by sandflies. "Screw it, cowboy," Maurice counsels me. "Let's just go."

Five minutes later, we reach Perú without incident and disembark into knee-deep mud.

The Peruvian fort is even more medieval than the Ecuadorian. There is a rather futile moat – barely two feet across and three feet deep – and a couple of bamboo barracks within the perimeter of a spike-tipped stockade. A sign above the main gate declares, *Victory or Death*, and beneath it a dozen crew-cut warriors slouch and cadge our sound man's cigarettes.

Alas, there is to be no debate of evolutionary theories in Peru this afternoon. The officer we meet is emphatic – this is a war zone, not a stage set. He waves the cast and crew of *Darwin Returns* out of the Republic.

But our Maurice is a crafty veteran. As we skulk back toward our flagship, he waves the camera around and surreptitiously records the striking Incan faces of the teenage draftees. I congratulate him on his cleverness.

The Ecuadorian family never gets out of the boat.

When Harry met Sarah, it was at the Chelsea Arts Club in London, six months before our expedition to these latitudes. Back in Toronto, he excitedly told me about her, and I agreed that *Darwin Returns* was a can't-miss idea for a television documentary.

I authored an effulgent proposal to be shopped to broadcasters around the world, then crammed Darwin, day and night. Gripped by the excruciating odyssey of "the most important man of the nineteenth century," I burrowed deep into the evolutionist's life of sickness, doubt, grief, toil, and triumph. I read *The Voyage of* HMS *Beagle, On the Origin of Species, The Descent of Man*, biographies, letters, journals, snatches of treatises on barnacles, earthworms, climbing plants.

Meanwhile, broadcasters around the world declared my proposal to be insufficiently effulgent to invest in.

Oh, well, I told Harry, quoting W. S. Gilbert: "Darwinian Man, though well behaved, at best is only a monkey shaved."

"Should we abandon the idea?" he asked.

"No! Press on!" I counselled. "Think of it – Darwin in the Galápagos!"

So we pressed on.

"Five minutes to Dolphin Lake!" shouts Mónica Amazónica, early on Day Three. We're back in the canoe, and just around the bend, we have been promised, lies an unforgettable encounter with one of the rarest aquatic mammals in the world. No one knows how the freshwater dolphins of Amazonia got stranded so many miles from the sea. Some scientists postulate that the creatures migrated inland from the Pacific, only to find their return trip blockaded as the Andes Mountains rose. But this is mere conjecture; the animals are real.

The Ecuadorians start stripping to swimsuits and preparing to dive with the dolphins. Our crew checks gear and loads tapes. The sun is satanically bright. The river is smooth, the birdsong symphonic, flocks of parrots chortle overhead – and our boat is hopelessly stuck in a raft of floating vegetation. We're marooned.

Immediately, Mónica and the boatmen and even the Ecuadorian father and sons leap into the muck. They yank twisted, mossy logs from the underside of the canoe, sweating and groaning with their effort, while the rest of us rock from side to side, nearly capsizing it – and Maurice's $100,000 camera – into the soapy slime.

Forty minutes later, we steam into Dolphin Lake. Someone spots a slight ripple on the surface, a hundred yards ahead.

"There they are!" I scream.

"That's a fish," Mónica explains.

When the canoe gets stuck for the eighth or ninth time, I suggest to Miss Darwin that it would make a fine scene for our film if she would kindly jump into the river along with the alligators, leeches, and the nice Ecuadorian family. She agrees and, clambering decisively over the rail – Sarah is not a small woman – plummets into the lukewarm *leche* of the Lagarto Cocha and immediately sinks to her armpits in quicksand.

"Now you've got to *deliver*," Maurice commands, and, nearly drowning, Miss Darwin gamely essays a "stand-up," informing the camera that the boat is stuck and that she can see, within arm's length, at least a hundred different species of spiders. Then the great-great-granddaughter of the most important man of the nineteenth century climbs back into the canoe, unbuttons her blouse, and announces, "I've got half the Amazon in my bra!"

But by this time, Maurice has stopped rolling.

When we finally see the dolphins, blowing and spouting, their shining flanks of silver arching from the stillness of this tiny lake, it is a wondrous, incongruous sight – leviathans in a fishpond.

The Ecuadorians splash into the water, and for a moment I am tempted to join them, blue jeans and all. But this is the Amazon, not Marineland, and, when the splashing starts, the dolphins vanish. For a few minutes, Maurice perches at the bow of the canoe, scanning for the beasts, but his meagre reward is a shot or two of distant ripples.

By now, it has become clear that we are not exactly collecting a feast of compelling televisuals. We have heard, but not seen, howler monkeys in the soaring jungle canopy, and we have walked for hours in the forest without ever managing to film a snarling jaguar pouncing on a luckless kinkajou. Our best image of a freshwater dolphin is on a poster Harry purchased at a souvenir stand. And Sarah Darwin is showing few signs of becoming the next Marlin Perkins or even Anthony Perkins. Unfortunately, as an on-camera performer, she reminds me of me.

"I feel like all of you are hovering over me all the time," she confides one maudlin evening.

"That's the whole idea," I reply.

After four days in the rainforest, we decide to abandon the lowlands and return to Quito. This will mean ten more hours in the motorcanoe, overnighting in a rough, raw oil town called Lago Agrio – Sour Lake – then a full day in a chartered bus, climbing the cordillera 10,000 feet to the capital.

Halfway up the Río Aguarico, fighting our way against the rushing current, we reach a settlement called Zábalo, home of the indigenous Cofán people and their blond American chief, Randy Borman. The son of missionaries, Chief Randy was born in Ecuador, speaks fluent Spanish and Cofánish, battles oil companies seeking to exploit his paradise, and conducts Christian worship services every Sunday in a basilica on stilts.

A radio message has been sent in advance of our vessel, but when we dock at Zábalo we are greeted only by a couple of elders in colourful tribal smocks, dozens of well-behaved children, and a bug-eyed, caterwauling monkey that leaps into Sarah's arms and begins discharging fleas.

"Quick, Maurice!" I command our cameraman. "Darwin and the Ape!"

I follow Mónica Amazónica to the Borman hacienda. There, after taking a few direct hits from the water pistol of the chief's son, Federico, I find the *yanqui* and inform him that we would like him to meet a direct descendant of the great Charles Darwin.

A few moments later, Miss Darwin and Chief Randy are

strolling through the village, past the soccer field and the school, when Harry comes dashing over – in his insulated vest and Gore-Tex socks – saying excitedly that he has heard a wonderful quote from Mr. Borman along the trail.

"He said he could see speciation going on all around him," Harry enthuses. "Did we get that on tape?"

"Did we get that on tape?" I ask Bill.

"Get *what* on tape?" Bill replies.

Just after noon on New Year's Eve, having struggled up the eastern slopes of the Andes in a full-sized bus piloted by a teamster who appears to be no more than 12 years old, the cast and crew of *Darwin Returns* pause for lunch in a town called Baeza. Six of us sit down to chicken, rice, and beer and two of us get food poisoning. Executive producer Harry wisely restricts himself to two bags of popcorn, but by the time we re-embark for Quito, he is stretched out across the genuine imitation red-leather seats of our luxury coach, holding his head and moaning.

He is missing a spectacular show. As we climb from the steaming forest toward the treeless, snowclad summits, we travel through an ever-changing stage set of foliage, rocks, and birds. Ethereal mists and the smoke of cooking fires mingle in the canyons, and, now, for the first time, we spy the gleaming vanilla cone of one of Ecuador's great volcanoes, Coyambe, three miles high.

A few minutes later, sliding into Quito, we pass a Pizza Hut, then a Burger King. The heroes of the Amazon have returned.

At nine o'clock on New Year's Eve, we bundle into a couple of taxis and head down to Avenida Amazonas to ring in 1996.

The boulevard – Quito's Broadway – is crammed with festive Quiteños, a few Teutonic tourists, and conga lines of serpentining drunks. On each block, dioramas have been erected, featuring life-size papier-mâché dummies of Ecuadorian politicians, to be set

aflame at midnight. In this way, the infamy of the old year is atom-
ized and the slate wiped clean for fresh scandals.

"How are you feeling?" I ask Sarah, who has been absent for a
few minutes, vomiting.

"Much better," the great-great-granddaughter of Charles Darwin
avows. "But I keep getting fondled in the crowd. Someone just
sneaked up from behind and pressed his hardness against me."

"Then it couldn't have been any of us," I tell her.

Suddenly we find ourselves on stage with a souped-up salsa
band. A fat little man is pounding a brace of conga drums, trumpets are blaring, and Sarah Darwin is doing the lambada with the
master of ceremonies.

"Well done!" I cry, rushing to praise her, but before I can reach
her through the madding crowd, she has gone off to be sick again.

"No doubt it is a high satisfaction to behold various countries and
the many races of mankind," Charles Darwin wrote when, finally,
he returned to England after five long years at sea, "but the pleasures gained at the time do not counter-balance the evils."

I'm coming back from a tough day of souvenir shopping when
Sarah Darwin stops me in the hotel lobby and says, "They're
taking Harry to the hospital. They're testing him for dysentery
and typhoid fever."

I hurry upstairs to tell the crew that our mighty captain has
fallen.

"Oh, God," says Maurice.

"He must be allergic to Gore-Tex," says Bill.

Five days out of the jungle, just before six in the morning, all
but Typhoid Harry are assembled at Quito airport to scatter and
say goodbye.

Our colleague, we are told, is going to pull through. He has
been intravenously rehydrated and already he has asked a travel

agency to get him a flight to the Galápagos Islands as soon as he is discharged. There, he will pursue stories on the ravages of introduced species in Darwin's desolate paradise.

Now I am standing in the doorway of the departure hall and an ocean of passengers is parting around me. I am thinking about the speedboat in the thunderstorm, the toucans in the trees, Coyambe in the setting sun. Maurice is here, with his camera, and Bill, with his sound gear, and Sarah, with her knapsack and hiking boots. We are weary and feeling a bit maudlin, as all travellers do when the adventure ends.

We snap a few photographs and promise solemnly to mail them to all concerned. Then Sarah and I move away from the others to share a final embrace.

"I'm sorry it didn't work out," I tell her. "It was such a wonderful idea."

"Come to England in the spring," she smiles. "I will take you to Darwin's house."

– Saturday Night

It Happens Every Winter

At 7:45 a siren screams behind first base and, as if startled from hiding, a full moon leaps out of the scoreboard, blowing hot air, tousling the palm trees. The baseball players, half-dressed, half-grown, slouch in careless circles on the crew-cut grass, tossing the ball around. The grandstand is filling. It is early January, the night before the Day of Kings.

The visiting team is called the Azucareros – the sugarmen – though it is, in fact, this game they play that keeps them out of the cane fields, for a time. Avoid Vice, the billboards warn, Say No to Drugs; and the message screen scrolls their names: Ramos, Rosario, Guzmán, Castillo, Jiménez, Hernández, Moreno, Meléndez, Manny Lee. A pink-faced pitcher, imported from another planet, sits alone in the dugout, counting the days toward home.

In a city of much history and little latter-day charm, on an island of sugarmen and dazzling beauty and, on the Haitian side, unmitigated grief, the lights come on and a siren wails again and the home team takes the field. These are the Escogido Lions – red-hatted, beefier, big leaguers in a small way – the icons of Santo Domingo on the island of Hispaniola in the Caribbean Sea. The peons in the bleachers rumble and root with concerted lunacy.

A few blocks away, outside the spike-tipped barricades of the presidential mansion on the Avenida Máximo Gómez, hundreds of women are encamped in voiceless supplication, awaiting the dawning of the Day of Kings. Then the aged, half-blind licentiate Dr. Joaquín Balaguer, obeying custom, will distribute small toys and trinkets to the children of the poorest of the city's poor, the blackest of the darkling races that scratch out a living in the Dominican Republic with a machete, or a baseball bat.

At the ballpark, on a stage set from 1953, the begging is only for base hits, for a ticket to the polished, perfect diamonds of the northern democracies. Bucking the air traffic of Dominican *peloteros* flying north to immense wealth or tragic disappointment, a soured fan jets south and finds that he has come all this distance only to arrive back home, in a boyhood reverie, at Ebbets Field in Brooklyn.

Last night, I was in Toronto, watching *Nature* on Channel 17, buried under a granny-square afghan. Now, suddenly, I am short-sleeved, air-dropped into a humid Third World coliseum, being stalked up and down the aisles of Quisqueya Stadium by a rabid peanut boy.

"*Maní, maní, maní,*" he wails. He is limping, stunted, tattered, silver-toothed, beaming. Cornered in the cheap seats, high above third base, I reach into my pocket and hand him all my high-school Spanish. His name is Julio. He is 16.

"*¿Juegas tú béisbol?*" I manage.

"Oh, yes," he sighs, in English, "second base."

Julio the peanut boy produces a sackful of white paper tubes with twisted ends that look like oversize joints. Each holds a couple of kernels of maní, a penny a tube.

"They scouted me," Julio expounds. "They said I'm not good enough yet. They said, 'Maybe next year.' They said, 'Go to school.' But I don't want to go to school. I want to play second base."

The arena is barely half-filled on a holiday eve in the latter stages of a winter's campaign. The adolescent militiamen in their grey soup-bowl helmets patrol the terraces; a man who has caught a foul ball during batting practice tries to sell it to me for a dollar. The big coastal resorts are crammed with tourists, but I seem to be the only alien in the stands.

I lope down the ramp, queasy from nostalgia – the green grass, the feeble lights, the wooden benches, the perfection of the setting for this antique game – to get some fried *pica pollo*, and a heavy-set man in a red T-shirt grabs me by the arm.

"Are you married?" he asks. He is standing in the doorway of the concessionaire's kitchen, bobbing this way and that to let the sausage vendors pass, brandishing a metal microphone the size of a Louisville Slugger. Two hours in the Dominican, and already I'm on the pregame show.

"Where do you come from? Did you fly here? How many sons you have?" he pleads. His eyes have the desperate glint of a man with airtime to fill and nothing to say.

"*Yo estoy* looking *por una* scorecard," I inform the nationwide audience. I visualize straw-hatted campesinos in thatched sugar shacks, barefoot women milking goats.

"How you like my country?" the drowning Tom Chico exasperates.

"Your country," I tell him, "is the best."

At Quisqueya Stadium on the night before the Day of Kings, the Lions and the Sugarmen go runless through six innings, at which point the home team pushes across half a dozen. I am getting up to leave when Julio runs over, leading by the hand a worn-looking woman who appears to be in her mid-20s, a beer and rum vendor whose take this night, she informs me, is about US$3. The name on her stadium identity tag is Esperanza.

"This is my sweetheart," Julio says. The woman doesn't understand his English. "Look at her eyes. Such beautiful eyes. Esperanza. That means 'hope.'"

At nine the next morning I pound on the door of Armando the alligator trainer, on the third floor of the old Hotel Hispaniola, where

Juan Perón lived out part of his exile as the guest of the dictator Trujillo, two reptiles of a different sort. Armando's Alligators are, in truth, the last-place Caimanes del Sur of the Dominican Winter League; they could play all summer, too, and never catch up. Armando is an Italian physiotherapist from Stoney Creek, Ontario.

The Alligators are scheduled to play today at Santiago in the fertile region known as the Cibao, a three-hour bus ride from their base at the Hotel Hispaniola. The Gators are, in an indirect sense, the lowliest link in the Toronto Blue Jays chain. Their roster is under the managership of Epy Guerrero, the Dominican scout who found Tony Fernández, Nelson Liriano, and many other Blue Jays wunderkinder on the rocky fields of Hispaniola. While I am pounding at Armando's door, Epy is on the telephone, informing his trainer that this is the Day of Kings and the match in Santiago is an afternoon game and no one has remembered to charter a bus.

The Alligator trainer begins a frantic roundup; the Caimanes, who are virtually bankrupt, do not want to be fined for forfeiture. (They draw few fans at their home park in the small nearby city of San Cristóbal, Trujillo's hometown.) The players already are afraid that their next paycheque may bounce like a Baltimore chop, though they make only about $100 a month while they essay their national *esperanza*.

The lobby begins to fill with thin-boned, yawning saurians: Corcino, Caraballo, Brito, Martínez, Vásquez, Olivares, Cabrera, de la Cruz. Armando the trainer slouches around, proffering pinches of whisky-soaked snuff from a puck-size tin. An outfielder accepts a dripping fingerful and stuffs it in his lip. "I've got two hits in 30 at bats," he says. "I might as well be drunk, too." The team mascot, an undersize imp, is sent across the street for *pica pollo*.

At 12:30 the bus arrives and we head north to Santiago, up the Avenida Máximo Gómez, past the slowly moving line of indigent women wending toward the presidential home, climbing, belching, honking, careering up the sierra until the sea is just a sparkle in the distance and the right-handed pitcher in the seat next to me nods into sleep. The countryside beyond the curtained

windows of the day cruiser is a verdant blur of banana plantations, cane fields, small towns and toothy mountains stretching
westward toward brutal Haiti.

"Knots of men and women, mostly coloured, and busy in
talk," the American journalist Samuel Hazard observed in 1872.
"Odd-looking stores, with still more odd-looking assortments
of goods, entirely open to the gaze of the passer-by . . . gaily-
coloured walls . . . broad-brimmed-hatted horsemen on small,
compact, quick-moving horses contrast with the dusky urchin
who, naked of everything but a shirt, bestrides an immense
straw-saddle on the back of a very diminutive donkey. . . ."

The donkeys remain, and the gaily coloured walls, and when
the Alligators pause for lunch at a highway cantina where the road
crests before descending to the Cibao, here are the dusky urchins,
three of them, the traditional merengue, scratching out a rhythm
for the rich men on the Day of Kings, naked of nearly everything.
When the music and the feasting cease, we board the bus again
and glide to a halt at the Santiago stadium at 20 minutes to game
time. "No problem," Armando says, gleaming.

The lack of batting practice doesn't bother the Gators; they can't
hit anyway. Their dressing room is a slat-floored shanty under the
stands; their opponents are the formidable Águilas (Eagles) of
the Cibao; their manager is tight-lipped, taut, wearing his game
face. He is a small man named Eddie Dennis, who handles one of
the Blue Jays minor-league clubs during the northern summer.
Fifteen years ago, Eddie Dennis, a carpenter's son from the town of
La Romana on the southern coast, was a professional infielder; in
the Dominican, these are as common as coffee trees.

"My father loved the game," Dennis says on the steps of the visitors' dugout. "We were quite poor, but he would not let me work
– only go to school and play baseball. He wanted it so badly."

Six rows behind the Caimanes bench, in a straw hat, his jacket
folded neatly in his arms, the old carpenter settles in for the ball
game. I hadn't even noticed him on the team bus; now, saying
nothing, the manager's father looks out at the green field and

the light towers and the gold plains of the Cibao. He comes to every game.

"I played eight years in the minor leagues," Eddie Dennis is saying. "Eight years, and I didn't make the majors. Okay, I accepted it. The Blue Jays gave me a chance to stay in the game. I'm very thankful now. But my father wanted it so badly. He has never said it – he never would say it. But I think I have broken his heart."

The Republic of Dominican Baseball, a substitute state of immense hope and intense devotion, was founded in the autumn of 1891 by two Cuban brothers named Alomá. With the aid of some American residents, the first teams were formed. On a half-island whose history presents a lamentable pageant of colonization, abandonment, massacre, invasion, liberation, and insurrection, the quadrangular principality of the four bases has managed to rise and prosper. There has never been a revolution during the baseball season, but the professional baseball season in the Dominican Republic only lasts about four months.

The dictator Trujillo liked the sport; before they shot him in 1961, he caused to be constructed the big Quisqueya Stadium and similar ballparks, now quaint, perfect visions of the true game before the domes and the plastic grass and the mouthy millionaires, in several other towns. While the tyrant ruled the realm beyond the outfield fences, the baseball republic came of age under grand dukes named Marichal, Cedeño, Carty, Alou, the first from the island to make it in the United States.

In the 1980s, the ministate exports all-stars named Bell and Fernández while the rest of the country sinks into the molasses of a feeble world price for sugar and the consequent collapse of the peso. Even the Republic of Baseball feels the pinch: last winter, the Caimanes hit bottom, the bank account of the Escogido Lions was frozen for a time for a lack of collateral, and even the mighty Licey Tigers, the other team based at Quisqueya, dipped some $20,000 into the red. The pro league contains six clubs. Each plays

60 games before a playoff determines the Dominican entry in the Caribbean World Series against Venezuela, Puerto Rico, and Mexico. It is all done in time for spring training.

Unemployment outside the ballparks is estimated as high as 30 per cent. "They did no work," a Spanish conquistador of the 15th century observed of the copper-skinned indigenes, "passing their lives in the greatest idleness. They danced a greater part of the day, and when they could do that no longer, they slept." Replace dancing with baseball and this is what you see on the sandlots of the Dominican Republic. But this is not idleness.

"You can see we are a subdeveloped country," says the manager of the Águilas of the Cibao, the former major-leaguer Winston Llenas, now a Blue Jay coach. "In the States, in Canada, if a kid doesn't make it in baseball or hockey, he's still got an education, he's still going to have a good life.

"But these kids here, three-quarters of them won't make it – I don't lie to them; I tell them; that's the facts. In this country, the hardest thing in the world to do is to tell a kid he's finished. Because here, he's *really* finished. He's back to zero."

Riding the wave from zero to zero, or from zero to everything, Dominican boys by the tens of thousands swat all day at balls of rags with broomsticks and barrel slats. When they fail, they sell peanuts in the grandstand or merely stand gaping at the gates as the fans file by.

The capital of the Republic of Dominican Baseball is the city of San Pedro de Macorís on the south coast, located about halfway between the opulence of the tourist resort at Casa de Campo and the queue of penniless mothers outside the presidential home in Santo Domingo. The region produces sugarcane and shortstops, just as Northern Ontario once was good for minerals and Mahovliches.

Behind the centre-field wall of Tetelo Vargas Stadium, the home of the Eastern Stars, is the home of Tony Fernández, the Blue Jays' devout and fragile nonpareil. The stucco house is substantial by the standards of its environs; other families dwell in shacks of boards and sheet metal clapped together at the base of the light towers of the ballpark of dreams.

A more bourgeois street, away from the stadium and the noise and the lights, boasts the capacious residence of George Bell. There is a Mercedes with Ontario plates in the driveway and, on the roof, a satellite dish huge enough to pull in broadcasts from the Venusian League.

Bell isn't playing on the winter circuit. The dusky urchins who perch on the outfield walls at Tetelo Vargas rub their fingers together and say that he wants "a million pesos for a month." Fernández has been recovering from an injury; most of the other big Dominican names have similarly absented themselves. In the evening paper, Matty Alou, the old Giants outfielder, is decrying this treason, but Matty Alou never made $940,000 from April to October.

At the San Pedro ballyard in place of the demigods, the ordinary Eastern Stars trot to their stations: Delgado, Sabino, Cuevas, Ramírez, Paulino, Bautista, Padilla, Carreón. I take a chair behind the third-base dugout and immediately am confronted by the King of the Coconuts.

The King of the Coconuts is a smirking little fellow named Reino Ismael Thomás. Like most of the very black Dominicans with English-sounding last names, he is a descendant of men brought in from other islands to work the big sugar plantations by the Americans, more than 60 years ago. The King wants to do some tricks. He punches the metal pipe holding up the backstop as hard as he can, bare-fisted, just for practice, and smiles.

Reino Ismael Thomás wasn't born of royal blood; he earned his title in a strong-man competition when he opened 50 coconuts in one hour . . . with his teeth. For this, he won 1,000 pesos – about $250 – and the right to inflict himself on the baseball fans of San Pedro de Macorís.

The King now takes a foot-long length of thread from his pocket, inserts one end in his nose, and inhales until all the string is sucked in. Then he takes three ordinary sewing needles, places them on his tongue and closes his mouth. Meanwhile, we all stand for the national anthem. A man comes by selling popcorn. The militiamen lean in and stare.

Reino Ismael Thomás sniffles and snorts, wiggles around, blows his nose without a handkerchief and out comes the foot-long length of string . . . with the three needles threaded on it! I grant him 20 cents and he bows and bounds away, in the Vatican of the Republic of Baseball.

In Santiago on the Day of Kings, the Alligators are shaded, 14-0, by the Águilas of the Cibao. At 7:45, in utter darkness save the naked fire of a roast-meat vendor in the stadium parking lot, they climb onto the bus again for the three-hour ride back to Santo Domingo. The manager, Eddie Dennis, sits by the door, his father, the old carpenter, beside him; they say nothing, beaten by two touchdowns in a baseball game. My slumbering right-hander of the outbound crossing had lasted two innings. One of the home runs they hit off him is still flying north over the cordillera toward Puerto Plata, where the tourists play.

The man next to me is a middle infielder named Julio Paula, 28, far too old for this game, far too young to abandon it. When he was 17, Epy Guerrero signed him for the infant Blue Jays. They mailed him to Medicine Hat, Alberta, without an overcoat or English. Julio Paula lasted three years in the Blue Jays system, was released, caught on with farm teams of the New York Mets, was released, played in Colombia, was released, hurt his ankle, tried a semipro league in Santo Domingo, begged a Detroit Tigers scout for one last chance and was signed to play in Toledo, class AAA.

"I don't do drugs," Julio Paula says in the darkness, the only voice on the bus. "I don't drink. Other players, they go to the casino and gamble until seven in the morning. I go home and have a good, nutritious dinner and get good sleep.

"I have a promise from God," he says. "God told me I'll make it.

You see, everybody is allowed one dream to come true in his life. And this is mine."

He is slim, well-muscled, the prototypical Dominican, lost in the middle of a pyramid that balances Tony Fernández at its crown and 100,000 dreaming Julios at its base. I ask him what he will do if he does not make it to the major leagues. He says, "But I will make it. I try so hard. I will never give up." I doze off until I am awakened by the halting of the bus. Julio Paula is getting off. His home is down an alley too dark for me to see.

"I will make it," he says. "God has promised. When I make it, come to me. I will shake your hand."

– Destinations

The Forgotten Species

·

GALÁPAGOS ISLANDS

The wild life of the Galápagos Islands doesn't get going until about 9:30 p.m., when they fire up the strobe lights and start spinning salsa at La Terraza, dockside on a distant sea. From a perch on the balcony, I can see the cruise ships lolling at anchor in Academy Bay, riding the heaving swells, some passengers feeling swell and others heaving. It's a lovely evening – the equatorial stars beaming, a warm wind flowing, tourists momentarily extinct. I order another Cerveza Pilsener. It seems a natural selection.

A few couples get up to dance, vibrating among the stucco trellises and palm-stump bar stools of the most popular night spot in Puerto Ayora, the largest town of the oddest archipelago in the Pacific. West of mainland Ecuador, east of a great ocean of emptiness, the Galápagos are a curiosity of evolution to scientists, a seafaring safari to rich foreigners, but to 12,000 Galapagueños, they are, simply, home sweet home.

"Another feature in these isles is their emphatic unhabitableness," Herman Melville wrote in 1856 of islands known then as the Enchanteds, but a century of emigrants and exiles has proved him erroneous. I like lizards well enough, but I'm no sailor. It's the people I came to see.

Attached firmly to solid ground, I am stationed at Hotel Galápagos, whose owner, a Californian named Jack Nelson, says that La Terraza is famed as the best place to pick up "white chicks" from Panama to Peru. This is not my aim – my wife, Linda, is along – but the nautical motif of the discotheque is a pleasing reminder that I can fly home from here without having to get on another boat.

The deejay plays "Speedy Gonzales." Linda leans over the railing, as she had done during much of the four-hour voyage from Isla San Cristóbal, across the cresting waves, and espies two locals dancing on the cargo bed of a pickup truck as the music carries across the only paved street in town. And that's about it. Jack Nelson had predicted brawling seamen and crashing rum bottles, but as the music ebbs and the small crowd scatters, it seems that another theory has been proved: as any zoologist will tell you, the wild life of the Galápagos Islands is the tamest on planet earth.

Next morning I am back in the harbourside plaza of Puerto Ayora, principal settlement of an island group most folks think of as not being settled at all. This particular volcanic remnant is Isla Santa Cruz, formerly known as Indefatigable, a cruel joke on the sun-sapped yanquis who are struggling under the broiling glare to get from their craft to the research station a mile yonder, where they can have their photo taken with a tortoise. This being Latin America, they are scrutinized by a recruit in full battle fatigues at the portal of the Ecuadorian Naval Detachment, who is cradling a large black gun.

It is hot as hell. The shops are shuttered; the seawater is bobbing blue; stray dogs are prowling. Two nuns in streaming habits walk purposefully churchward. A crippled launch, towed in from Isla Santa Fé, lies half-sunk in the waves. And music is playing.

It's the radio. Santa Cruz, an island of about 8,000 inhabitants (and ten times as many cows), has no television, no telephone link with the rest of the galaxy. Six flights a week arrive from Guayaquil on the distant mainland and one radio station provides home-grown entertainment, a smooth voice droning "the hits of yesterday, today . . . and forever."

The voice is Rosa Irene's. Of all the subspecies of the Galápagos, she is perhaps the most typical: the landlubbing Ecuadorian who came out once for a holiday and saw not reptiles, not sea lions, not blue-footed boobies, but a blank slate on which to try a new life.

I have climbed the stairs above the bus-ticket bureau to meet the voice on the air. She is behind the microphone and a glowing control panel, wiggling knobs, spinning platters. She is enormously pregnant, madly made up, beaming, eyes closed, living the music.

"I have come to meet the people of the Galápagos," I announce.

"Ah, yes," Rosa Irene sighs. "The forgotten species."

She tells me her story between 45s. She came from Los Ríos in 1979 for a two-week vacation. In a café she heard that Radio Santa Cruz was seeking announcers. She climbed the stairs above the bus-ticket bureau, passed her audition, decided to stay. She went home after three months to pack her things and say goodbye. Her parents wept. She left anyway.

"I fell in love," she says.

"With the Galápagos?" I ask her. "With a man?"

"No," she replies, tapping the mike. "With this."

Rosa Irene Sánchez Yovani is the biggest celebrity in the Galápagos. She has married the principal of the school, given him a Galapagueño son with another child on the way. She says, "We live at the pace of the tortoise, but it is paradise."

She used to sing. A few years ago, she made a record. Side A is "Bella Galápagos." Side B is "Peregrino" – the Pilgrim. She puts the record on and dedicates it to me.

"I don't play it every day," she says. "But, if people ask . . . 'Peregrino.' It's a song about people like me. They come here for a moment and never leave. 'Pilgrim, what do you want?'"

She tries to sing along, but she has had eight operations on her throat.

"People only think of the flora and fauna of these islands," she says. "They don't think of the people here who have made so many sacrifices."

"Why do you stay?"

"My home is here. My work is here. My husband is here."

"And your heart?"

"Here and there."

She flips on Dire Straits, reads a commercial for a seafood house, takes a request from a rancher for a love song, looks out on the sparkling sea. I ask for her autograph; she signs in a practised hand.

"Do you still like the animals?" I ask.

"Oh, yes," she replies. "Especially the little penguins. So far from home, so far from home. Like us. What are they doing here?"

I never saw any penguins in the Galápagos Islands. Boobies, yes – we sailed one day to Isla Española, where no man lives, and the rocks and tufts of straggling grass held whole curious colonies of wondrously unruffled birds. There were iguanas on the shore, crimson crabs, sea lions suckling, nuzzling pups so close I could count their toenails.

"The place is like a new creation; the birds and beasts do not get out of our way," the seventh Lord Byron (not the poet) wrote of the Galápagos in 1824, commanding HMS *Blonde*. There was still some of this. Flycatchers fluttered in our faces.

The penguins and famous flightless cormorants were on Isla Fernandina, a six-to-20-hour sail away. A Danish couple and some neo-hippies were going to charter a boat. We were lunching at Chifa Asia when they invited us along. We looked out at the bounding whitecaps – it was the "calm" season – and remembered my mother's favourite dictum: "Let's not and say we did."

I went in instead to talk to the cook who had made the chop suey. It was more in my line. The cook was a Korean named Choi. On the walls were moody photographs of Seoul. In 1980 Choi Yong-Do heard from a buddy in Buenos Aires that South America was heaven on earth. Choi was a factory hand. He said, "I thought everyone in Korea was a millionaire but me." He set out for Argentina but they denied him a visa. He was shunted off to Ecuador. Some heaven.

How did he get to the Galápagos Islands? He tried running a restaurant in Quito and teaching tae kwon do on the side. He was trying to make enough money to get back to Korea. After four years, he nearly had it. Four guys with pistols stuck him up, took 600,000 sucres in cash (why was he carrying it?) and a silver watch.

Choi tried again in the Ecuadorian Amazon, gave up, saw an ad, bought the Chifa Asia. Last year, he almost had enough saved to go home when he was robbed again, cleaned out, right here in Puerto Ayora in Byron's "new creation," across the street from the Naval Detachment, one flight below La Terraza.

His son and daughter wait tables, losing their language. He has lived eight years without kimchi, the Korean staple, searingly spicy coleslaw. When I mentioned kimchi, it was the only time Choi Yong-Do smiled.

"I am the only Oriental in the Galápagos," Choi said. "People here are very poorly educated. They don't like us. They don't understand."

He said he was hoping to have enough sucres to get home within six months. A relative had put money down on an apartment at the Olympic Village in Seoul. He was afraid of being robbed again.

Most visitors to the Galápagos Islands fly into San Cristóbal or Isla Baltra, just off Santa Cruz. They are loaded into a cattle truck, rumble a couple of miles to port, and get on a nice boat. They then cruise around for a week or so, visit islands, eat and sleep on board, walk the lava trails to the iguanas' indifferent stares, and visit Puerto Ayora for half a day to buy T-shirts and see the tortoise reserve.

The giant tortoise was once so abundant, fleets of whalers lived for years on its flesh. It was said to be the most delicious animal in the world. There were hundreds of thousands of them. In 1813 the USS *Essex* put ashore four goats on Isla Santiago. Now there are more than 100,000 goats; also dogs, cats, rats, pigs, horses.

Non-native animals annihilated the endemic fauna. They ate tortoise eggs and hatchlings. Settlers brought in more than 200 new species of plants; blackberry vines, lantana, cinchona, guava. In 1923 an expedition of the New York Zoological Society found exactly one tortoise living in the wild. They captured it – not a difficult feat – took it aboard their vessel, tied a rope to it, threw it into the ocean to see if it could swim. It could. Seven days later, it died. Salt inhalation.

One of the members of that New York team, William Beebe, wrote a book – *Galápagos: World's End*. Although Beebe said that Indefatigable "made Purgatory look like the Elysian Fields," the work made a strange impact in Norway, of all places. It inspired a group of Norwegians to migrate to Santa Cruz, and there they cleared ranches and farms and they were still represented until 1983, when the last of the originals, a man named Alf, electrocuted himself while untangling some fallen wires.

Foreigners had been arriving since long before. On San Cristóbal, Beebe met a certain "Johnson, of London," who had been in the Galápagos for half a century. Johnson, of London, described himself as a peregrino, but, Beebe wrote, "anyone who has stayed anywhere, especially the Galápagos, for 50 years can hardly be said to be consumed with wanderlust."

A few years after the Norwegians arrived, a German family named Angermeyer packed up for Puerto Ayora and founded a small settlement now known as the Colonia Alemán. Karl Angermeyer, the patriarch, lives in a fine house above the harbour with a corrugated metal roof on which sprawl dozens, if not hundreds, of marine iguanas, which he feeds from a doggie dish.

Just up the beach is Hotel Delfín, owned and operated by Erna Sievers, whose original home is Schleswig-Holstein. In 1957, Erna Sievers's daughter and her husband, a dentist in Hamburg, saw a photo essay on the Galápagos and decided, just like that, to

move there. This dream ended in a thicket of Ecuadorian paperwork, but in 1962, when Karl Angermeyer made a speaking tour of
Germany and extolled his volcanic valhalla, they decided to try
again and succeeded in obtaining a visa.

This had them on a banana boat sailing for Jacksonville,
Florida, when they were swept into the Bermuda Triangle by a
raging hurricane. Erna Sievers smiles at me and says, "I remember
I was saying to the others, 'So this is the end of our life?'"

It wasn't. She receives me on the patio of the hotel that over-
looks the foaming inlet that leads to Puerto Ayora. Today, the
Colonia Alemán is not entirely German: the de Roys, from
Brussels, have been here for decades, and there are a few Swiss,
although one Swiss woman shot herself not long ago when her
Ecuadorian husband left her and went back to the mainland.

"What were we running away from?" Erna asks the sky. She is
in her 70s, widowed three years ago, still blue-eyed. "Well, it wasn't
really my idea to come, but I am happy here now. I will never go
back to stay in Germany. When my husband died, my friends
said, 'Now you will come home.' And I said, 'Why? To sit alone in
an apartment?' I will never go back."

She remembers when her husband would set off for the hills to
shoot goats, when they lived in a leaking shack, when the supply
boat came four times a year and those who got no letters from home
sat on the lava and wept. She says, "They call this the German
Colony, but we are not guests here. This is our home."

Fewer than a hundred Europeans live on Santa Cruz. On San
Cristóbal, where a man named Cobos ruthlessly ran a sugar plan-
tation with convict labour until his employees shot him (in 1904),
the 3,000 inhabitants are mostly Ecuadorian seafarers, shopkeepers, ranch hands and bureaucrats.

A small settlement lingers on Isla Isabela, the largest by far, home
to 200,000 head of cattle. On Isla Floreana, four foreigners, including the (self-anointed) Baroness Eloisa Bosquet von Wagner,

mysteriously disappeared in the 1930s. A few hundred souls persist today, among them a woman named Wittmer, now in her 90s, whose role in the disappearances has always been rather unclear.

On the other nine principal islands and the dozens of scattered rocks and shoals live naught but birds and beasts. "Like dross, worthless, because it has not the power of raising a little grass," wrote the first European to see the islands, Tomás de Berlanga, bishop of Panama, to the king of Spain in 1535. But the Galápagos are far from worthless. Although tourism is restricted, the islands lure about 25,000 foreign tourists annually to a laboratory of nature's creation and man's destruction.

Even a traveller who blanches at the sight of a ship in a bottle can fly to Santa Cruz and see this. On the rocks at Puerto Ayora are specifically adapted marine iguanas and, all around them, empty bottles of 7UP.

"To the conservationists, it's disaster, but from the people's point of view, it's jobs and food," a Galapagueño tells me. He is José Luís Gallardo; we're on his farm in the Santa Cruz highlands. Gallardo came out from mainland Ecuador 30 years ago, married Jack Nelson's sister, lived in Los Angeles for five years, and came back.

He shows me his Simmental herd, his Brahman bulls, his tomato plants, his lemons large as softballs. Ten miles up the dirt road from the *puerto*, halfway up the hillside of the dead volcano that once spawned Indefatigable, we are feeding the chickens left-over salads from Hotel Galápagos.

Gallardo says, "Some people want to throw all the settlers out, leave the islands to the animals. But it's too late. Even if we left and let things go wild, it wouldn't be the original Galápagos. It's too late. Why should they blame us? Why didn't the scientists come sooner?"

"They did," I tell him. "They threw tortoises in the ocean to see if they could swim."

José Luís Gallardo has 325 acres on Santa Cruz and two sons at college in the United States. He is a small man, thick-chested, waving a machete, shirtless, loping through the elephant grass brought in by the Norwegian who first cleared away the endemic flora. The soil is a russet powder. It hasn't rained in three months.

Someone once sensed here the key to evolution, but today we're witnessing the result of species, not their origin. Something is killing off Gallardo's papaya trees; rats are munching on his onions. "Other farmers are not educated," Gallardo says. "They plant anything. The wind scatters the seeds."

Far below, I can see the Pacific, the town of Puerto Ayora, the tower of Radio Santa Cruz. "Man and wolf alike disown them," Melville may have hissed, but these islands were already man's, even in Herman's time. And man's they will stay, a province of impoverished Ecuador, a port of call for penguinists from the First World, a job site for cowhands from the Third.

"You didn't expect this, did you?" Gallardo asks, puncturing the silence of the shade.

We are stopped for a minute in a copse on a mountainside in the Enchanteds. The trees soar over us. Mahogany, planted by the Norwegian.

"No," I tell him. "I didn't."

"These are my trees," the Galapagueño says. "God, I love this place."

– Destinations

AFRICA

Previous page: Kalahari Bushmen (Agata Motyczyńska)

There was a time when I divided all travellers into two camps: those who had been to Timbuktu, and those (like me) who hadn't.

The city seemed so mystical, so inaccessible, that anyone who returned, alive and with snapshots, wore a mantle of heroism that never would fade. Even after I had reported from Dum Dum, India, and the village of Map on the Pacific island of Yap, Timbuktu held its mythic sway in my mind.

A documentary crew from CBC's The Journal *had been there in the early 1980s, the nonpareil correspondent Ann Medina walking dolefully through the spreading sands to the banks of the dying Niger. As ever, I was jealous of her skills, but it was her dateline that made me weep.*

Then, in 1999, I was sent to cover a presidential election in Nigeria, and I knew that my chance had come. That work completed, I bought a ticket from Lagos to Abidjan to Ouagadougou and on to Bamako. But these teeming African capitals were only roadhouses along the way.

Then, the day before departure for Timbuktu, I began to cough up red-flecked phlegm – the first time I had ever been ill while on foreign assignment. "Le sang a toujours sa raison," said the Malian doctor – there is always a reason for blood. And he sent me for a chest X-ray to a clinic on a street of stray dogs and mud.

I flew anyway, and never told my mother about the sickness. Now, I divide all travellers into two camps: those who have been to Timbuktu, and those who haven't.

Timbuktu

———————— • ————————

MALI

In Africa (a quarter of the world),
Men's skins are black, their hair is crisp and curled;
And somewhere there, unknown to public view,
A mighty city lies, called Timbuctoo.
                          – William Makepeace Thackeray, 1829

The journey to the sand castles of a wanderer's soul commences at 5 a.m. Outside the Hôtel de l'Amitié, a towering relic of the Kremlin's mad dreams of a Soviet Africa, the city of Bamako, capital of the Republic of Mali, barely stirs. There are a few bush taxis huffing on the Martyrs' Bridge across the doleful Niger, and yesterday's beggars – fewer here than in Toronto – lie swaddled in Patrice Lumumba Square. The moon is up, and Mars is with her, but I do not know these stars.

At the stale airport, groggy, a melee. Squadrons of fat Americans; Korean businessmen; Dogon and Bambara duchesses in sweeping robes; silky French snobs. A formless crush at the counter; then, paperwork, passports, more queuing, departure taxes – all the sapping nuisances, excused in exultation of the goal.

Giddy, I leave the desk. My red Air Mali boarding card, hand-lettered, reads: Tombouctou.

Up a spiral staircase, then, to a lounge where passengers and carved and woven handicrafts, equally immobile, garner dust. A barman brings tea and sugar, fries eggs, swats flies. The Malian tricolour – green, yellow, red – slumps from a pole outside, dreading the coming day. There is no search of baggage or of person. Twittering swifts flee the eaves at the first sight of dawn.

Precisely at seven, with the sun already boring its way through the helpless atmosphere, a small twin-jet screams to a stop in front of the terminal. The plane has been whitewashed except for an eagle rampant on the fin with the world in its talons. I envision Leonid Brezhnev alighting, or Chairman Mao, ill-suited to the heat, greeting the grinning murderers of the National Liberation Front. But Mali is today the world's poorest democracy and neither commissars nor tourists get off, or on – this is not the ship for Timbuktu.

Instead, a prehistoric Antonov-24 with two propellers, oval portholes, and rectangular tires heaves to. Four pink Russians climb down through the cargo hatch and begin walloping away at the understructure with hand tools. This is Air Mali's "big plane," a 50-seat Aeroflot orphan, the weekly camel's-milk run bound for Mopti, Goundam, and, should the rivets hold and Allah will, for the fabled oasis where, George Chapman wrote in 1600,

Deep in the lion-haunted inland lies
A mystic city, goal of high emprise.

From the air, I spy no lions. (There are elephants and hippos here, but hiding.) The flight path follows the petering Niger, rainless these four months, past settlements of sand, then trackless scrub, then goats and cattle white against the dun. At Mopti – a substantial town – we disembark to be besieged by Marlboro and shoeshine boys and dagger-sellers, while the Russians whap and pound the plane once more. At Goundam, the same: on the unpaved runway, we squat in the shade of the Antonov's wing and gulp at the gritty sky.

That somewhere in the void of Africa stood a citadel of scholarship and gold, Europe dreamed for centuries. And it was true.

A Moor baptized by a Renaissance pope as "Leo Africanus" crossed the Sahara in 1512 and saw it with his widened eyes. "Instead of coined money, pure gold nuggets are used," he reported to the Vicar of Christ. "The king has a rich treasure of coins and gold ingots. One of these ingots weighs 970 pounds [436 kilograms].

"There are in Timbuktu numerous judges, teachers, and priests, all properly appointed by the king. He greatly honours learning. Many handwritten books imported from Barbary are also sold. There is more profit made from this commerce than from all other merchandise."

"Timbuctoo [sic] held African commerce in her fist," a later voyager would write. "She was at the crossroads where Saharan trade from Morocco and the salt mines of the desert met and exchanged with the exotic goods of Negroland. . . . No city had saints more ascetic, nor women more lovely. . . ."

Yet no pink-skinned man had ever gained its baked-mud portals, and Jonathan Swift could fairly mock Europe's poverty of knowledge:

> Geographers, on Afric maps
> With savage drawings fill their gaps
> And o'er unhabitable downs
> Draw elephants for want of towns.

For 300 years, the Islamic El Dorado kept the Christian world at bay. In 1824, the Geographical Society of Paris offered a prize of 10,000 francs to any man who could gain the gates of gilded Timbuktu. The bursary was superfluous; the quest itself was enough to fire the blood. In 1826, a Scot named Gordon Laing succeeded, by going southward from Tripoli. Coyly, the sultan humoured the heathen. As he left the city, his servants slit his throat.

In 1828, a Frenchman named René Caillié, masquerading as a Muslim, passed several weeks in Timbuktu, and lived to return home and tell what he had seen. The "mystic city," he despaired, was a hovel, a pile, a hole.

"I looked around," Caillié wrote of his arrival, 3,000 miles on foot from the slaving ports of the Guinea coast, "and found that the sight before me did not answer my expectations. I had formed a totally different idea of the grandeur and wealth of Timbuktu. . . .

"The city presented, at first view, nothing but a mass of ill-looking houses built of earth. Nothing was seen in all directions but immense plains of quicksand of a yellowish-white colour. The sky was pale red as far as the horizon; all nature wore a dreary aspect, and the most profound silence prevailed . . . Timbuktu and its environs present the most monotonous and barren scene I ever beheld."

For all his heroism, Caillié did not understand – that Timbuktu is not an earthly city, but the letterhead for all our lost horizons. He had come 300 years too late, or a century too early.

Our prehistoric, twin-prop Antonov-24 has touched down at the Timbuktu landing strip – the sand is ankle-deep on the tarmac – and sleek Land Cruisers are swallowing our luggage. The Russians are wrapping tarpaulins over the engine cowlings. Like us, the Antonov-24 will sleep tonight at world's end.

"Call me Halice," a young man says, and he hands me a business card that reads Guide Saharien. His brethren sit on sheets outside the terminal and hold up necklaces and leather sandals with "Tombouctou" across the toes. Our hosts are Tuareg, the dashing, Caucasian, nomadic "blue men of the desert," robed, turbaned, veiled, and reduced – after centuries of raids and depredations – to the obsequious indignities of the tourist trade.

We motor into the town on a paved highway, passing the tidy compounds of United Nations agencies and European charities. Beggared by decades of drought and Marxism, Mali has a foreign debt of $2.8 billion (all figures U.S.), a per capita gross domestic product of $600, and an average life expectancy of 47. Stragglers and donkey carts are honked aside. Then, the mystic city gained, the pavement ends in a littered sandbox, all are put out into the sun-blast, and this is Timbuktu.

A boy comes running up and begins chattering to me in Chinese, then Japanese, then Italian. Now there are a dozen youths, flies in their ears, mouths, noses. No one smiles or laughs – it is all just business – there is no joy in Mudville.

Halice conducts me, shoeless, into the mud fantasia of the mediaeval Djinguereber Mosque, points out the oven-like tombs of two especial saints, then stands glum and impatient while I eagerly climb a stucco turret, look out over the rooftops, climb back down. At the entrance, a boy who has been guarding my shoes laces them for me and groans at my paltry tip.

There is little else to see. ("In a word, everything had a dull appearance," reported the crestfallen Caillié. This hasn't changed.) Women are pounding millet in stone mortars. Goats are gnawing gainfully on trash. A few of the two-storey houses bear plaques in memory of European men of high emprise: Laing, Caillié, the 19th-century ethnologist Heinrich Barth.

"In contrast to the conventional wisdom of his time," reads a panel in the home where the German scholar passed part of 1853, "Barth believed that Africa did indeed have a history." But history would soon conclude; by 1893, mighty Timbuktu had been subjugated into the French Soudan, its toy forts reduced to humus by cannon fire and sappers from Senegal.

A century later, an outpost of sovereign, multi-ethnic Mali since 1960, Timbuktu is a town of 15,000 Bambara, Fulani, Songhai, Dogon, Berber, and other groups, settling into an indolent peace following the conclusion – or at least the suspension – of the most recent Tuareg war of independence. (Hundreds of innocents were slaughtered in this region before an armistice was signed in 1995.)

To the north are the massacres of Algeria, and farther afield the ceaseless agonies of the two Congos, Sierra Leone, Rwanda. By comparison, Mali – West Africa's largest state in area, but only 2 per cent arable – is stable and serene.

"A city like this in the middle of the desert with all the peoples living together," Halice the Tuareg says through the folds of his tunic, "*il n'y a pas partout. Pas partout.*"

In the courtyard of the Azalaï (Caravan) Hotel where we are quartered, there are a few dusty trees, and in those trees a chorale of wine-chested finches is singing for all they're worth.

I wander around the town for a while, find a pharmacy stocked with Parisian remedies, buy some syrup for my sand-stormed lungs. I note that, in a Timbuktu grocery in 1999, it is possible to purchase Moroccan couscous, soap from the United Arab Emirates, Nestlé powdered milk, sacks of mint candies from China, tins of butter, bubblegum, and Crown brand mayonnaise manufactured in Metairie, Louisiana. There are a few satellite dishes, but nobody I see on the street is wearing Tommy or Gap. Everyone is in flip-flops, or barefoot. Coughing is the national sport.

"In the city is too much," Halice offers, when I ask his opinion of the metropolis. He is a country boy from the deep wells of Araouane. "Pearl of the Sahara," seven days' trek due north from the ends of the Earth. "In the city, you must have a good car, good watch. In the desert, you only need a good camel."

"What about a good wife?" I ask, trying to get a rise.

"The camel is more important," he replies. "A wife is the last ambition."

"Why do you stay here?" I wonder. (If it were up to me, as Marvin Gaye might say, I wouldn't be Dogon – I'd be long gone.)

"I want to return to my village," the nomad sighs, from somewhere deep within his cloak. "I wish only to go home."

Now we are to saddle up ol' *Camelus dromedarius* and lope off into the Sahara to watch the Tuareg women dance.

This is timed for late afternoon, in a pleasant breeze, as the sun starts to set behind the thorn bushes, which are festooned with every plastic bag that has ever been thrown away in the history of Africa. We slog to the field where the bleating creatures are tethered; dozens of men and boys tug at our arms, cajoling us with "Please, mon patron, I have very good camel." And no doubt they do.

My mount, a vanilla female, conveys me for 30 minutes without mishap to the dancing ground, which is the summit of a virgin dune as soft as icing sugar, rippled and pure. Beneath us, to the west is a collection of Tuareg huts and tents, surrounded by middens of trash, and to the east is the Timbuktu skyline, René Caillié's "mass of ill-looking houses," with TV antennas poking through.

The women are in a semi-circle, clapping their hands and chanting. Hooded and loosely veiled, all are wrapped in indigo, save one rebel in key-lime green. No walls imprison their wailing. Behind them, the sons of Timbuktu spread their simple wares for sale on the sand.

– National Post

Election Day in Ijebuland

NIGERIA

"Would you like to go down to Waterside?" asked the Roman Catholic priest.

Democracy was stirring anew in the Giant of Africa after 15 years of military manhandling, and Rev. Father John Patrick Ngoyi had not slept all night. Now it was Saturday morning in the district known as Ijebuland. The priest's parishioners would be going to the polls at midday and one of his principal benefactors – the Canadian taxpayer – had come to audit the proceedings.

There had been little on the 95-kilometre drive from Lagos to indicate a stirring of electoral passions. Senators and representatives were to be chosen across the 36 states. There were to be 111,430 separate voting stations, none of them computerized. Next week, they would have to do this all over again, to choose a president.

To forestall the hijacking of ballots, all road and air traffic had been banned for the day. (Racing to beat the 6 a.m. deadline, a truck overturned on a northern highway. *The Sunday Vanguard* reported 15 people killed in a single vehicle.) Only diplomats and journalists were permitted to travel. Boys kicked soccer balls in the empty roads. Women laid their washing out to dry on the tarmac. Lagos enjoyed a lull in its lunatic din.

Out along the coastal flats, halfway to Ijebuland, the road forked at a place called Epe, like the sword. In a bare, sandy compound, away from the town, there was a row of derelict concrete dwellings. Three thousand people were living here in unmodified desperation. They were Ilaje people, refugees from a little-noticed Nigerian civil war.

A man named Olesegun, a fisherman from Ondo state, came forward from the press of boys and teens and nursing mothers. The Ilaje had been set upon by a rival ethnic group, the Ijaw, he claimed. (I suspected the Ijaw would have their own version of events. It is they who have been warring with the mighty oil companies down in the Niger Delta, fighting for a fraction of the oozing wealth.)

Olesegun borrowed my notebook and began to write down the names of the villages from which the Ilaje had fled. Ubale, Odunugo, Odofada, Ekeporo, Jinrinino, Oretan . . . I stopped him at number 18 of 85.

"All our houses were bombed down," he said. "There is no place for us to go. Everyone came here on three or four big vessels. First when we came here, good Samaritans gave us food. Lagos state government gave us food. Now, no cash, no food."

The Ilaje's right to vote had not been abrogated, despite their displacement. An empty schoolhouse was being used for the poll. A green box with glass sides like a small aquarium was in place to hold the ballots. (No one could allege that it had been illicitly stuffed.) A dozen people were waiting patiently to have their thumbs marked with indelible ink manufactured in India by Mysore Paints & Varnish Co. Ltd.

I wandered through the empty classrooms while they voted.

"Where are you staying?" Olesegun asked me when I came out. He meant, "Where do you live?"

"In Canada," I replied.

"I was born in Canada in 1951," said the fisherman.

"Where?" I asked.

"I do not recall," he said grimly.

East of Epe a small, white monument stood in silence in a rough-hewn lay-by, an artifact – like representative democracy – of Britain's African dreams.

Two rusted cannons were still attached to the top of the stela, and bas-reliefs of big negro warriors brandishing bows and arrows had been left untouched. The original plaques on either side had been torn off and replaced by newer ones, dedicated in 1992 by one of Nigeria's thousands of parochial noblemen, His Royal Highness the Awujale of Ijebuland. They read, in part:

"This war was fought by the gallant people of Ijebu against the British colonial army. . . . It was a war which having been won by the British paved the way for the establishment of the Southern Protectorate of Nigeria."

In 1914, the plaque explained, all Nigeria was united by British whim into a single colony, overriding the linguistic, cultural, and religious chasms that divided Yoruba from Hausa, Christian from Muslim, East from North, Ijaw from Ilaje. Thirty years ago, these enmities led to the secession, slaughter, and starvation of the Biafran war. Now they were to be militated, in theory, by the little slips of inked paper in the green fish tanks.

Father John Patrick was dedicated to seeing this happen. He was in his office in Ijebu-Ode, a market town stifled for the afternoon by the election-day travel ban. He had sent his people all across the district to watch over the balloting in the name of his Justice, Development & Peace Commission. Canada had given him $250,000 toward that goal and had spent more than $1 million on other electoral projects, including the publication of a handbook that was to be distributed to all 111,430 polling booths.

Waterside, the priest said, would be worth a visit. The village was another hour's drive away, at the head of the lagoon that led to the Gulf of Guinea. The deserted highway, smooth as syrup, cut a straight slice through the palms.

At a town called Oni, they were voting on the verandah of what might once have been a handsome two-storey home or school. Now, like nearly every other substantial edifice in Ijebuland, it was a mouldering shell. Upstairs, a zealot had chalked on the wall, "God is above and also God is merciful."

At the north end of the house, a rectangle of bricks marked out what might have been the garden. Some older men, having voted, were idling there.

"This is a rich man's house," one of them said.

"Where is the rich man?" I asked.

"You are standing on his grave," they replied.

At Waterside, the road to democracy ended in a cul-de-sac where fishermen hauled their nets ashore and a motor launch of the Nigerian Marine Police Force lay beached and bleaching, unlikely to be of use in the event of invasion from Togo or Cameroon.

A soft, sandy path led along the shoreline to a collection of slate-and-metal houses. Men were tying small chunks of dried white cassava into their nets as bait. Women were sitting under the heavily laden mango trees, weaving on ancient looms.

In the shade of a large, roofed shed, two men were applying layers of pitch to the hull of a wooden pirogue and children were coming up with trays of kola nuts and fried plantain. This, too, was a polling place and the tabulation was available for anyone to see: 750 voters registered; 128 voted; and this was about the average nationwide.

A little inland, at another voting table, a man named Chief Moses Odufeso was overseeing the affair. (His title identified him as the head of an extended household or clan, subordinate to a local oba, prince, or king. And there were five obas in Waterside alone.)

Chief Moses said, "We want the military to go. Let's have a change of hand to restructure our country."

At 57, he could remember British times.

"It was nice then," he said, and he sang "God Save the Queen."

It was Chief Moses and the men at Waterside who mentioned the paper mill.

"The biggest in the world," they said. "Only in Canada is bigger." They said it was "over there, six kilometres," and pointed to the jungle. They made it sound like El Dorado. Which, in a way, it was.

Exactly six kilometres down the road, a white gate and a block-house ratified the mystery. Beyond rose one of the most gargantuan industrial enterprises I had ever seen, useless and inert. Giant boilers and pipelines, conveyors and coolers – an Erector set on a galactic scale, covering perhaps a square mile – an impossible (and obviously failed) experiment in megalomania for such a place.

But men were walking down the path, and beyond them were neat rows of decaying company flats, and sitting in a car outside one of them was a white man.

In Ijebuland, this was rare as freezing rain.

"Where are you from?" I asked him, astonished. From the waterside town of St. Ives in Cornwall, England, he said, and as we walked in the tropical sun, he began to recite:

As I was going to St. Ives
I met a man with seven wives.
Each wife carried seven sacks.
Each sack carried seven cats.
Each cat carried seven kits.
Kits, cats, sacks, wives
How many were going to St. Ives?

"Only one," I answered. And there was only one John Page at Waterside, an engineer hired to refit for service (almost single-handedly) the largest pulp and paper mill in Africa. Several of his workers, in coveralls and construction helmets, were hammering away in the equipment yard. The megalith was not abandoned, after all. It just didn't make any paper.

Mr. Page had been 20 years in Nigeria and he was married now to a Hausa woman from the north. He went into his office and showed me some of the original engineering plans from the plant's inception, more than 20 years ago: Piping from Flexonics of Brampton, Ontario, welding specifications from Stearns-Roger of Edmonton. Who built this place? He had no idea.

"My job here is to help these people learn to do it the European way, the British way, and not the Nigerian way, which is fatal," he said. "The biggest problem I find in Nigeria is that the word 'maintenance' is missing from the culture."

"How long will you stay here?" I asked the Cornishman.

"Probably until I die," he replied.

On the highway back to Ijebu-Ode, I thought I saw a bundle of clothing in the roadway, but it was not a package, it was a human corpse.

The driver did not even slow down.

Back at Father John Patrick's office, the priest passed around bottles of Fanta. He was waiting for calls and faxes from the voting sites. He said, "Not a single issue was ever raised. I did not see one single person campaigning. I never saw one. But let us not throw the baby out with the bath water. For now, the basic thing is that there was an election."

I mentioned the body I had seen on the highway from Waterside.

"Human sacrifice," he said. "They take some of the parts for eating and throw the rest on the road.

"We are talking to the rulers about this," he went on. "We are trying to get them to stop this, and the burying of wives when the husband dies. The only way out is poverty reduction. If people do not value their own lives, how will they value some other person's?"

– National Post

The Lost Words of the Kalahari

SOUTH AFRICA

*Perhaps this life of ours, which begins as a quest of the child for
the man, and ends as a journey by the man to rediscover the child,
needs a clear image of some child-man, like the Bushman,
wherein the two are firmly and lovingly joined in order that our
confused hearts may stay at the centre of their brief rounds of
departure and return.*

         – Laurens van der Post, *The Lost World of the Kalahari*

They are murdering a donkey for his meat as we arrive. The
roar of our pickup on the corrugated road drowns out the final
cries, so that when we get out and walk toward the place of execution – it is in the grudging shade of a camelthorn tree, where some
of the slayers are encamped – the beast is already lying dead in a
lake of claret in the sand.

There is no wind and the sun is without mercy, but evening
soon will come to bank the furnace of the veldt. Around us,
beneath us, containing us, is a landscape whose name whispers its
isolation. Kalahari.

As the daylight fades, a few men and a small boy surround the carcass, bickering. Two of the men are drunk and lurching. One of them reaches deep into the animal and smears himself with blood in gruesome finger-streaks. The others go about dressing the flesh, ripping off the hide, hauling out the intestines, severing the forelimbs at the knee.

Dogs tear at the discards. Someone hoists the liver aloft as if it were the World Cup. The lad jabs a knife into the bulbous offal and spatters us with half-digested mulch.

A dowager in a pink headscarf with sunken cheekbones rises from the shadows and begins to chant and clap over the meat. Hearing this, a much younger woman, who has been making beads from fragments of ostrich eggs, gets up to join her. But the matriarch has lost the words, and the sight of a gutted jackass does little to fire her passion. The singing fades and the women stand mutely for a moment, then wander away.

Dancing with extinction, reduced to a sad pantomime of The Hunt, these are the remnants of one of the world's most skilled and specialized peoples, the last Bushmen of the Republic of South Africa. As the Southern Cross glitters and May's new moon grins, they carve their kill and carry off the bounty to mud and metal shacks across the road, travelling a landscape that was theirs alone for 20,000 years.

Of South Africa's many cruelties, the Bushmen were spared none. Hunted from horseback by white and non-white intruders, bound into slavery, cast in plaster for museums, and set up in straw hovels at fairs and shopping malls, they were classified as marginally human – van der Post's "child-men" – by a state obsessed with complexion and caste. Today, the country advertises itself as a reborn Rainbow Nation, but the Bushmen suffer still. The gods, they say, are not crazy – but they, like the mortals they watch over, are bitter, and bent with shame.

One small group of Bushmen – or "San," as they are called by outsiders who judge the more graphic name demeaning – has been on exhibit for the past decade at a private game park in the treeless Cederberg Mountains, a four-hour drive from the Cape Town waterfront. Another band, evicted from their immemorial homeland a generation ago to cleanse the Kalahari for a national park, clings to charity and craft-making in a desert shantytown.

The members of these groups rotate every few months, exchanging the marginally better economic prospects of the cold, rocky highlands for the red, red dirt of home and a shack and a slab of fresh-killed goat or donkey. In 1994, two Bushmen – a pregnant woman and a fourteen-year-old boy – were killed when their overloaded four-by-four flipped on a gravel highway during one of the transfers. An elderly man renowned as a diviner suffered irreparable brain damage.

With apartheid dead in theory and a few white liberals warming to their cause, the Bushmen had been pressing a legal claim for a patch of Kalahari thirstland with limited success until last November, when an exuberant young activist and linguist from Montreal discovered what was hailed as a "lost tribe" of click-talking Kalahari San. The tribe was not really lost, of course. It was the world that had gone deaf.

In the clucks and chatter of one impossibly ancient woman named Elsie Vaalbooi, Nigel Crawhall glimpsed proof that the phylogeny of the hunter-gatherer – the link with Australopithecus, the very atom of our humanity – still flickered, however feebly, in today's South Africa. It was a jolting and poignant addition to one of our era's most troubling equations: the debt owed by "modern" people to the "primitives" who, against our engines of progress, somehow endure.

The prevailing academic consensus had been that South Africa's pure-wool Bushmen were totally defunct and that those who claimed the right to a San homeland were merely half-breed, tan-skinned "Coloureds." (Several thousand other Bushmen survive in Botswana, Namibia, Zimbabwe, and Angola.) Elsie's palaver, and Crawhall's subsequent discovery of a dozen more speakers of the same "dead" language, changed everything.

Government officials immediately declared the tongue "official," vowed to teach it in the public schools, and made the day of its discovery a public holiday forever. "The lost tribe of !Kabee Bushmen trance-dance into a future of hope," declared Johannesburg's *Sunday Independent*.

This sudden attention to the Bushmen was welcomed by their defenders. But no one needed to educate the Quebecker, Nigel Crawhall, that language is the axle around which the wheels of pride and culture turn.

His logic was irrefutable: anyone who spoke !Kabee or N/u, as the old language was variously named (the symbols stand for the Bushmen's famous clicks), had to be 100 per cent bona fide Southern Kalahari San, and thereby more thoroughly and primordially South African than any of the browner men who were now running the country. (President Nelson Mandela himself, the San's defenders aver, carries a trace of Bushman blood – the hue and shape of his face announce it.)

And there was more – a Prophecy. Old Elsie growled to the Crawhall that a distant relative, called "Kaffir" by his Afrikaner overlords, had informed her, half a century ago, that a messenger would cross the ocean to rescue the Bushmen and their land. Now the time had come and the courier turned out to be a doctor's son who had once run for the presidency of the McGill University Student Society on a platform of Maoist revolution, economic divestment, and cheaper cafeteria food.

Six months later, as we watch the last of South Africa's Bushmen drag home their dinner, tail-first, the land claim proceeds, but the provincial legislator who owns the swath of desert the "lost tribe" covets vows to shoot them if they win in court.

Recently, even more !Kabee-speaking souls have been found living in the wretched "locations" of the Northern Cape to which apartheid consigned them when the old hunting grounds were fenced off and farmed. And the Canadian rescuer, who is bucking the drift of white flight and is committed to South Africa after ten years below the Equator, sighs and tells of his first conversation months ago with the ancient lady who altered and enriched his life.

"In her mouth and in her brain was the end point of twenty thousand years of experience," Crawhall says, as we pass the night in a four-star thatched tourist hut. "All the loves, the tastes, the fears, the violence, the desires that shape a language were fused inside her. We were touching on the very origins of South Africa.

"I was haunted by this. I could hardly sleep at night. I wanted to open her mind, and cast the light backward."

The first time Nigel Crawhall made history was in 1980, when he invited a young man to be his date for the Mount Royal High School senior prom. They were, he says, the first openly gay couple to dare such an appearance in Canada. There was a hubbub, he recalls, and a photo in the paper, but nobody got bashed.

"We could always judge the level of violence at Mount Royal High," Crawhall says dryly. "When the Greek gangs needed somebody to beat up, the Jews got hit before the fags."

He had come out to his parents at 15. His father, Dr. John Crawhall, a clinical researcher at the Royal Victoria Hospital and, later, the Notre Dame, remembers that he and his wife, Pamela, "always accepted his inclination, as we did with all three of our children."

Nigel's sister, Nicola, works for a Third World aid group in London and his brother, Robert, is a member of the technical advisory board at Northern Telecom in Ottawa. For years, they believed they were the Last of the Crawhalls, until Nigel searched the Internet White Pages and found three distant clanmates in New South Wales.

The archives of the *McGill Daily* depict Nigel Crawhall, Class of '85, as a committed campaigner against "the racist regime," soliciting funds for Mandela's African National Congress, and joining what he remembers as a "huge protest that shut down the Port of Montreal" when a shipload of Namibian uranium was being unloaded.

He was captivated, back then, by Africa in general rather than South Africa in particular, though he had never set foot on the continent. He trumpeted the socialist strongmen of progressive Tanzania and benighted Guinea-Bissau. But with the apartheid government in Pretoria under intense attack by Brian Mulroney and most of the Commonwealth – and with the issue bubbling so prominently on First World campuses that Columbia University's administration building was renamed Mandela Hall – Crawhall found himself drawn deeply to the cause.

In the fall of 1985, as president of McGill's South Africa Committee, Crawhall led demonstrations that demanded the school withdraw all investment from corporations doing business with the pariah regime. In November of that year, McGill's Senate voted to press the governors to divest. Only one person, a white South African professor, voted against the motion. Two of the senators who voted in favour were Nigel's father and brother.

After McGill, Crawhall intended to study African languages in South Africa itself, but found the political climate unendurable at a time of martial law and severe repression. He spent three years at the University of Zimbabwe, gaining a master's degree in linguistics, picking up Shona and later Xhosa and Afrikaans.

Now 35 years old, Crawhall lives in a fashionable Cape Town beachfront suburb. His work with the South African San Institute and other NGOs is partly funded by CUSO and the Canadian High Commission. He thought himself clever when he mastered conversational Greek during a three-month holiday. Then he heard of a friend who picked up Samoan in one day, from a book.

Think of the Bushmen. Think of the two men and the two women who have been exhibited around England for some years. Are the majority of persons . . . conscious of an affectionate yearning towards that noble savage, or is it idiosyncratic in me to abhor, detest, abominate and abjure him?

– Charles Dickens, 1853

The Kalahari Gemsbok National Park, a fingertip of South Africa wedged between the borders of Namibia and Botswana, was created in the 1930s ostensibly to protect the country's last free Bushmen, but not long after that they were rounded up and thrown out. The park encloses the valleys of the Nossob and Auob rivers, which are dry most of the year, and a number of boreholes that attract springbok, wildebeest, and exquisite platinum-coloured gemsbok and the lions who lunch on them.

We are driving through the park in a Toyota four-by-four with a quartet of Bushmen squatting in the cargo bed. One is Anna Swarts, the old woman in the pink scarf who attempted to dance around yesterday's dinner. Joining her are a young mother and her daughter, aged about six, and Anna's nephew Dawid Kruiper, aged sixty or more, who is often called the Bushmen's "traditional leader." He has come to show us the dune where he was born, and where he begs to die.

Dawid Kruiper is an enchanting and well-seasoned raconteur who has been exhibited to white audiences for decades at various fairgrounds and shopping centres wearing a loincloth and a quiver of arrows. The heir to a thousand hunters, he does not speak Elsie Vaalbooi's near-dead language, but he is prone to come out with whoppers in Afrikaans such as his description of his recent journey to Geneva, where he was invited to attend a United Nations conference and photo opportunity on the plight of the world's vanishing indigenous tribes.

"We flew and flew and flew," he says, as we pause for water and a Jet-O-Matic Portable Flushing Toilet break, thirty miles into the park. "It was my first time on an airplane. I was worried that they had made a mistake and we would run out of petrol. It was all water underneath us – you can't just stop and get petrol!

"I went to sleep and when I woke up, we were still flying and flying. There was water, and after the water there were more rocks and mountains. 'Oh!' I thought, 'the world is big!'"

The conference was a success. And Swiss Customs was sufficiently distracted by its unorthodox visitor not to scrutinize

Kruiper's suitcase, which was stuffed with cannabis, the Bushmen's favoured spliff since the dawn of time.

"When I got to Europe," he continues, "I looked for the stars to find north and south but I couldn't find anything I knew. Then the sun came up in the wrong place and made a small loop and set in the wrong place. All the Bushmen who were there said the same thing – the sun was in the wrong place."

We drive on, watched by a brace of white-faced owls in a tall acacia tree, ignored by the black-backed jackals and butterscotch antelope who graze in the sere yellow valley. A cluster of tourists' cars announces something worth seeing, and we pull up in time to watch a cheetah drag a springbok's haunch from under a thick green bush. Round, ripe tsamma melons – the Bushmen's staple fruit and source of liquid – litter the sand. But the rules of the park forbid us to get out of the Toyota and gobble them.

"When I was young, it was an open world," Anna Swarts laments. "There were no fences. You couldn't see houses. We just walked on and on. The Father above protected us. That's why we could sleep anywhere. The lions would not bother us."

At the waterhole where Dawid Kruiper was born, perhaps in 1935 as his apartheid passbook estimated, the Father has placed a Do Not Enter sign.

"Gee, man," Kruiper says, "I used to walk around in this park. Today, I can't even walk to that tree. I'd be breaking the law.

"I feel absolutely trapped. There's been so much lost in all the children's knowledge. This little child – she names things incorrectly. When we saw the jackal, the child said, 'There's a cat!' It was the first time she'd ever seen one. This makes me very sad.

"If we can't use the land like we used to, we're going to lose the knowledge and it's going to be lost forever – what we can eat, what is good, what is dangerous. The women have to teach the little girls the foods of the veldt, where to get wood, how to find plants. The men must teach the boys where to get water, how to follow spoor and find game.

"A Bushman is a totally different thing. I can see into the future what will happen. Out of a hundred springbok spoor, I can pick one and follow that one and tell you if the animal is male or female, young or old, healthy or sick. That is what I must teach the young boys."

"Why have the gods permitted the destruction of your people?" I ask him, as if the gods had a choice against the rifles of the Boer.

"The situation we find ourselves in is a punishment," Kruiper replies. "Part of the punishment is that we have to live among other people. That's what the old people say. We're trapped among the Coloured people. We must wear our ≠gaib – our loin-cloth – underneath our clothes when they are around us. We are ashamed – they laugh at us. But the ≠gaib is there – and the soul of the Bushman is there – hidden underneath. I hide it, but it is always there.

"The old people would like to take the children into the veldt and bring the children's hearts back to the dances and the music and the stories – the stories that make them scared, that enable them to sit still and quietly listen.

"The day that the children feel the spirit in the dances, that is the day that the Father will forgive them. That is what the punishment is for. For forgetting the dance."

In our comfortably furnished rondavel, with a speckled little gecko perched motionless on the wall above our beds, Nigel Crawhall tells of his first visit to Dawid Kruiper, who was going to teach him a few words of a living click-language called Nama that is spoken by thousands of "Coloureds" in Namibia and South Africa's northwestern tip.

(No one knows why Bushman languages evolved to employ a unique cacophony of dental, palatal, lateral, and alveolar clicks as their commonest consonant sounds. Crawhall suspects that they aided a hunter's stealth, sounding more like snapping twigs than human voices. Early travellers thought the languages proved the Bushmen to be more animal than human. A Frenchman named

Tavernier wrote in 1649 that "When they speak they fart with their tongues in their mouths.")

"Dawid told me," Crawhall says, "that his parents had spoken the old language, and that there were Bushmen deep in the desert who still spoke it. I knew the language had been declared extinct – I had read the academic papers. But I said to the people who were doing a census of the Bushmen for the land claim, 'If you run across anyone who speaks this language, let me know.'"

In a cinderblock dwelling in a Kalahari hamlet called Rietfontein, the impossible happened. A man named Petrus Vaalbooi, whose name means "pale boy" in Afrikaans (as opposed to Swartbooi, or "black boy" as the darker races were often called), announced that his own mother, Elsie, aged 96, could remember an ancient tongue that no one else in the village could comprehend.

Crawhall was informed and he contacted one of South Africa's most prominent linguists, professor Tony Traill of the University of the Witwatersrand, who hastened to Rietfontein as fast as the region's loose-sand freeways would permit. (It was he who had pronounced !Kabee or N/u officially kaput.) He brought with him some scratchy recordings made in the 1930s, when a number of Bushmen, including three sisters dubbed the "Hottentot Venuses," were shipped to Johannesburg for public delectation at the Empire Exhibition.

Elsie Vaalbooi listened to the tapes and said they described the ceremony that marked a young woman's coming of age. Traill, delighted that his obituary for the language had been premature, estimated her comprehension at 80 per cent. The Canadian's fantasy had borne fruit. He headed for sun-kissed Rietfontein, which was becoming quite a mecca.

"When I met Elsie," Crawhall says, "she was sitting under a tree beside that little house. She was completely dignified, and I was so nervous that I could hardly speak. I knew that this woman was a speaker of a language that her ancestors had spoken for centuries – as far as we knew, she was the last speaker. It would die with her.

"I didn't know what to do. Certainly I couldn't speak it with her. Then it came to me in a bolt. I was there to explain her constitutional right to the protection and promotion of her language by the South African government.

"Suddenly, her antiquity caught my imagination and I got completely freaked. We were touching on the very essence and origins of this country. These people moved across this land before any other human being. It was they who named the plants and the trees and the features of this land. South Africa is them first. I got this sense that, in her, was everything her people had ever done. Now she was the end product of all that.

"Before this, when people talked to me about language death, I thought, 'Well, the language dies, but life goes on.' But with Elsie, I understood that I was wrong – when you lose the language, it's more than that. *You lose the whole thing.*

"What was I supposed to do? I thought, 'She's the only person on earth who can understand herself.' I had a bit of a flash of inspiration. I asked her, 'Do you want to tape a message to the National Language Board?' She made a message in N/u and I played it back to her. She laughed and had a conversation with herself – perhaps the last conversation that would ever be held in that language.

"There was this incredible weirdness about the whole thing. In the academic world, they swore on their mothers' graves that there were none of these people alive in South Africa. Now I was sitting under a tree with Elsie Vaalbooi."

The saga became even more bizarre. Petrus told Crawhall his cousin's wife's sister also could speak the language. This person lived in a township called Rosedale outside the town of Upington. Until 1994, of course, only whites could live inside the town of Upington. A siren chased the Coloureds and Blacks out at 10 p.m.

So Crawhall went to Rosedale and found a woman named Anna Kassie, also known as Uintjie, or "Little Onion." Anna Kassie was talking !Kabee into his tape recorder when a neighbour named Griet Seekoei strolled in and she started speaking it, too.

Griet, Crawhall soon learned, knew of three sisters in a nearby location called Swartkop. All spoke the ancient language. And, yes, they had been the Hottentot Venuses in Johannesburg, so long ago.

Within a few weeks, Nigel Crawhall had tracked down a dozen Khomani speakers. He asked them, "What do you want to do? You are a people. You have rights." They told him they wanted a piece of land that was irrevocably theirs, where the women could teach the girls which plants to gather, and which to shun.

"There was a sense of explosion of identity, a rising tide," he says. "I was listening to people who had spent their whole lives having to hide what they were. These people had been destroyed, and now suddenly there was light and air.

"I was sitting by the Orange River one day when I twigged. The way these people talked about their identity, they sounded like they were going to a Gay Pride parade. I identified with them completely, because coming to terms with my own sexuality had been the same journey they were on – a journey toward who you are.

"I knew exactly what they were going through and what would come next. You awaken to this passionate sense of what you are. I understood the anxiety, the fear, the shame.

"To be ashamed of what you are is a very frightening thing. To walk away from fear is pride and that can get very militant and all-consuming for a time. The ultimate thing is you settle down to your life."

A Boer from Graaf Reynet being asked in the secretary's office, a few days before we left the town, if the savages were numerous or troublesome along the road, replied, he had only shot four, with as much composure and indifference as if he had been speaking of four partridges.

– J. Barrow, 1801

The Bushman land claim was in the works more than a year before Nigel Crawhall sat under a tree with Elsie Vaalbooi. A human-rights lawyer from Cape Town named Roger Chennells already was collecting what turned out to be 175 registrants who were, or claimed to be, the human potsherds of the ancient vessel of the Southern Kalahari San.

"If it was just five or ten, I'd have told them, 'Bad luck, chaps,'" Chennells says. "But they are a community. It's not just one hundred and seventy-five individuals – they symbolize so much more. They stand for a class of people and a spirituality – the most ancient, most non-materialistic people I have ever known. These people have been murdered by South Africans for centuries. The land claim is a symbol that we didn't annihilate them all."

Roger Chennells is sitting in the lounge of the venerable Savoy Hotel in the city of Kimberley, where diamonds grow under-ground. A conference is taking place here to discuss the claim, which Chennells confesses was his idea and not the Bushmen's.

"The Bushmen are very much like your Inuit," he says. "They tend to belong to the land and not the land to them. They say, 'We don't own the land, we merely utilize it.' *I've* imposed the notion of possession. It's quite a curious notion for them, but now they rec-ognize that, without land, you don't have the power to be yourself."

"This is my first client in 20 years," the solicitor adds, "in which my professionalism is diluted heavily by emotion."

There is a subtle irony in the case that is not lost on the Bushmen's adversaries in government and the National Parks Board. (The claimants are also seeking hunting and gathering rights within the park.) The deconstruction of apartheid was sup-posed to eradicate the link between race and residence. The trans-parent "tribal homelands" of the P. W. Botha years have vanished from the national atlas. But now here is a tiny group of stragglers (with a very prominent lawyer) announcing, "We are a people. We want our land."

"The facts are true," Chennells says. "The old languages had been declared dead by Tony Traill in 1974. We had found 175

claimants but we needed to prove their links to the land. Serendi-
pitously, Nigel came along. He found Elsie Vaalbooi, a speaker of
pure N/u.

"This was a tremendous assistance to the land claim. Suddenly,
we could say that not only do these people look like Bushmen,
they are Bushmen. We could say, 'These people belong to a club
that no one else belongs to. And the people who belong to this
club are going to get their land.'"

The Bushmen will get their land, Piet Smith vows, over his dead
body. Smith is a major Kalahari landowner and a duly elected
provincial legislator from the Mier Coloured Settlement, as the
sheep and cattle ranches adjoining the fence of the Kalahari
Gemsbok National Park are known. When I find Mr. Smith at his
handsome Kimberley home, he is far pinker than I am with my
Kalahari tan. But Coloured he was born and registered, and
Coloured he adamantly remains.

"We won't lose," Smith says, as his wife, Mary, translates from
Afrikaans. "The government can't give our place to the Bushmen,
because there are no Bushmen."

"They're Coloureds, just like us," Mary smiles. She has been
with her man for 35 years, scratching out a living in an infernal
region the Afrikaners call *tussen erens en nerens* – between
somewhere and nowhere. They shuttle between the provincial
capital and her husband's waterless riding in a magnificent new
Land Cruiser that waits outside the Kimberley house like a
grazing rhinoceros.

"They wear clothes, just like us," Mrs. Smith goes on, "but when
people come from overseas, they take their clothes off. When the
people ride away, they put their clothes back on. Real Bushmen
have no clothes."

"What about Dawid Kruiper?" I ask. "Isn't Dawid Kruiper a
real Bushman?"

"Dawid Kruiper is a Bushman," Piet Smith allows.

"And Petrus Vaalbooi?"

"He's a Bushman for money."

The land in the Mier Coloured Settlement has been the Smiths' since 1930, when Piet's father took it over from whites who had given up on the Kalahari and returned to more livable climes. The problem, he says, is outside interference; "People come from outside and give them money."

"We can't just give our place to them," he declares. "They must buy a place for the Bushmen and not just take our place."

"And if the Bushmen win?" I persist.

Without saying a word, Legislator Smith raises his arms, squints as if aiming a rifle, and pulls the trigger.

So many pilgrims now travel to Rietfontein to sit at the feet of Elsie Vaalbooi that she should open a Journey's Inn. The settlement, surrounded by a vast expanse of absolutely nothing, is hard by the Namibian border, a collection of small houses scattered erratically in the satanic sunshine. I am sitting on the porch of Elsie's dwelling, waiting for her to muster the inclination to talk to me, when another Bushman drives up in a battered blue Mercedes 350SE.

This man is named Harold, and Harold declares, in English, "The true can hurt but the true must come out! God sent us here! The San must start again where he begin! South Africa belongs to the San! It does not belong to anybody else! It belongs to the San!"

This expostulation, translated into Afrikaans, serves to inspire Elsie, who is reclining on a divan in the shade and crushing a handful of cheesies into powder between her strong, bent hands for lunch.

"It's all ours!" she yelps.

Her son, Petrus, comes out of the door with a folio of maps of the Mier Coloured Settlement and the word list of Kalahari birds and animals Nigel Crawhall drew up during his meetings in Elsie's little house on the prairie.

"We hear that South Africa is free," Petrus says, mounting his soapbox, "but the Bushman is not yet free. My greatest longing is for the land of my grandfathers, the language of my ancestors, and the traditions of my Bushman people."

He surveys his territory, which is a yard of bare dirt and a small tree from which his goats have nibbled all but the uppermost leaves.

"Look at my little bunch of animals," he cries. "They have to eat stones because they have pushed us out into the hard, hard veldt."

"If you win the land claim," I ask him, "what will you do?"

"I'd move there today," Petrus replies. And his 96-year-old mother (or godmother, for Petrus does not appear old enough to be her biological son) pipes up: "My name is known everywhere for speaking about the land. Why wouldn't I go?"

"It's high time!" Harold the Mercedes man inserts, uninvited. "The Bushman must go back to where his dead bones lie!"

Things are warming up. Elsie licks at her cheesies and sends Petrus into the house to fetch the hand-tinted portrait of the man who told her of The Prophecy.

"This is my sister's child, I carried him on my back," she says, cocking her one operational eye when the framed picture is brought to her. The long, long story begins. The man, she says, was called Kaffir. He went to work in the diamond mines but was sent home in tears without being paid. Then the train on which he was returning to Upington came to a sudden halt *tussen erens en nerens*.

"The train was stopped and there was nothing wrong with that train," Elsie bellows. "A witch doctor came and saw the little Bushman sitting there and he said, 'He stopped the train.' The witch doctor tapped him on the shoulder and said, 'Do your work, little Bushman,' and the train magically went on to Upington.

"The Lord told that Bushman to go everywhere in the land and tell his story and not to fight or swear or drink or kill the caracul lamb. He told me, 'Auntie, things will come right. The Lord gave me a microphone to tell the whole world. The help of the Bushmen will come from over the sea. The newspapers will speak. The radio will speak. Then there will be a solution for the Bushmen.' And now what he said is coming true."

"What do you seek for yourself?" I ask her.

"I want to pick up the blood and the bones of my mother's mother's mother and my father's father's father and give them to my children's children's children," she declares. "Now just give me some money."

"What we know about language death," Nigel Crawhall says, "is that the post-ethnocidal generation feels a tremendous guilt.

"I know that Petrus Vaalbooi is driven absolutely mad by this. He doesn't blame his mother. He blames himself. He told me, 'I am useless. I am dirt, because I don't speak my mother's and my father's language.'

"What I am doing, I hope, lets some of this guilt fall away. I'm not here to resurrect the language. It's for the community to understand what happened. It's for the community to get the guilt off their shoulders.

"When a language dies, it shows that conditions were so extreme that people were willing to murder their language – to swallow it right back into their belly and not stain their children with it.

"A Nama midwife once told me that the women she attended believed that speaking Nama to their children would make them retarded. With the Bushmen it was more than that. It was a fear that their children would be hurt or killed."

We go up into the Cederberg to visit the private game park called Kagga Kamma – "The Place of the Bushmen." Crawhall brings along his list of words. He wants to introduce them to the tiny children who are kept occupied for a few hours each day in a newly opened schoolroom while their parents sit topless and nearly bottomless in an adjoining longhouse, making necklace beads and hunting bows for fascinated vacationers.

This is where it all started, where Dawid Kruiper told Nigel Crawhall of the survival of the ancestors' language, somewhere in the wilderness, and Crawhall dedicated himself, as he elegantly puts it, "to snatch this coal from the fire of their pre-colonial past." Now he sits on a bench with his precious little dictionary, wearing a green McGill windbreaker against the snapping autumn gales. Three men and three women, who are passing around the broken neck of a wine bottle stuffed with hemp, intently study and pronounce the ancient words for aardvark and ostrich and bat-eared fox. The Montrealer is jubilant and redeemed.

"Dawid Kruiper's father was a great Bushman leader," Crawhall says when we walk away. "He was a very bright, very honest, and very just man.

"In his world, to be a Bushman was a very dignified and whole experience. This language is the last link to that world."

The men passed the whole night doing strange and wonderful posturings, with leaping, hopping and dancing; but the women made a continual hand-clapping and did other such rare antics, and sang only ha, ho, HO, HO, until one almost lost hearing and sight because of the terrible noise.

– Johan Christian Hoffman, 1672

Having eaten their fill of donkey flesh and hung the rest to dry, the men of the lost tribe are going to do the old trance-dance for us, and for themselves. This is the pathway to the spirit world and the gift of healing, to an alternative, but no less genuine, reality in which animal and human souls merge and energies flow like the rivers of the Kalahari after the late-summer rains.

A space has been cleared and a campfire ignited in front of "city hall," which is an open-fronted structure built of bales of straw, stuccoed and painted the deep red of the desert beyond. Four adult men, led by the old diviner who was injured in the highway crash coming back from Kagga Kamma in 1994, are joined by a few young boys.

Dawid Kruiper, injured in the same accident, has pins in his knees and cannot dance. He stands on the sidelines and smokes a cigarette made from a rolled-up magazine.

In the western sky, Orion props himself on his elbow to watch the pageantry. To the east is the Botswana border fence and to the north is the national park and Piet Smith and his rifle. A few chickens peck around the courtyard. All the rest is silence and history.

The dance begins. Wearing rattles on their ankles made from the dried cocoons of moths who live on the camelthorn trees, the men and boys stutter-step around the fire. The women, meanwhile, sit with their babes in their laps and clap their hands and sing ha, ho, HO, HO.

We take a few photographs. When we leave, someone says, the dancers will become even more frenetic. Their spirits will fly to the realm of the eland where the Bushman is ever free.

– Saturday Night

THE MIDDLE EAST

Previous page: By a Bedouin Tent East of Jerusalem
(author on left, next to friend Avi Lev)

The first time I went to the Holy Land, I was sitting in the Church of the Holy Sepulchre in Jerusalem when I noticed an English tourist pointing to the tomb of Christ and heard him asking a guide, "Is the body still in there?"

"The body is no more," the attendant replied, casting his eyes heavenward. "He rose on the third day."

"Ah," said the visitor, nodding. "Was this church here then?"

That was in 1985. I went back in December 1999, on the eve of the end of the world. My assignment was to document millennial hysteria in the provinces of the Book – Sinai, Bethlehem, Megiddo, Galilee. Then I would fly back to Times Square in New York City for the final drumroll to oblivion.

In North America, in those days, there were citizens stockpiling food and water, and lighting candles against the dark nights to come. But in Jordan and Israel and Palestine and Egypt, I found what there always had been – pilgrims and searchers, apostles and acolytes.

In a red Sinai sunset, some saw the Second Coming, but I held that the mountains were far more real than the passing fears of men. Swept up in the spindrifts of history, I felt I could climb to the sky.

Mount Sinai

•

The freighter captain from Bombay, shipwrecked 7,000 feet above the sea, stared at me with doom in his eyes and said, "Breathing is coming too fast. Chest is paining." He slumped onto a boulder and began to clutch his breast and moan.

I offered him my Bible and climbed on.

We were nine-tenths of the way up Mount Sinai, where there went up Moses, and Aaron, Nadab, and Abihu, and 70 of the elders of Israel, and they saw the God of Israel. But now, instead of holy men, we were tourists and travellers, anxious to reach the tiny stone chapel at the peak by sundown, then to descend 3,000 chiselled steps by the acetylene light of a winter moon.

The seaman, a Roman Catholic, a heavy man, past 60, had ascended this far by faith alone. He said, over and over, "It is very tiresome. It is very tiresome. It is very tiresome." And it was. But I had failed to reach too many summits in my life to turn from this one, so close to the goal.

Fifteen minutes later, I was at the peak, with the red rocks of Sinai far below me. There were Bedouins up here, selling mango juice and Snickers, and a loud party of Italians, snapping photographs as the sun dipped beyond Suez and the night wind seized the small remainder of my breath.

I was just turning to start back down, hoping to get beyond the most treacherous defile before complete darkness, when the freighter captain from Bombay reached the top. A young Bedouin man was walking with him, gently nudging him up the final flight.

"Praise the Lord!" shouted the captain's son and daughter-in-law, who had gone up ahead, as they saw them approach. And the seaman smiled at them, and at me, and said, "Praise the Lord."

My escape from Egypt had been easier than Exodus; there's a highway tunnel under the Suez Canal. On the east bank, and all along the road, Pharaoh's army – young conscripts in thick black winter uniforms – lolled listlessly, starved for food and nicotine at noon on the tenth day of the fasting month of Ramadan, in their year 1420.

Every few miles, a battered oil drum, painted green and white, had been trundled to the centre of the pavement.

"What your country?" a soldier barked, as we halted at each one.

"Canada Canada," our driver, an affable and witless Cairene named N——, would say. And the two sons of Moses in the back seat (I am travelling with a former Israeli paratrooper who served in the bunkers at Suez after the Six-Day War) would prudently remain silent, for the Lord had sent angels to this place, and warned us to beware of him, and obey his voice; provoke him not, for he will not pardon your transgressions.

"What your country?"

"Canada Canada."

Then, at one barricade, they decided to examine N——'s bona fides instead of ours, rifled through his papers, hauled him into the commandant's cinderblock headquarters, and fined him one hundred Egyptian pounds – a week's pay – because Cairo taxis are not allowed east of the Suez Canal.

The morning after the triumphant assault on Mt. Sinai, I hiked into the valley where the angel of the Lord appeared unto Moses in a flame of fire out of the midst of a bush, and he looked, and, behold, the bush burned with fire, and the bush was not consumed.

I passed turbaned men on camelback, and their women, veiled, high on the hillside, urging their coal-black lambs up the harrowing slope. Behind me was the flatland where the Israelites, despairing of Moses' return with God's commandments, forged their golden calf, and brought peace offerings; and the people sat down to eat and to drink, and rose up to play.

At the head of this wadi, 1,530 years ago, the Emperor Justinian ordered the construction of a great walled monastic fortress. This still stood, consecrated to Saint Catherine, a fourth-century martyr from Alexandria whose beheaded body was carried by angels to Sinai's highest peak.

Three centuries later, guided by a dream, the monks of the cloister of the burning bush found what my guidebook calls "the sweet fragrance of her sacred remains" on the mountaintop, and placed them in a golden casket, before which the faithful still come to kneel and weep.

Within cedar doors half again as old as our flickering millennium, I entered the body of their incomparable church. Censers and candelabra hung from ancient chains that also held the silvered eggs of ostriches.

Icons dating to the sixth century lined the walls, and we ceaseless throngs of impertinent penitents shuffled in our Timberland boots and bent under our Invicta rucksacks to peer and gawk and mumble beneath a ceiling brilliant with gilded stars.

A tall, slim, bearded man in glasses and a long black robe and high black cap was standing in beatific calm amid the touristic horde. He was one of the Greek Orthodox monks of St. Catherine's, the pious handful who still lived and prayed and worked here, irrevocably dedicated to the laws inscribed on two stone tablets, on the mountain above their cells.

Not knowing whether he would, or could, speak, I timidly approached to ask about the turning of the calendar.

The monk turned out to be a sympathetic ascetic from the United States of America, one of only two here not of Greek nationality. He gave his name as Father Justin, and when I asked his hometown, he smiled broadly and, pleased with himself, answered, "Here!"

Father Justin outlined the daily details of a monastic life little changed since Byzantine times: the awakening, to 33 chimes from the bell tower, for matins at 4 a.m., the first of three communal services, to be augmented by hours of private prayer; the tending of the gardens and the bookshop and the herding of the tourists; rare visits to Cairo for an eye appointment, and to Jerusalem to meet his parents, every few years.

I asked if he found the life punishing – he seemed as soft a baby boomer as myself – and he said, "I guess it's like a military training camp. At first, you think you can't do the sit-ups and the push-ups and the running, but gradually you become accustomed to the ardour."

My mention of the coming of 2000 set him off on an obtuse expostulation about the Greek Orthodox year having already begun in September, and the monkey wrench the adoption of the Julian calendar in the 18th century threw into everything, and how Christ was born in 4 BC anyhow. But finally Father Justin gave up this line of argument and allowed that he was delighted to be living two thousand years after the birth of his Saviour, whenever it was.

His was a cycle of rigour cushioned by certainty: that Justinian's walls would not crumble; that, when life ended, he would be interred in the tiny burial ground behind the church, but only briefly.

After one year in the dry earth of Sinai, his body would be exhumed and the bones scraped of flesh. Then, like the relics of the saint to whom he had pledged his celibacy and sacrifice, they would be placed in an ossuary a few yards up the valley – the skull in one pile, the femurs and tibias in another, a heap already six feet high – and that would be the end of Father Justin.

The freighter captain from Bombay, Master Mariner Mervin John Lobo of ss *Normar Progress*, noticed me staring at the elbow bone of Saint Catherine in a small display case. He fixed me in those eyes again and said, "There will be catastrophes!"

It was the first time on this journey that I'd heard anyone forecast the Apocalypse.

"I am very much worried that – what is his name? – Bin Laden will light a few bombs," the seaman said.

"It is advisable to stay away from large gatherings of people."

This was an admonition Captain Lobo did not seem to be heeding, as the Monastery of Saint Catherine was by now overflowing with at least a thousand tourists. (I had asked Father Justin why the monks permitted visitors at all and he had replied, "We have many things of importance here, but we want to be a monastery, not only a museum.")

Captain Lobo had been married at the Church of the Holy Sepulchre, kept an Israeli flag in his wheelhouse, was descended from Hindus converted by Saint Anthony, and was headed for Christmas in Bethlehem, then Bible college. He had applied for special dispensation to view the preserved roots of the burning bush itself, which are kept in a small, private chapel behind the Holy Altar, on the very spot where God said, "I am the God of thy father, the God of Abraham, the God of Isaac, and the God of Jacob."

He let me come with him; the more, the holier. In the presence of sacred relics – Saint Catherine's golden casket was back here as well – the mariner went a bit overboard, chanting and praying and making videotapes and flash photographs and dabbing balls of cotton into various holy waters and oils.

Then he said, "In Saudi Arabia, they tried to destroy my Bible, but I told them, 'If you destroy my Bible, you destroy your Koran, because it is the Bible of Abraham and Isaac and Jacob, and they are in your Koran, too.' And when I said this, and I prayed to the Lord, they said nothing more."

We went outside to a bower where the burning bush – a lovely, flowing shrub – had been transplanted.

Tourists were plucking the lower branches clean. It was less than two weeks until the Third Millennium; we were Jews and Christians at the foot of a holy mountain in a Muslim land.

"Praise the Lord," said the freighter captain. He asked if I would join him for Christmas in Bethlehem, and I said that I might, but that it wasn't written in stone.

– National Post

Armageddon

·

MEGIDDO, ISRAEL

On the hilltop where the seventh angel of Revelation poured out his vial of doom, the tumbled ruins of ancient palaces await the end of the world.

This is the address, in the north of the State of Israel, where God assigned one corner each to Good and Evil, and then announced to all His children, in a roar that broke the universe, "Let's get ready to rumble!"

Those who expect the battle to begin on Friday night will have no trouble finding a ringside seat. The only hotel within walking distance of the arena of the Apocalypse is barely half-booked for New Year's Eve. Reservations still are being accepted for bed and (one can only hope) breakfast. The management would prefer full payment in advance.

"And he gathered them together into a place called in the Hebrew tongue Armageddon," says the 16th chapter of the Bible's last and most terrifyingly incomprehensible book. ". . . and there came a great voice out of the temple of heaven, from the throne, saying, 'It is done.'

"And there were voices, and thunders, and lightnings; and there was a great earthquake, such as was not since men were upon the Earth, so mighty an earthquake, and so great. And the great city was divided into three parts, and the cities of the nations fell. . . . And every island fled away, and the mountains were not found. And there fell upon men a great hail out of heaven."

But on the day I come to Armageddon – the hill of Megiddo, in modern Hebrew – there is not a hailstone, a thunderbolt, or another tourist in sight. If the Lord really is planning the Fight of the Century, He has failed to tell Don King.

Awaiting its sixth turn of the millennium, Megiddo National Park is an archaeological layer cake, the site of one of the most important fortresses of the Iron Age. In this high, thick hill are compressed the pulverized fragments of 17 separate civilizations, dating back to the infancy of imperialism and organized warfare.

Compared to the living stones of Jerusalem, Megiddo only faintly evokes the ancient world. A few reconstructed walls, a deep, round silo from the reign of King Jeroboam, and an ingenious subterranean aqueduct that allowed access to a water source beyond the walls in times of siege are the principal attractions.

The fortified mountain was abandoned in about 400 BC. Most of its ivory and gold treasures are at the Oriental Institute of the University of Chicago, leaving only the stubble of stables and palaces, a few struggling palm trees, and numerous small, grey lizards to watch me as I walk around the ruins.

The rest is left to the imagination of the traveller, and to the echoes of the stirring Song of Deborah in the Book of Judges: "I will sing unto the Lord . . . the kings came and fought; then fought the kings of Canaan by the waters of Megiddo. . . ."

It was here that Pharaoh Thutmose III sent his armies to suppress a provincial rebellion in 1468 BC, and King Solomon's cavalry kept watch over the wide, flat valley beneath Mount Carmel that served as the granary of Israel.

And it is here that, some Christians believe, God will descend to weigh the righteous and the wicked on the Day of Judgment, according to their works, and whosoever was not found written in the book of life will be cast into the lake of fire.

Last week, a busload of ministers from New York City came to Megiddo, wearing T-shirts that identified them as "Triumphant Christians Breaking the Barriers of Sin."

One of them was the Reverend Bennie Wright, Jr., of the New St. John Baptist Church in the borough of the Bronx. Reverend Wright, a man of appreciable girth and passion, dressed entirely in black, wearing a crucifix monumental enough to serve as a ship's anchor, was waiting for his return flight to the American Babylon from Tel Aviv when I approached and asked about Armageddon.

"To SEE the place where the end of the world is prophesized," Reverend Wright bellowed (he was just warming up). "When you look at the news, IT'S JUST A MATTER OF TIME.

"We went up to the Golan Heights and, man, when you see all the military bases up there, you think, 'IT COULD BEGIN AT ANY TIME. It could happen before we get back to the HOTEL.'"

"How do you think the end will come?" I asked him.

"When Christ comes to CONQUER," the minister said, "He will have to get everybody together in one spot, and that spot is Armageddon.

"Just as it says in the Bible, 'And the lion shall lie down with the LAMB,' Jesus will gather all the military leaders. Syria and ISRAEL shall lie down together. AMERICA and Israel shall lie down together. In America, black and WHITE shall lie down together."

"Will the leaders themselves be there?" I wondered.

"All of them – Clinton, Arafat, that Syrian guy, the Israeli president – ALL OF THEM," said the Reverend Wright, Jr. "That's where PEACE will begin."

The reverend described himself and his fellow pastors as "gas stations on the road of life where you can fill up when your soul is empty." He said that his own spiritual refuelling began on a battlefield in Vietnam in 1970, when he was serving with the Seventh Armored Cavalry, the motorized descendants of Solomon's mounted warriors of Megiddo.

It was there that he began to experience mystical visions not unlike those that the imprisoned John of Patmos transcribed into the Book of Revelation, with its women with the wings of eagles, and its scarlet-coloured beasts with seven heads and ten horns, and its vials of the wrath of God.

Back in New York, he told me, he "ran and ran and ran from the ministry," but after having his legs broken in a race riot, he turned to the Church. Now he was returning home from Megiddo with a thermonuclear New Year's Eve sermon detonating in his brain.

"Armageddon tells us that Christ is ALIVE," he said. "And when THAT happens, there will be PEACE in the VALLEY."

Five days before the main event, Good and Evil are already in the house. Just below the mound of Megiddo, where the Jerusalem road meets the highway from Haifa and the Mediterranean Sea, guard towers and concertina wire surround a maximum-security prison for Palestinian militants. At the entrance to Megiddo National Park, four Jeep-loads of Israeli policemen slouch beneath the evergreens, lest someone break free of the jail.

No one ever has, but a few months ago, a Jewish man and woman hiking in a nearby woodland were murdered by an Arab from a village on the Haifa road, leaving the neighbourhood nervous and edgy for reasons that have nothing to do with Biblical prophecy.

Adjacent to the national park is one of Israel's trademark kibbutzim, the agricultural and industrial communes that epitomized the socialist fervency of the young, encircled nation.

Fifty years on, Kibbutz Megiddo is showing its age, and its plastic-sheeting factory is barely keeping the membership in the black. Trying to reverse the downslide, the membership has opened a new block of 40 spotless guest rooms in expectation of a millennial onslaught.

"We kept hearing on the TV that this is one of the places where crazy people would come to commit suicide," says Iris Ziv in the booking office of the kibbutz B&B. "But we haven't seen any of them yet."

Ms. Ziv has taken only four room reservations from non-Israelis for the coming weekend. A small pub, downhill from the communal dining hall, will be the scene of a party for the 150 kibbutzniks and the young, gentile volunteers from Denmark, Britain, Brazil, South Africa, and Japan who have joined them here as kitchen workers, gardeners, and cleaners. Should the world not end before Saturday, they will be back at their posts come the dawn.

"I met an American preacher who says that all the world leaders are coming to Armageddon," I tell Ms. Ziv, trying to cheer her up. "Clinton, Arafat, Assad, Barak – they're all going to be brought here by Jesus Christ to make peace."

The woman looks up from the empty account books of the Final Reckoning.

"That's great," she says. "Maybe they'll all stay here and we'll make some money."

– *National Post*

A Silver Platter Marked "Peace"

We had driven halfway up a winding mountain road in the once and future Syria when Avi took my hand in his and placed it on the back of his head.

"Can you feel the lump?" he asked, and I could, easily – a small, solid object embedded beneath the skin and my friend's short, greying hair.

"They took out two and left one in there," he said.

"A quarter-inch deeper – maybe much less – and I'd be a quadriplegic."

The route we were following was threading its way up a steep slope in brown winter plumage, with the Sea of Galilee far below us and snow-capped Mount Hermon hidden somewhere in the clouds.

Between those two Biblical landmarks lay the few thousand square miles, and the few dozen Israeli settlements, that virtually everyone in the Middle East expects to be handed back to Damascus in the very near future, on a silver platter marked "Peace."

We climbed higher, past banana and date-palm plantations, vineyards and apple orchards, factories, cattle pens and farms.

Until June 9, 1967, this was the westernmost quadrant of an Arab
state sworn to Israel's destruction. Then, suddenly, after barely 24
hours of combat, it was the Jews', and the Jews' it has remained.

I began to notice the scattered debris of that war, and the one
that followed six years later – rusted vehicles, abandoned pillboxes
and bunkers, a tank half-buried in sand. Then we came around a
bend in the highway, and Avi stopped the little Peugeot and said,
"This is where it happened."

We had arrived at Eli Al, a minor battlefield of the 1973 Arab-
Israeli war, when Egypt and Syria attacked on the holiest day
of the Hebrew year. That afternoon – Yom Kippur, the Day of
Atonement – Avi and his fashion-model wife were at home in Tel
Aviv with their month-old daughter. The next day, he was lying
face-down at Eli Al with shrapnel in his skull.

A white stucco monument in a garden of yucca plants marked
the spot. Standing beside it, Avi spun out the story.

Called up from the reserves six years after serving at Suez and
Jerusalem in the Six Day War, he had been assigned to a signal
corps on the Golan front. Here, after a sleepless night helping to
co-ordinate the radio communications of the Israeli blitzkrieg, he
and his platoon were resting and preparing lunch, three miles
behind the lines.

A woman named Aya, with whom Avi had trained in 1964, was
up in a supply truck, slicing cheese for sandwiches, when the
Syrian rocket hit. Four men were killed instantly. Avi was knocked
down by the concussion, but rose quickly and began to assist the
wounded – a man with both his feet blown off; another with
the bone sticking out of his leg.

Aya was lying next to Avi, softly gurgling. They rolled her over
and saw that part of her skull had been blown away and that her
brain was seeping out through the wound. A medic looked at
her and waved his hand, indicating there was nothing he could do.

A fragment had punctured one of the tires of the ambulance
that took the wounded, down the road we had just driven, to a
field hospital on the Galilee shore.

It was there that my friend discovered that the back of his uniform was bathed in blood from the shrapnel blast he had been too stunned to feel.

We studied the names on the monument – Friedman, Wechser, Laschick, Freed. I felt humbled and ashamed; my entire experience under fire was limited to ten minutes in a van in Romania, ten years ago, to the day. But Avi had bled, and his friends had died, for this morsel of land that had become as negotiable as a Pokémon card in the Holy Land's unending game of revenge and reconciliation.

Then he had moved with his wife and baby to Canada, to become a documentary editor at CBC-TV.

"How do you feel about giving the Golan back to Syria?" I asked him.

"If it means true peace," he replied, "they can take everything. Just leave me Tel Aviv and the beach."

We drove down to one of the new Israeli settlements in the Golan to visit the daughter of Avi's sister. Iris was at home with her three-year-old son in a small community called B'nei Yehuda – the Sons of Judah – which received government approval yesterday for the construction of up to 58 new homes.

I asked about the likelihood that she would have to relocate, and she answered, "If that happens, we are finished with Israel."

The town had been founded in 1972, and before its 30th birthday it was probably going to be abandoned by the Jews. We wondered who would be living in Iris's house, and whether the Arabs would demolish the little monument to the dead at Eli Al.

"War is a family business," Avi said. "We want to believe that they think the same as us. Maybe they will show us some respect."

Farther down the hillside, right on the Galilee littoral, was the place where Christ performed the miracle of the swine. According to the Gospel of St. Matthew, two men here were possessed by evil spirits: Jesus cast the demons out of the men and into a herd of pigs, which then "ran violently down a steep place into the sea, and perished in the waters."

A Byzantine monastery and cathedral had been built for pilgrims in the 5th century, and their ruins, including an exquisite mosaic floor, had been excavated and conserved by the Jews in a national park called Kursi. (Before 1967, the Syrians used Kursi as a base from which to fire on Israeli fishing boats in the Galilee.) The Israeli curator had inculcated the rumour that a certain wooden bench in a grove of eucalyptus trees near the church somehow was capable of transmitting mystical healing energies.

"If you have a fight with somebody and you sit there," the man told the *Jerusalem Post* in 1996, "then you feel calm."

The man was Iris's husband, Nissim.

Like all the holy sites within a thousand miles of Golgotha, the ruined church at Kursi had been made the object of millennium exploitation. An outfit in New Jersey was selling "Jubillennium" candles on the Internet for US$10 each, to be lighted at the sacred site. But a triple-decker repository held only a dozen of the candles, and all of them had gone out.

We walked around the site for a few minutes, admiring the mosaic, and then went up to Iris's for lunch. Her little boy, Ariel, was playing in the driveway. I watched him pick up a lemon that had fallen from a tree, and throw it as far as he could.

"Practising for the anti-Syrian Intifada," his mother said.

To close the chapter, we sought to visit Aya at her kibbutz near the crusader bastion of Acre on the Mediterranean coast. She had not died in the Syrian attack. Somehow, her horrible wound had been closed and she had gone on with life, functioning as best she could in a wheelchair, in the land for which she had fought. Avi had last tried to visit her four years ago, but she was not in her room when he called.

In a city called Katzrin, the administrative capital of the Israeli Golan, we hunted for a phone. Soon, this town also would belong to Syria, and the Soviet emigrés who seemed to make up the bulk of its population would be rootless once more.

We went into a small shopping centre, and I darted off for some ice cream while Avi made the call. When I came back, he was ashen.

"She's dead," he said. "Two years ago. Heart attack.

"They don't know if it was related to her wounds."

We walked back to the car for the long drive to Jerusalem.

"At least she had 25 more years," I said, trying to comfort him. "And so have you."

At a checkpoint along the Jordan River highway, we picked up two young Israeli soldiers who were hitching their way home to the Holy City.

"My girlfriend left me," one of them said. "She couldn't accept it when I told her that my country would always be my first love."

Avi told him where we had been, and why.

"We'll *never* give the Golan back," the soldier vowed.

– National Post

The Fires of Kuwait

•

In May 1991, just after the conclusion of the Gulf War, I reported from Kuwait for CBC Television on the attempt by firefighters from Alberta (plus several teams of Texas wildcatters) to douse and cap hundreds of oil wells that had been set ablaze by retreating Iraqi troops. The Canadians were employees of a firm called Safety Boss, led by a man named Mike Miller. Our camera operator on this assignment was Maurice Chabot, who four years later would be hired to film the ill-fated "Darwin Returns" in the Ecuadorian Amazon (page 48)

As this excerpt from my book Scaring Myself Again *begins, we've been in Kuwait for less than a day, and have hired a local playboy named Aboud to chauffeur us through the hell-fire. Amid the rubble of Kuwait City, he's the only man we can find with a working car.*

Filled with courage, swaggering and drawling like the heroic Houstonians we saw at Ahmadi House, we decide to take the silver Audi out into the oil fields to shoot some wallpaper and look for Team Canada. We are out of al-Ahmadi, following a sticky two-lane blacktop toward the blazing orange fountains when I remember an item in one of the Toronto faxes and I realize: this is how those British journalists got themselves killed.

I don't remember many of the details; it was part of that thick pile of background articles I read while we were in Frankfurt, lounging on the sofa on Sunday morning while listening to Aerosmith warble "Love in an Elevator" on the satellite TV. What I do recall is that two correspondents from the *Financial Times* were driving, unescorted, down one of these long, straight oil-patch access roads when they lost their way in the impenetrable smoke, slid off the pavement, and were engulfed in the horrible flames. Maybe this is the road. If Aboud wants to motor like Parnelli Jones around here, I promise to myself, I will get out and walk home. I'm scaring myself again.

In this mood, we enter the inferno.

Now the landscape we had seen from the descending jumbo spreads out before us, as flat as some satanic Kansas, the limb of the horizon broken by dozens of vertical orange jets, as if a crust of sand had fallen over an ocean of flame that, here and there, had managed to burn its way to freedom, leaping out from narrow vents. Hypnotized – we all are – I get out of the car and stare at the closest fire. It is about a hundred yards away, screaming like the engine of a Boeing on a taxiway, captivating yet terrifying, as if the whole surface of the earth might blow apart at any moment. Maurice is set up and shooting, his big body hunched over the viewfinder, twisting the focus ring, then, satisfied with the framing, turning to me and saying, "It's unbelievable, what they did."

No one else is in sight; from here, it doesn't appear that anyone is trying to put the fires out. Then, behind us, a pickup truck zips by. It's some American soldiers. Leaning from the windows, they snap some souvenir photos, turn around, and drive away.

We continue ahead, a little farther into the alien world. There are fires on both sides of the road, not big ones – it is easy to tell that some of the gushers are more powerful than others – but even more menacing, because one of the burning wells sits in the centre of a pool of leaked oil and all around the perimeter of this jet-black lake are little wispy flits of dancing flames, as if the ground itself is burning away. We are so close now that even with the windows rolled up and Aboud's air conditioner set at its maximum, the ferocious heat first warms my cheek, then pinches it with pain.

Outside, a little distance away, it is hot but not uncomfortable, even when the billows of smoke abate for an instant and the full Kuwaiti sun falls through. A stiff wind is blowing from the north-west – from Baghdad – and when I face it, I can watch more of the tiny black specks accumulate on the lenses of my glasses.

A mile or so south of the Safety Boss trailers, with us still unable to see anyone at work anywhere in the fields, the road curves slightly and around this bend is a wall of the blackest smoke we have yet encountered, an opaque cone of ebony rising, narrowly at first, from a fire just a few feet from the pavement, then expanding to completely cover the roadway, blown horizontal by the whipping winds. I, for one, am not going to try to punch through this wall in anybody's car, certainly not Aboud's Audi – but there appears to be a detour around it, a pair of wheel tracks leading onto the sands, bright white marks in the blackened soil. We're about to test it.

"Would anybody know a land mine if he saw it?" I ask, and, hearing this, Aboud wheels his baby around and we head back to al-Ahmadi, Kuwait.

Maurice Chabot and Chris Davies climb into Miller's four-by-four and I get into another vehicle with Ken Rose, a Safety Boss engineer who, if this is possible, is even more gentlemanly than Miller. Rose, a father of three, soft-faced, shy, aw-shucksy, is looking forward to the end of his first tour of duty here. Miller's men are working 28 days in Kuwait without a break, then being sprung for 28 unpaid days off – with a plane ticket home if they choose to go that far. Ken Rose, as we drive out of the equipment yard, tells me that he is looking forward not to four weeks of alcoholic debauch, as I'd expect, but to visiting his aging mother in Orillia, Ontario.

Our truck follows Miller's, down the paved road we had taken this morning in the Audi, to the lake of oil where the burned-out skeletons of a small car and two big water-tanker trucks rest, half submerged, in the lifeless sea. This is where the two British journalists and three Egyptian teamsters lost their way, left the road, and died. It is exactly the spot where, with my jest about land mines, I convinced Aboud to turn around.

The lake of pure crude oil, as we stand by its shore, stretches a couple of hundred yards eastward from the paved road. Miller says that it is only about five feet deep, a mere puddle compared to the black oceans that lie farther into the desert. The surface is calm, flat, reflecting the flames and smoke that arc through the furious sky. Beyond it are more of the giant squashed soda cans, a storage-tank farm the Iraqis torched. A bewildered swallow flits and darts over the oil and the wreckage, as if this was some prairie pond and these were boulders, not twisted metal tombs.

The bodies have been removed and a bulldozer has created a dam of sand along the shore of the oil pond, to keep it from running onto the pavement. No one will ever know what really happened. One theory is that the heat of the engines ignited the oil into which the vehicles sank. It may have been a sudden conflagration. Or the men may have had time to try to escape, frantically jamming the gears as the honey-thick oil ensnared them and the flames began to rise. With so much other work to be done, the wreckage has been left where it is, a reminder, as the fire fighters drive past each evening, that they have made it through another day; a hint, each morning, of what may lie around the next bend in the road.

The smoke today is as thick and impenetrable as it must have been the day the five men died. The fire from which it erupts is not a simple jet of flames surging from a severed pipe, as some are, but a miniature volcano of sand and rock and the molten metal fragments of one of the nine hundred wellheads the Iraqis blew up, or tried to. Dousing and capping the cleanly cut wells will be simple, a walk in the park, Miller says. But a fire like this one, seething through a small mountain of glass and coke from a pipeline that might have been sheared away twenty feet underground, will require months of labour. It will be several years, he predicts, before all the treachery is undone, the oil flows, the skies clear, and expatriate executives once again loll on the porch of Ahmadi House, sipping Shirley Temples and foamless Islamic beer.

The detour around the roadblock of smoke leads us right onto the desert sand. The trail has been well blazed; we rock and roll deep in white-yellow ruts that have been carved into the black-crusted soil. After just a few hours here, our arms, necks and hands are polka-dotted with little spots, and my favourite baseball cap, bright green, with the insignia of the Estellas Orientales (the Eastern Stars) of San Pedro de Macorís in the Dominican Republic, has been ruinously blotched. But after three months of unceasing carbon rain, the fragile earth itself shows the most awful evidence of torture. All around us, the ground is thickly coated with a layer of fallen tar. Grasses and low bushes, specialized for this dry ecosystem, are matted and soaked. Yet uncountable thousands of anthills have been pushed up through the crust, forming bright little circles on the dark lunar tableau.

Just to our right is a half cylinder of beige plastic, about four feet long, lying on the ground. There is some English lettering stencilled on it, but I can't make it out as we bump and grind along.

"What's that?" I ask Ken Rose.

"Cluster-bomb casing," he replies, yawning.

Every few hundred yards, heading back toward the oil field known since the 1930s as al-Burgan ("the Volcano," an apt, if innocently given, appellation), we pass a well either on fire, gushing oil or, occasionally, wired to explode but still intact, either through equipment failure or the premature departure of the troops assigned to blow it. We can see the sandbags piled around the well-head – the dynamite was packed down in a hole dug around the pipeline – and from there, a thin wire leads across the sand to one of the abandoned bunkers. (There never were towering derricks or nodding pumps here, as in North American oil fields. The Arabian reserves are so rich, the oil under such high pressure deep underground, it vaults out of its epochal confinement as soon as a pipe is sunk, the world's easiest exploitation of fossil fuel.)

The destruction of the Kuwaiti oil wells was not a decision hastily taken. In the war of kept promises – George Bush vowing that "this aggression will not stand"; Tariq Aziz calmly assuring the world from Geneva that Israel would certainly be attacked – Saddam Hussein declared that he would have his innings with the al-Sabahs, and in that game he has been victorious. The sandbags, the wires, the pillage at al-Ahmadi speak of studious planning and malevolent genius – a Professor Moriarty, a Lex Luthor – wreaking terror on a grand, cartoon scale, and though the men in these meagre little fortifications were merely the instruments of evil, it was they, not their commandant, who huddled here, in the bombsights of the enemy's computerized killing machines, until the order came to light the fuses and flee. The fact that the man who gave the order still sits unharmed in Baghdad makes Ken Rose sicker than the smoke.

But the pollution, as we dive back into it, has Rose concerned as well. He says he sometimes feels a tightness in his chest, "like I had when I used to smoke," and that other men have been complaining about difficulty in breathing. One morning early in the work – before Miller decided to move to the edge of the field – they were trying to cap a gusher just outside al-Ahmadi town, the smoke was so thick they couldn't see ten feet in any direction, and everyone, Rose says, felt edgy and lethargic. He puts it down to "lack of oxygen." It might have just been fear.

We are in the heart of the fire zone again, parked, it seems, at the edge of a great body of water. The tracks in the sand run toward the sea, enter it, and vanish. But this is not the Persian Gulf. It is the giant of all the oceans of oil, so huge I can't see the opposite shore; how deep it is, no one has waded in to find out. It must be more than a mile on each side. It will take months, at least, to drain. And there are dozens more.

As Maurice pans across the unbroken smoothness of the oil, capturing the reflection of the burning wells that mark its perimeter, Mike Miller says he's heard that some of the Texans plan to go sailboarding on this petroleum pond, and then send the tape of their exploits to *America's Funniest Home Videos*.

The idea is so loopy, today's whole adventure so ridiculous, I decide to mention that back at the International Hotel, the other reporters told me there is even a herd of wild horses roaming this Kurt Vonnegut range.

"Yes," Miller says. "I've seen them."

He has seen them, but they do not run free. In the centre of the al-Burgan field, there is an oasis. At this oasis the al-Sabah family has built a small palace, a holiday retreat. At this kingly cottage on the Arabian sands, the monarch has kept his thoroughbreds, feeding them on the finest grass.

Now the oil field is a raging tempest, but the country palace still stands. We approach it, carefully, cautiously, threading our way toward the distant walls and towers in a little-trodden landscape of cluster bomblets and shallow lakes of oil that splash the door-frames and splatter the windshield as we slowly motor through them, hubcap deep. Ken Rose navigates a little nervously in the wake of Mike Miller's truck. We are just about to tiptoe through another swamp of oil when we notice that Miller's tail pipe is on fire.

It's too late – there's nothing we can do. The lead vehicle is already in the black lagoon, but the oil does not ignite. The fire in the pipe goes out. I start to breathe again.

Miller has been out here once before – he saw some horses nibbling at oil-sodden trees beyond the yellow-brick palace walls – but the falling tar has covered his tire prints. Bouncing and bumping on the unbroken sand, passing in and out of blinding smoke, the heat of the fires burning my face though the window

– looking around, I count 79 burning wells within my range of vision – we circumnavigate the palace enclosure, searching in the darkness for the gate.

Along the southern wall of the compound, an ornamental door stands open. Beyond it, I see palm trees, hanging heavy with shiny oil; a driveway lined with ornamental bushes, some of them with bright pink blossoms erupting from blackened mats of leaves; garbage, wreckage, some small outbuildings and garages trashed and burned, a smashed and overturned Jeep. The main building of the palace – about the size of a modest Rosedale mansion – has been violated and sacked. And at the end of the garden pathway, a grey-haired man in a stained blue shirt is holding a little green bird.

The wind roars. The sky turns orange, white, black, purple, impossible colours in an impossible place. Two parallel rows of towers in a side garden look like light standards, but they are dovecotes; a single pigeon, last of the emir's racing flock, perches on the ledge of its nesting hole, glistening, soaked in gum. The Iraqis ate the others.

We climb down from our trucks.

"The set for David Lynch's next movie," Chris says.

The man who is holding the bird stares at us through the swirling smoke. The disbelief is mutual. While Maurice hurries to film the pigeon houses, the sodden trees, the wild, windy sky, I introduce myself to the man in the blue shirt. He is a Bostonian, John Walsh, representative of the World Society for the Protection of Animals. He has come to rescue the horses.

Walsh has been in Kuwait since the first week of March. He is weary, exhausted, a little confused. His first priority had been the Kuwait City zoo. The Iraqis had shot some of the animals, fed others to the lions for sport and dined on the deer and the antelope themselves.

"I took 56 animals out of al-Ahmadi when I first got here," Walsh says. "This is April . . . May . . . this is May . . . back in, early in March, we took out cattle, sheep, goats, donkeys."

This is May 4. I suddenly realize: today's the Kentucky Derby.

When he arrived in the emirate, Walsh didn't know that any of the emir's thoroughbreds had survived the war. A photographer had been here and had seen them, oil-soaked and shrunken, muzzling the blackened arbour for edible morsels of green. The photographer had told John Walsh.

A water pipe had been laid years earlier, from the coast to the monarch's pleasure garden. The horses had found the outlet. The water had kept them alive.

Four horses survive. Walsh has moved them into a stable behind the main house. Fodder has been flown in from Canada, not only for these helpless victims of sabotage and ruin, but for the few remaining livestock animals – about fifteen hundred out of twenty thousand – in the country. Tomorrow, Walsh will bring a truck down here, through the lakes of oil, the cluster bombs and the swirling blackness, and try to get the four horses out.

We set up for a quick interview, the setting sun painting our faces briefly golden as it searches for a passage through the smoke, then, the sun defeated, everything goes grey.

"Can you describe the extent of the devastation?" I ask John Walsh.

"It's affected everything," he answers, speaking very rapidly; as with all on-camera interviews, I'm measuring his words, editing in my head, listening for useable clips, in-points and out-points, the antithesis of normal human conversation. Even here, we are focused on lighting, battery life, sound bites.

I ask Maurice for a close-up of the bird in Walsh's hand. It is a bee eater, robin sized, iridescent green, but its beak is clotted with tar and it is barely alive, not fighting to break free, slowly blinking. It has come from Africa, bound, possibly, for Iran.

Walsh says, "The birds that are migrating through are dying. I'm seeing large numbers of them here in the trees that are unable to fly. I think everything migrating through that's going to be lightly oiled will continue on its migration, will have cleaned itself, preened, ingested the oil, and will die later on during its migration."

The Bostonian leads us around the palace to the stable behind it. We pass heaps of wrecked furniture; lawn chairs; a basketball. The former residents of this Xanadu draw no sympathy from Walsh; he is horrified that the government, which is the al-Sabah family, has shown no concern for all the animals of Kuwait.

"The government says they have other priorities," Walsh says.

He is reluctant to put on a pony show for the sake of the CBC. The interior of the stable, a low stucco building, is far too dark for Maurice to enter and shoot. We prevail upon Walsh to bring one of the horses out into the weakening daylight. There is a little exercise yard, a walking ring where Walsh has piled up some hay.

The animal that slowly steps out of the building is a chestnut mare, smallish, subdued, with darker patches of matted oil along her flanks and twisted clots of tar in her tail and mane. She stands stock-still, makes no sound.

What is she thinking, I wonder, of this world of men?

- excerpted from *Scaring Myself Again*

EUROPE

Previous page: In the Catacombs of Paris (Agata Motyczyńska)

"*Fifty years ago this spring,*" I wrote in Maclean's *magazine in 1995,* "*my father liberated Europe. . . . Later that summer, he was in California, about to be reassigned to the Pacific war, but when the Japanese heard that Sgt. Ben Abel was on his way westward, they surrendered, too.*"

I have only a basic understanding of how my father routed the Nazis, fighting house-to-house and hand-to-hand with a division of the U.S. Army called the Timberwolves. I know that I have phoned him from various points on my own easy, civilian travels – Aachen, Liège, Dortmund – and he has perked up at the names of these places and revealed that he had been there in another time, a guest of his Uncle Sam.

This always made me feel small, and guilty for the leisure of my life.

He has told me a little of the terror of those times, of watching friends fall headless in sudden spouts of blood beside him; of riding on the outside *of tanks, exposed to sniper fire, during the great push to the Rhine. Then of returning to New York, and writing across the continent to the mothers and wives of the men of his platoon who never would come home.*

When I was a boy, I would open the lid of the case that held his Purple Heart, and stare at the sternness on Washington's face, and wonder if – in the same circumstances – I would have found my father's courage.

Thank God, I will never know. My own European travels have been a merry lark. But never do I forget what he went through, and all the soldiers of all the ages, on the continent of our crimson ancestry.

In Search of the Year 1000

—————————— • ——————————

"Already, people are coming to me and saying, 'Father, I am afraid of the Millennium,'" the Canon of Autun tells me, as we sip crème de cassis in his panelled study, across a narrow lane from one of France's great cathedrals. Abbé Denis Grivot is 76, a renowned scholar of medieval lore. "The TV, the newspapers play it up so much," he sighs. "'The year two thousand! The year two thousand!' People come to me – they see catastrophes on TV and they think the world is coming to an end.

"I think we are in an epoch of decadence, yes, but we are not the first," he says. "Egypt, Greece, Rome – after every one, there was a renaissance.

"I tell them of the year *one* thousand. There were catastrophes, yes, as in every age. But there was no terror. It was an *optimistic* time. It is exactly the same thing today.

"I believe in a progression of history. I don't believe the world will ever end. The world evolves. It does not end. I must show the people that I am not afraid. On New Year's Eve 1999, I shall give a very optimistic sermon."

I have spent the past 12 months in search of the Year 1000 AD, seeking to learn how much of the soul of the ancients we retain, unsuspected, in ourselves. The trail has taken me across Christian Europe, from Yorkshire to Poland to the Pyrenees, to cathedrals and abbeys and mouldy archives and the holy bones of saints. I have slept in the cradle of the Middle Ages and marched to battle with a Saxon king.

It has been a marvellous journey, spurred by a love of history and by the thousandth anniversary of a thousand years ago – the looming, dooming Millennium that has already sent lunatics flying off to Comet Hale-Bopp aboard Starship Suicide. Yet this is only the prelude to our own generation's rendezvous with wonderment and fear. So we ponder how they handled it the last time around.

Our intuition tells us that a thousand years ago, the Millennium must have weighed heavily on the minds of men and kings. The priests had kept the calendar and read the Book of Revelation:

> Then I saw an angel coming down from heaven, holding in his hand the key of the bottomless pit and a great chain. And he seized the dragon, that ancient serpent, who is the Devil and Satan, and bound him for a thousand years, and threw him into the pit, and shut it and sealed it over him, that he should deceive the nations no more, till the thousand years were ended. After that he must be loosed for a little while.

The thousand years were ending. Surely, nations trembled at the darkest hour of the Dark Ages. "A general consternation seized mankind," the Scots historian, William Robertson, wrote in the 18th century, describing the late tenth century. "Many relinquished their possessions, and abandoning their friends and families, hurried with precipitation to the Holy Land, where they imagined that Christ would quickly appear to judge the world."

"Buildings of every sort were suffered to fall into ruins," another Scottish writer, Charles Mackay, claimed in 1852. "It was thought useless to repair them, when the end of the world was so near."

"The Millennium of the supposed birth of Christ brings fear of the Last Judgment and the end of mankind throughout the Christian world," reports the entry for 1000 AD in a popular reference book called *The Chronicle of World History*, published in 1993.

But looking backward across a hundred decades is not so simple. What filled the minds of men and women in Anno Domini 1000, no living person really knows. For first-hand reportage, our only source is a French monk named Rodulfus (Ralph) Glaber, whose chronicle, written close to the year 1030, complains that:

A thousand years after the Lord was born on earth of a Virgin . . .
Fraud, theft and all infamy reign supreme in the world . . .
The sword, plague and famine rage all about,
And the impiety of men uncorrected spares no one.

All the symptoms of the Last Judgment were on display. In 993, Glaber wrote, Vesuvius erupted and "almost all the cities of Italy and Gaul were ravaged by flames of fire." Also, "a horrible plague raged among men, namely a hidden fire which, upon whatsoever limb it fastened, consumed it and severed it from the body." As if this wasn't enough, "a most mighty famine raged for five years throughout the Roman world . . . so fierce waxed this hunger that grown-up sons devoured their mothers and mothers, forgetting their maternal love, ate their babes."

Yet mankind did not abruptly end on 1/1/1000. It survived to engender Joan of Arc, Rembrandt, Newton, Jefferson, Chairman Mao, and Shania Twain. Nor were most people consumed with dread as the date approached. There were, most scholars now believe, no terrified crowds huddling in soot-blackened chapels as the clocks tolled the knell of Doomsday on New Year's Eve, 999. For one thing, there were no clocks.

And today, we have had Mount St. Helens, the Kobe earthquake, flesh-eating disease, alien abductions, and Rwanda. But when the fearful clamour and the New Agers quake, they come to the Canon of Autun and he calms them with tales of the turn of the first Millennium. "Those people really *loved*," he says. "They built those amazing cathedrals. There was a *passion* and I have a passion. They believed in love and I believe in love."

In the year 1000, the Italians had no tomato sauce for their linguine (and no linguine), tea was unknown in England, the Jews endured Hanukkah without potato pancakes, and the benighted Swiss had never heard of chocolate. In Egypt, nobody smoked Camels. King Macbeth was about to bleed Scotland; in Denmark, Prince Hamlet had just begun to be. The Arabs had Spain. The Vikings were on the road in western Newfoundland, versus the hometown redskins.

Christianity was spreading north-eastward. It had reached Kiev by 988, Hungary and Poland by the end of the century. In Britain, most of the Norsemen had converted willingly, giving up on Odin and Thor. They arrived in Yorkshire with boatloads of herring and were told by the Saxons that they only did commerce with Christians.

"Vell den, ve are Christians, too," the Vikings cheerfully agreed.

The weather was balmy. Mean temperatures were two or three Celsius degrees higher in 1000 than in our own ozone-depleted age. It was the Early Medieval Warm Period. The polar ice caps melted slightly, making exploration, settlement, and pillaging easier around Greenland and the Arctic bays.

The Roman Empire was dust, the Byzantines were splitting permanently from the Western church, and the Pope was a Frenchman.

In America, unaware of the First Coming of Christ, let alone the Second, the pagans were constructing magnificent pyramids in the jungles of Guatemala and four-storey apartment buildings in the deserts of New Mexico. The most cosmopolitan city in the world was probably Kaifeng, China. In 1000, most Europeans lived and loved in wattle-and-daub huts.

But high in the mountains of Catalonia, a holy man named Oliba Cabreta was etching his name into the altarpiece of a miraculous new church. He was the son of a count, yet he cast off his title and his estates to answer God's subpoena. Perhaps the approaching Millennium inspired him to call his broker. Perhaps it was a tax dodge. We will never know.

Oliba's graffito endures, as does the abbey for which he abandoned his earthly wealth. It is the Romanesque masterpiece of Saint-Michel-de-Cuxa, a working Benedictine monastery on a slope above the river Têt at the very bottom of France. The nearest major city is Perpignan, whose homely railway station Salvador Dali, for some surrealist reason, once declared to be the Centre of the Universe. Two miles below the abbey is Prades, where Pablo Casals lived in voluntary exile from the Franco regime for about 20 years.

In the faltering daylight of November, I arrive at Cuxa in a rented Fiat smaller than the Mars Pathfinder. With me are a Monsieur Calm from the Prades civic administration and a Mrs. Hicks from the local tourist office. As we negotiate the narrow alleys of the town and climb toward the abbey, Monsieur Calm discourses on the history of the region.

"They talk of great fear in the year one thousand, *la grande peur*," he says. "That is a romantic idea that we think they had. But there were two much greater fears – the Arabs coming up from the south, and the Vikings coming down from the north. Those were the true terrors of the year one thousand. I don't think they really had the idea of the end of the world, because so many people were building houses around here."

"Maybe so," says Mrs. Hicks, a Welshwoman who has lived in Prades for 20 years. "But there are people today building fallout shelters who think they'll be the only ones who'll survive, aren't there?"

Saint-Michel-de-Cuxa is announced by a peach orchard, a graveyard, and a long, low wall that, Monsieur Calm explains, was manhandled into place, stone by stone, by one of the monks. Above it, one of the finest surviving monuments of the tenth century pierces the mist – the tall, square tower of the abbey, begun in the 970s, sheltered by the folds of Mount Canigou, the Catalonian Everest.

The abbot, a very slender and charming Barcelonan named Father Ramón, awaits us at the portal. He has been resident at Saint-Michel for 32 years, roughly half his life. He leads us through the courtyard, pausing to let us admire the surviving columns and portico. The rest of the quadrangle, he explains, was scavenged by the Rockefellers and installed in Upper Manhattan – the cloister at the Cloisters is the cloister of Cuxa.

Father Ramón extracts a key from the pocket of his chinos and opens the door of the church.

"*Voici l'an Mil*," he says. Here is the Year 1000. And the abbot asks me, "Why would they have built a church like this if they thought the world would end?"

The architecture of the church is so heavy – the columns are as round and thick as sequoias – that I feel the ceiling will fall in. But I am comforted by the knowledge that the archways have been standing for 1,025 years.

"Sometimes," he says, "I am thinking about other things, and then it hits me as I enter here that I am the continuance of *une tradition ancienne*."

In addition to living history, the Benedictine monks at Saint-Michel-de-Cuxa – all seven of them – harvest peaches and nectarines, make jams and cheese to be sold at the market in Prades, breed German shepherds, tend several hundred sheep, and sell their wool, maintain the grounds, and try to keep the ancient buildings in decent repair. A music festival in memory of old man Casals fills the great church every August.

We walk up to the altar and Father Ramón shows me where Oliba knifed his name into the slab. The stone has not been in place throughout the entire millennium, however. It was being used as someone's balcony in the village of Vinça when a travelling scholar fortuitously spotted it from the window of a bus and retrieved it for Saint-Michel.

"A thousand years ago," Father Ramón says, "the abbots from Cuxa went to Jerusalem and brought back a relic from the Holy Manger of Bethlehem. For them, relics were the most important thing."

"They had more than two hundred relics around here," Monsieur Calm inserts. "One church had a bag of hair from the Virgin Mary, and Cuxa had a piece of the Holy Crèche."

"Today," says Father Ramón, "we'd be saying, 'Is this really the wood? Can we test the wood?' It's the evolution of man – we study more, we learn more.

"But essentially, I think the same as the monks of one thousand years ago – somewhere inside each person is the love of God and the most important thing is love."

I inquire respectfully whether the abbey accepts overnight visitors. I have visions of a garret high in the ancient tower, with hooded monks chanting and the moonlight tumbling in through the Lombard arches.

"Come back at nine o'clock," the abbot nods.

That evening, precisely on time, I haul up to the doorway of the abbey and my knock is answered by a tiny old monk who leads me to my quarters. "*Je suis Joseph*," he whispers. All else is silence. The wind puffs gently down from Canigou.

My "cell" – it is merely a standard bedroom – contains a cot with fitted green sheets, a map of Catalonia circa 1680, an icon of Jesus, and a prayer book in the Catalan vernacular open to the Twenty-third Psalm:

El Senyor és el meu pastor,
no em manca res . . .

Outside my window, there is a direct-broadcast television satellite dish.

At precisely seven o'clock in the morning, I join the seven men – Ramón and his monks – for matins and then head for breakfast. "I was young, once upon a time," Father Ramón tells me, over toast and Lipton tea and the abbey's white peach confiture. "At 17, I felt the calling to become a monk. I have had crises, like everyone else, but I'm accustomed to this life. Imagine you are part of a couple – of course, there are times when you wish that the other wasn't there. This is like a man and a woman – it's not so easy to break up. You remain in the couple."

There are casualties. Ramón's brother tried the monastic life, quit, moved to Chicago, and became the father of two.

"It's a vocation, rather than a job," the abbot continues. "When I was young, I felt an *inquiétude* about religion and God. To me, my life and everything I do is part of this *recherche de Dieu*. I am searching, yes, but unfortunately, you don't find God by looking around with a flashlight.

"One monk came here around the year one thousand and wrote 'I can stand the heat and the cold.' He did climatic studies and based it all on angels. The monks of one thousand saw angels everywhere. I don't see them, but that doesn't mean they are not there.

"I don't know what the face of an angel should look like, but the images on art are very suggestive. Angels are like the wind – you don't see it, but you see the traces the wind leaves behind."

A history of Saint-Michel-de-Cuxa, written in 1881 by the abbot of the day, had suggested that the great Oliba himself had taken to the monastery in trepidation of the impending *fin du monde*. But by the middle of our own century, Western historians were dismissing that sort of thinking as a lot of hooey, decreeing that the Panic Terror of the Year 1000 never happened at all.

Even the chronicle of Ralph Glaber was said not to be worth the parchment it was written on. In 1931, in his four-volume *Life in the Middle Ages*, the Cambridge fellow, G. G. Coulton, had pooh-poohed "certain exaggerated deductions" drawn from Glaber "as to the overwhelming significance of the year AD 1000."

"It was not only at and about this date that our forefathers expected strange events," Dr. Coulton sniffed. "The medieval mind was perpetually haunted by the expectation of Antichrist."

But that hasn't stopped Professor Richard Landes of Boston University, a maverick medievalist who is convinced that nearly every tenth-century Christian – even the illiterate farmers – knew exactly when to expect the Year 1000 and the cataclysm that was sure to accompany it. Spurred on by Glaber and other sources, Professor Landes has become today's lone horseman of the Apocalypse, publishing extensively and firing off a series of essays on the Internet to prove his case.

"The historian who sails through this period ignoring what he thinks is the apocalyptic flotsam, has, without knowing it, already sunk on the edges of an iceberg he has not seen," he writes in an enormously long treatise on tenth-century angst posted on the Web site of his Center for Millennial Studies.

(The fact that there are very, very few apocalyptic references that survive from the tenth century may be due to one of two causes. There may have been little awareness or apprehension of the Millennium to write home about. Or, later generations of monastic scribes may have shredded the old manuscripts, since their reports of "panic terror" had proved embarrassingly wrong to the church. How many bookstores still carry *The Coming Crash of 1992?*)

On the telephone from Boston, Dr. Landes makes his case for the widespread expectation of the *fin du monde*. "If you believed that the Millennium of Christ was going to usher in the Last Judgment," he thrusts, "wouldn't you go to the village priest and ask, 'How much longer, Father?' Every priest knew the correct Anno Domini. They had to know, to calculate the date for Easter."

As further proof, Professor Landes cites an assemblage near Amiens, north of Paris – peasants, noblemen, and clergy united in a campaign known as the Peace of God movement – a sort of medieval Million-Man March in 1033. If the world had not ended in 1000, our ancestors believed, surely it would terminate that year, a thousand years after the Crucifixion. Hence a series of pacifist marches, convocations, rallies.

"It was the first major movement to combine elements of the popular and the elite," Landes says. "Such an extraordinary event would take place *only* under the fear of the coming Last Judgment."

Rodulfus Glaber described the assemblies in colourful detail:

> At the millennium of the Lord's Passion . . . the bishops and abbots and other devout men of Aquitaine first summoned great councils of the whole people, to which were borne the bodies of many saints and innumerable caskets of holy relics. . . . Such enthusiasm was generated that the bishops raised their croziers to the heavens, and all cried out with one voice to God, their hands extended: "Peace! Peace! Peace!"

"By and large in the historical profession, we are trained not to take this thing too seriously," Landes gripes. "I'm really, basically, the first historian to re-examine the dossier. The evidence is clear – from the second century onward, Christians believed the end of the millennium would bring the Second Coming of Christ."

"Don't the French accept this?" I ask.

"The French have it right under their noses, but they don't see it," the Bostonian huffs. "They're all so constipated over there."

After three days of Camembert and snails, I am, too.

To Britain, then, and decent food.

At the base of the ramparts of a ruined castle, hidden in a grove of pines, we wait for the summons to rise, to fight, to die. Some of us lie quietly in the late summer grass, picking at the hems and seams of our handmade raiment. Warriors test their wooden shields, and file the points of their swords.

We are Saxons, led by brave Godwin Haroldson, son of Harold the King. Our England is no longer our own. On the rise beyond the forest, the usurpers await us – garlic-eaters from Normandy.

Beyond them, camp followers and countrymen have gathered in the forecourt of Old Sarum to watch the combat, out of range of the arrows and javelins.

It is a holiday weekend and Godwin Haroldson and I – along with Edgar the Atheling, Lady Godgifu, Wulfgyth the peasant, Eadnoth the Staller, Gunnhild, and a cast of hundreds – are tilting in the Wiltshire countryside, three miles from Stonehenge. I have been given a red and blue banner to carry onto the field of battle – an emblem of locked arms and clasped hands. Hundreds of tourists have paid five pounds each to watch.

"We'll try to protect you," Godwin Haroldson comforts me, "but if somebody gets through and wants to fight you, just say 'non-combatant' and fall down dead."

Such is the fate of a rookie in The Vikings Norse Film and Pageant Society. (Today, the Vikings are acting the parts of Normans *and* Saxons.) I have been taught the rudiments of medieval swordplay – "we *never* hit anyone in the head" – and have been given a helmet, a chain-mail glove, and a plywood shield, but they will not let me actually take part in hand-to-hand mayhem without a further 20 hours of instruction. So I get to carry the flag.

My mentor is a biochemist named Deborah Hodges. Like most of my fellow re-enactors, she is an educated professional, obsessed with the minutest details of costume and weaponry, and enraptured by the romance of a thousand years ago.

"I was walking down the street in Cambridge," she tells me, "when I saw a young woman with a knife in her belt. I had read an article about kids bringing knives to school and I thought, 'Hmm – she's rather nasty.' Then I saw a guy in chain mail carrying a Dane axe. That looked like fun."

Joining The Vikings Norse Film and Pageant Society, Dr. Hodges and her husband, Dr. Ben Davis, another Cantabrigian biochemist, found themselves increasingly consumed by a passion for historical exactitude. The Vikings make their own hobnailed boots, forge their own armour, sew their own costumes, and thrash their weapons about with such panache and ferocity that it is amazing that only one person has been killed in the past few years.

"It was during a stage show," Dr. Davis explains. "An actor was demonstrating sword-fighting when his opponent's sword broke. The jagged edge cut through the main artery in his thigh."

He opens the trunk of his car and shows me a thick iron helmet with a deep dent in the crown.

"A five-year-old did this," he says.

In search of the Year 1000 – and in search of an educational and comradely hobby – thousands of Britons and North Americans have taken up the lance. Some groups are rather amateurish – "they use plastic swords and wear American football helmets," Dr. Davis sniffs. But all are stymied by ignorance of the epoch of Eadnoth and Lady Godgifu.

"Audiences expect horned helmets and bare chests – well, the truth is, the Vikings *didn't* wear horns in their helmets and a woman could divorce her husband if he bared his chest. That's why they wore these brooches at the neck of their cloaks, to keep from exposing the chest."

For accommodation, I am provided with a canvas tent, a couple of goatskins, and all the fleas and black ants I can swallow. Luckily, there is a pub across the road, an anachronism even the most dedicated Vikings tolerate, as a chilly English fog is cloaking the battlefield. Late in the evening before the battle, I order a jacket potato, which was unknown in eleventh-century Britain, and hard cider, which wasn't.

"Why this obsession with the past?" I ask a couple of archaeologists who are taking part in the exhibition.

"Because it's there, and it has always been there," says Mark Randerson, a specialist in pre-Conquest field work who goes by the nickname of Trixie. (He plays Eadnoth the Staller – keeper of the king's horses – in the pageant.) "We are a very thin skin of bubbles on top of the deep well of human history. I challenge anyone not to find a facet of history to fascinate him."

"It's a profession for dreamers," his colleague Caroline Buckley says. "At least when you start off. Then the hard work begins."

"History gives you a set of rules you can define yourself by," Trixie muses. "It's a window on human behaviour and human values – and it teaches us that human values have not always been the same as they are today.

"Just because we think this way now doesn't mean that people a thousand years ago thought this way. But the way they *did* think influences how we think now."

When it is time to go into combat, I am five paces behind Godwin Haroldson as the first volley of (rubber-tipped) arrows flies toward us. We cower under our shields. Don Cherry would decry it as "turtling," but after all, we are Scandinavians.

Six caparisoned horses charge, their riders flaunting spears. Some of the men (and women) in our front rank are annihilated. The rest of us courageously run away.

Then comes the full force of the Norman infantry. The next few minutes are a blur. (They won't let me wear my glasses.) Valiantly defending our banner to my last drop of cider, I am drowned in a crescendo of metal on metal, iron on wood, blades piercing flesh, groans, shouts, cries, sweat, confusion, orders, rallies, and retreats.

The rules of engagement are these: if you are touched by an enemy sword or lance in the abdomen, ribcage, or head, you must fall down dead. If struck in the arm or lower leg, you may fight on. It is very poor form to jest, Python-like, "Hah! Only a flesh wound!"

About half our soldiers go straight to Valhalla. But no foe even comes close to me, and I am still standing defiantly with my red and blue flag when Godgifu and her ladies-in-waiting enter the field with bulls' horns full of water.

Suddenly, a single-engine airplane sputters over our heads, descending for the Salisbury landing strip.

"Don't worry, lads – it's one of ours!" cries Godwin Haroldson.

The next afternoon, now a full-fledged, battle-hardened, dues-paying soldier, I am standing outside the Marks & Spencer store at Coppergate in the English city of York. A chorus of ten-year-olds in bright orange T-shirts is singing the Monkees' immortal "Last Train to Clarksville," the square is as crowded as Hong Kong at Lunar New Year, and a poster is inviting me to "See How The Vikings Lived and Dyed."

In front of me, the goal of a considerable queue, is the Jorvik Viking Centre, a Disney-style, yet scientifically faithful, under-ground recreation of life in Viking England in the tenth century, AD. "They Raided and Slaughtered," screams a display at the entrance, but the rest of the exhibit concentrates on commerce and family life.

We clamber into driver-less battery-powered cars and motor through a restoration of the streets of Viking York. Thatched houses, a riverside quay, animal pens, and "lifelike" dummies illustrate the period. Sounds and smells are pumped in, most noticeably in a backyard where a man is squinting and squatting behind a low twig fence, creating what the guidebook calls "human stools (pooh)."

The theme of mundane Viking life continues in a museum at the end of the ride: ice skates, eel bones, combs, purses, shoes tanned in urine. A schoolboy examines some granules in a glass case.

"Look, Mum – human faces!" he exclaims.

"No," she corrects her boy. "That's human *feces*."

"When you think of the Vikings," Dr. Peter Addyman, the direc-tor of the York Archaeological Trust, tells me later, "you think of rape, pillage, all those macho things. But the truth is, we exca-vated for five years and took out forty thousand artefacts, and only five of them were in any way military. Even in violent eras, ninety-nine per cent of life is people getting on living, loving, dying, burying, taking out the garbage, and going to the loo.

"We built the Jorvik Viking Centre as a *corrective*. This was one of the most prosperous places in Europe a thousand years ago. It was, for its day, a tremendous success story. A great importing centre. A place where sailors came ashore and married local girls. If there was raping, there is very little record of it. If there was pillaging, there is little archaeological evidence. We hope that people will leave here with the understanding that this was a very important place. As was once said of the church, 'They go to mock and remain to pray.'"

Down in Wiltshire, Trixie Randerson had complained that the Jorvik Viking Centre portrayed "a Thatcherite view of Britain – small shopkeepers making their own way in the world." Dr. Addyman accepts this – to a point.

"What we see is that there must have been a Mrs. Thatcher saying, 'You *will* do this. You *will* re-lay the street system. You *will* put in a new bridge over the River Ouse. You *will* chop down every tree for three miles around.' You see the same thing in Denmark by the year one thousand – great bridges and causeways all over the country. The Vikings must have had quite a Minister of Transport organizing everything."

A few years ago, Dr. Addyman travelled to rural China and was dizzied by what he found. He says, "It had exactly the feel I imagined of eleventh-century Europe. I thought, 'Gosh – I'm looking at something I've been digging up back home.'"

But the Chinese are living and the Vikings are dead. "Archaeology has limits of inference," Dr. Addyman allows. "You've got the clothes, the textiles, the colours, the jewellery, the environmental evidence, the rotting vegetables, the trash in the street, the pig bones, the turds. You can go to something pretty close to the truth. We have their words, but we don't know how they spoke them. We have their musical instruments, but we don't know how they sang."

"What are we looking for in a place like this?" I wonder.

"The human universals," the scholar replies.

In AD 997, a prelate from Prague named Adalbert crossed the High Tatra mountains and descended to the valley of the Warta

River, where he pow-wowed with the newly Christianized ruler of the Polonians, Boleslaw the Brave.

"The world will end in less than three years," Adalbert may or may not have warned his host. "The righteous go to heaven. Sinners roast in hell. Think about it."

Then Adalbert moved on to try to proselytize the Prussians, who responded by axing off his head and slicing the rest of him into cutlets.

Boleslaw the Brave (ancestor of Boleslaw the Generous and Boleslaw the Wrymouth) had important company coming for the Year 1000 – the Holy Roman Emperor, Otto III. He ransomed Adalbert's body parts from the Prussians in exchange for their value in bullion, giving us our expression "worth his weight in gold." Duly impressed by these still-fresh relics, Otto responded by crowning Boleslaw with his own crown. Poland was born.

Adalbert's severed head remained an object of veneration at the cathedral in the Polish city of Gniezno until 1923, when it "became the booty of thieves," according to a pamphlet on sale at the site. To replace it, the Vatican reached into its vault of wholly owned holy body parts and shipped up a four-inch fragment of Adalbert's forearm, which you can still see today at Gniezno Cathedral, encased in a hollow silver model of the saint's right arm and hand.

A statue of Adalbert, reunited with his head, stands outside the church, bearded and melancholy, dressed in a cassock of stone. The story of his life and afterlife is told on the massive brass doors that have been mounted at the Gniezno Cathedral since the year 1175.

"Realize that you are standing before the whitness [sic] of our stormy national history," the pamphlet says.

Outside, the sun of post-Communist Europe warmly beams. Gniezno, five hours by car west of Warsaw, is alive with flowers and freshly painted cafés and hotels. Its cobbled streets are unlittered. Its gleaming new gas stations and convenience stores are open 24 hours a day. Shop windows display two of the defining icons of AD 2000 – Air Jordan running shoes and the Pentium PC –

affluence sweeping eastward toward the Russian steppes exactly a thousand years after the cross blazed the same pathway.

To the Poles, Adalbert of Prague is known as St. Wojciech, patron of a nation as homogeneously Catholic (since 1945) as all of Europe must have been in 1000. His red-brick cathedral, on a midsummer weekday morning, is thronged with native worshippers and German tour groups, hushed and kneeling, still drawn, after all these centuries, to the veneration of holy relics.

"We cannot see God, but we can see the bones of the saint," the archivist of the cathedral, a young man named Maciej Chosinski, says as we stroll around the church. "This is the proof to us that this person *lived*. This person is *real*."

He shows me some gilded manuscripts and royal proclamations by Boleslaw the Brave and his successors, kept under glass in the archbishop's office.

"My country may not be as rich as France or England," the young Pole says. "But when I look at these, I know that our roots go just as deep. We are poor, but we, too, have history."

"The man of the XIth century lived in fear," I read in an exhibit on the Dark Ages in the Romanesque church of Chapaize, on the Côtes du Rhône. "To exorcise the dangers and to merit eternal life, a pilgrimage to the tombs of saints was the best route." In Gniezno, a thousand years later, the pilgrimage continued.

Hope, fear, redemption: these were the human universals, then and now, as palpable as a Viking helmet in York or the forearm of a holy man.

"They were absolutely *consumed* with faith," a historian named Colette Chanay told me in France. "In the eleventh century, they were *terrified* by the power of God."

It would be the same a thousand years later for the New Age alchemists, the UFO warp-travellers, the gonzo Idaho militias, though few would invoke the name of the Biblical God.

"Power is always mysterious," explained a folklorist in

Philadelphia named Ted Daniels. "*That's* what the Millennium is doing – assigning a meaning to the mystery of power."

"And when the Millennium passes and the world is *not* destroyed?" I asked.

"They say, 'See? We *prevented* it,'" Daniels explained. "'We stayed God's hand. We *prevented* His wrath. But it could happen again – we must *continue* to pray.'"

In the year 1001, high on the slope of Mount Canigou in Catalonia, a day's travel west of the monastery of Saint-Michel-de-Cuxa, the Count of Cerdagne decreed that a new church be built, to honour, we may fantasize, the survival of the world. The *fin du monde* had not come the year before. But this was not a guarantee that it would not arrive tomorrow.

"If God's great pity did not delay his wrath, Hell would engulf them in its frightful mouth," Rodulfus Glaber wrote, in those days, of the "tyrants . . . faithless and foolish men" who governed his known world. Incessant and fervent prayer was required to fore-stall the Apocalypse. In the Pyrenees, they are praying still.

The church of Saint-Martin-du-Canigou was consecrated in 1009 by the great abbot Oliba. It was reduced by an earthquake in 1428 and as France fell into revolution it was abandoned. Rebuilt in the 1950s, it is reached today by a forty-minute climb from the end of the road near the hot springs at Vernet-les-Bains. A more beautiful setting for a Romanesque abbey is unimaginable.

You do not see Saint-Martin until, breathless, you are almost upon it. It sits on a shelf of the mountain, cradled, when I was there, between the snows of the highest crags and a garland of autumn leaves. Fallen chestnuts leave pocks in the path. There is no sound but the birds.

Saint-Martin-du-Canigou is the domain of a Roman Catholic congregation that calls itself The Community of the Beatitudes. About 50 devotees, men and women and children, live up here. Some are celibate priests. Some are married couples. They come and go, spreading the Word. They have an apostolic base in the Central African Republic. They have another in Beauceville, Québec.

They spend an hour each morning in wordless prayer, kneeling and bent and motionless, their long, white robes melting over them. A sign on the door of their thousand-year-old house of worship says: "Listen. God speaks in the silence."

I meet a member of the community named Guillem Farré, a former journalist from Barcelona. He and his fiancée have been here for two years.

"Why?" I ask him.

"The easy reason is 'the call of God,'" he replies. "You ask yourself two questions. 'What does God want from me?' And 'What do I want from God?'"

He invites to me to observe their Mass. The rituals are eclectic – there are bongos and maracas – some dress in priestly vestments, others shiver and sniffle in jeans and parkas in the damp, unheated vault of solid stone. Nearly everyone is under 30. A thick red Bible is paraded; the men and women line the aisle and kiss the holy book in turn, as Jews do with the Torah.

"I feel I am experiencing what men experienced here a thousand years ago," Guillem says, as we walk from the service. "It is different from a church built only in the last ten years.

"I think we all feel it. Perhaps it is strongest when you pray. You think, 'This chapel is a thousand years old.'"

We are at the portal of Saint-Martin, taking our leave. I have to go back to my century. He has to go back to his prayers.

"Are you afraid that the end of the world is near?" I ask, as I would have asked the abbot Oliba, exactly a thousand years ago, at these gates, on this mountain.

"The creed of our faith says we believe in death and resurrection," the young man replies. "In that sense, yes, this world will end, someday. But not in fire. Not in explosion. For each of us, the world must end. But we don't know when. Only God knows when."

– *Saturday Night*

The Last Brigade

·

The last of the soldiers made their way down a trail wet with history and blood. The rain was slashing and a band was gamely playing and a gale ripped the trees.

It was Sunday afternoon – a wretched day for glory – at the field where a regiment of Newfoundlanders had gone to battle and three-quarters of them had been cut down like cornstalks in less than half an hour. That was July 1916, in the slaughter of the Somme at the nadir of the First World War.

More than 80 years later, a shrunken brigade of their Canadian brethren came to whisper a final goodbye. That any man born in the 19th century and bled in war might still be alive and sensate and mobile on Remembrance Day, 1998, is almost beyond comprehension, yet here were more than a dozen veterans from seven provinces – most in wheelchairs; a couple of them striding, even hurrying, toward the trumpets and the trenches filled with autumn's last leaves.

Seventeen indestructible combatants, nearly all of them more than 100 years old, are here this week on a pilgrimage provided by the government of Canada, defying the actuarial tables, the climate, and their own desires to put the Great War behind them.

Most are small-town men whose long, long lives were built on daily labour. None is wealthy or otherwise famous. One is the last surviving Great War pilot. One had never been on a plane until he flew over here.

Saturday, they had been at Vimy Ridge to receive – more than eight decades after the battle – France's highest decoration, the National Order of the Legion of Honour. Tomorrow – at the 11th hour of the 11th day of the 11th month – they will be in the Belgian city of Mons, where Canada's 3rd Division found itself on the morning when the killing ceased. There will be more bagpipes, more benedictions, and more acknowledgement that, the next time, we will remember without them, if we remember at all.

"I didn't want to come," Fred Connett of West Vancouver was saying on the bus that brought the men down from Lille, where the veterans and the functionaries are staying. "You don't want to renew a lot of these memories. I didn't want any part of it – it's gone – why do you want some more of it?

"You try to forget it. You have forgotten it. Nature has constructed us to forget the bad things and remember only the happy things.

"But then someone at the institution where I currently reside told me, 'Oh, Fred, you must go – God ordained it.'"

Connett – born on April 17, 1897, precisely 20 years before Vimy Ridge – has outlived colon cancer and four heart attacks and talk of the Deity makes him squirm.

He survived his Great War without a scratch – a signalman, he never fired a shot – but he has little time for the "we'll meet again" sort of heavenly hopefulness that others find an antidote to grief. To Connett, war is satanic and purposeless. He learned that lesson 81 years ago, when a mate came moaning toward him with his intestines in his hands.

"The tombstones," he said as we drove by them in thousands, "make you think not only of your inevitable destiny but of your own knowledge of yourself. They remind you that you must try to do the best you can while you're living.

"I don't believe in 'life everlasting' the way we were all taught as children. I think when you're gone, you're gone. These men are gone. But we are like the 300-year-old pine tree that drops its cones on the ground – we live in our genes. Not in God, but in our genes.

"Do you believe in Santa Claus? If you believe in Santa Claus, then there is a Santa Claus. If you believe in God, then there is a God. We all need something to cling to, I guess, like a drowning man grabs a straw."

"Are you afraid to die?" I asked Fred Connett. At 101, one supposes the nearness is palpable.

"I don't fear the future," he replied. "I look at it this way. We drive, don't we? Sometimes we drive on a one-way street. I figure I'm on a one-way street and at the end, there's death. You can meet it at any intersection, but you cannot turn around and go back."

One in ten Canadians who fought in the Great War was blown apart or poisoned by gas or drowned in the clutching mire. In the general population, even in this age of medicine and miracles, barely one in 10,000 lives to see a second century. But Harry Routhier of Langley, British Columbia – gassed by the Germans and shot through the left biceps – was on the bus on Sunday, and so was Fred Gies of Kitchener, Ontario, although I had to help him adjust his blue beret because the shrapnel in his shoulder does not allow him to raise his right arm.

It was Gies who had never flown before; it was Routhier whose grandfather wrote the lyrics to "O Canada."

"My father didn't want me to enlist," Fred Gies remembered. "He told the doctor who was doing the examinations, 'If you see a boy named Gies, hold him back.' So I changed my name and signed up anyway."

Such was the spirit of the First World War; in Britain, some men rejected for enlistment committed suicide. In Dominion City, Manitoba, a teenage railway telegrapher named Tom Spear rushed to sign up. The whole town was emptying of men determined to do their duty, to help the cause, to play the game.

"I guess we didn't really see the horror until we got over here and started seeing the casualties coming back from the front lines," he said. "We realized it was pretty bad, but it didn't deter us. I didn't see a single soldier who didn't want to go to France."

"Honestly, I wasn't scared," Fred Gies said. "I never thought that I might get killed. I got wounded, but you had to expect that. I was the right-hand man on the line for the 13th Highlanders. We went through the barbed wire and I remember thinking, 'Gee, this is dangerous.' Then the shrapnel hit me and threw me right down in a heap.

"I crawled into a shell hole and there were 22 other men in there. The ones with leg wounds were on the bottom and I was in the pile on the top. Then the Germans came and said, 'Hands hoch!' and they took us prisoner. As we were marching out, four of our men who were carrying another man in a blanket were hit by a shell, and the man marching behind me got hit right in the jugular vein. It was our own troops who did it. Our men killed our own."

Gies spent two years as a guest of the Kaiser – he remembers the prison-camp food as "pig swill" – and went home to be a postman. They were all like that: Connett a labourer on the crew that rebuilt the Houses of Parliament after the 1916 fire, and later a bookkeeper; Routhier in the fresh air of the B.C. woodlands, where the asthma from the German gassing eased; Tom Spear with the CPR.

"I was getting too big for my mother to handle – a bit too rambunctious – so she sent me back to the farm, out east of Regina," Routhier recalled with lingering gusto when I asked why he had gone to war at all. "I figured I'm going to join the Army. My mother said, 'Wherever you go, I'll fetch you out.' I thought, 'I'll go to war – she'll never find me there.' I was 15.

"I was rarin' to get there. It was the thrill – the thrill. I wasn't scared. I wasn't frightened. I just wanted to do my part. After I was wounded, I was ready to go back."

He didn't have to. The Germans heard that Harry was fit again and they packed it in. It was 80 years ago this week.

"What if the Germans had won?" I asked Harry Routhier.

"We'd be working as slaves," he answered. "Not that we don't work anyway."

– National Post

Glamis Castle

·

Christ in a black hat, an apostle in eyeglasses, stuffed bears and otters and birds; spires and turrets and towers and the horns of hunted waterbuck and rhinos; coats of arms and suits of armour; strawberry walls and icing-sugar ceilings; a ship of silver and serving-plates of gold; chalices and chain mail and a secret chamber without doors where Satan, it is whispered, duels a pair of moaning ghosts in a game of cards that never, ever ends.

To all this, add Shakespeare's vivid imaginings:

All hail Macbeth, hail to thee Thane of Glamis . . .
All hail Macbeth, that shalt be king hereafter.

And, for a fraction of her country's history, yet far longer than the compass of our own lives: Queen Elizabeth the Queen Mother, born to the laird and lady of Glamis Castle on August 4, 1900, and raised through all her girlish summers at this breathtaking château in the Scottish mists.

Yesterday at Glamis Castle – it rhymes with "Brahms" – drawn to the moorlands north of Dundee and high above the Firth of Tay by the nearness of the royal centennial, by all the opulence and history and legend, we troops of tourists groped about and gaped. A fine fog blanketed the wooded hills and made spectres of the shaggy sheep and cows.

We walked through the bedroom where the newlywed Duke and Duchess of York passed part of their honeymoon in 1923, the Glamis girl never dreaming that her stuttering Bertie some day would be hurtled on to the throne of the empire because his brother sovereign was too in love to rule. We saw her childish crayons in a schoolbook, and the valence on which her mother embroidered the names of her ten children, of whom only this one accidental queen endures.

We saw the anachronistic renderings of Jesus and his disciples in a haunted chapel consecrated in 1688, and walked the vaulted corridors where Lady Macbeth ridiculed her husband's shrinking from the dagger that would make him Scotland's king:

Glamis thou art, and Cawdor, and shalt be
What thou art promised: yet do I fear thy nature,
It is too full o' th' milk of human kindness
To catch the nearest way.

This last was make-believe, our guides informed us; Macbeth was, in fact, a peaceable king from a far region of Scotland whose reign commenced in the year 1040, three centuries before a man named John Lyon was dubbed the Thane of Glamis. Those Lyons, with a fabulously wealthy English heiress named Bowes stirred into the mix in the 18th century, led eventually to 18 earls of Strathmore, to the Queen Mother, and through her to Elizabeth II and, someday, perhaps, to Charles III and William V, should the monarchy survive.

Yesterday, in the castle in the mist, I met the widow of the 17th earl (and mother of the 18th) for lunch. Mary Pamela McCorquodale, now a white-haired, blue-eyed, sparkling grandmother, was the untitled daughter of a Scottish printer when Fergus Michael Bowes-Lyon, first son of the fifth son of the father of the Queen Mother, married her in the 1950s. By then, the Glamis succession had been forced to detour around a scarcity of male heirs to one of her husband's cousins, a rather sickly man.

"So the cousin finally dies," said Mary Pamela over her quiche, "and suddenly my husband is Lord Strathmore and I'm a countess. We had to get on with it, and get on with it we did."

"Is it cool to be a countess?" I asked her. She is the sort of aristocrat who would graciously answer such an impudent commoner's crack.

"You don't feel any different," she said. "You're still the same person. It's the person you are, not what you're called or what you've got that matters. Perhaps the new aristocrats – the ones who think they've 'made it' because of all the money they make – think you can buy people, but you can't. You have to earn respect.

"In my case, I felt more like a cog in a wheel of history that has been going 'round and 'round for 600 years. You carry out your responsibilities and pass it on because, after all that time, you don't want to be the one to muck it up.

"When my husband died, I officially became the Dowager Countess of Strathmore. My daughter was 20. She said, 'I will not be the daughter of a dowager,' so I stopped using the word. But now that I'm 68, I guess I'll have to go back to it."

On display at Glamis Castle are numerous photographs of the Dowager Countess of Strathmore with Queen Elizabeth the Queen Mother. (She knows the private telephone number at Clarence House, but wouldn't give it to me, even though I paid for her quiche.) I suppose she knows the Queen Mum as well as anyone outside the nuclear circle, although, even when it's just the two of them, the loyal subject still curtsies and calls her "Ma'am."

The closer I get to people close to the royals, the more one theme is echoed and seems to ring true: that these people – the older ones, at least – are motivated by duty, tradition, and a lack of options for escape save the "nearest way" that Bertie's brother took.

"She had, I can't say an ordinary, upbringing in these castles and big houses, but it wasn't spoiled," the Countess said of her centenarian in-law. "She was raised by a very devoted mother to be unselfish and to genuinely help other people.

"What she does every day, it's not acting, it's not putting on a show. It's doing what she's done since she married into that family. Underneath is a very unchanged person. I don't think you can act for a hundred years.

"What I'm sure she is thinking – but would never say it, of course – is that she hopes she doesn't disappoint all those people and pop off before the big day."

At Glamis, the big day will bring fireworks and a philharmonic, a potential tonic for a sluggish tourist season dragged down by high gasoline prices – about $2 a litre – and the strength of the pound. The stories of the satanic card game and the spectral Grey Lady of the chapel are always an attraction, despite Lady Macbeth's mockery that "'tis the eye of childhood, / That fears a painted devil."

In the eye of her own childhood, Lady Elizabeth Bowes-Lyon peered up to these same parapets; saw the dusty old encyclopedias, the same warthogs and woodcocks and canopied beds. She rode her Shetland pony Bobs along the forecourt, and nursed the wounded soldiers of the Great War in these halls.

Now there are restaurants and gift shops. Anyone can walk here, or lease the grand salon for dinner for £1,000 (about $2,300).

"You don't really own it, you just do it," the Countess told me, as we said goodbye. That was what it was all about, at Glamis as at Buckingham Palace – play your part, and pass it on.

How many little girls dreamed of castles, I wondered; how many boys shot arrows from the eaves?

"How do you get to be a countess?" she laughed. "Be lucky enough to marry an earl!"

– *National Post*

Diana in a Day

·

Doing Diana in a day means a mad sprint for the 8:23 from Euston Station, London, bound for the lakeside resting place of England's fallen rose. The queue for first-class tickets is much the shorter, so I take the plunge for the extra few farthings (about $65 each way for a one-hour ride). One must not quibble over trifles, you know, if one is doing Diana in a day.

From Northampton Station, then – a quick five miles by big, black taxi to Althorp House and the Diana exhibition and grave. (I've missed the $5 double-decker bus by two minutes, but the cab costs only $20 more.) The home of the Spencers for 500 years and 20 generations, Althorp was just another staggeringly opulent country seat until the shy blonde daughter of the incumbent earl suddenly found herself betrothed to the Prince of Wales.

The admission fee at Althorp is $26, a buck more than they get at Windsor Castle. (Part or most of the Althorp fee goes to charity.) For this, one is admitted only to the lower level of the magnificent old mansion – poking around upstairs costs an additional $6 – and is allowed to hike the mutton-munched grounds, to view the tomb from a distance, and to see Diana: a Celebration, a tribute to one of the most singular lives of the 20th century, for which the Spencers have allotted their stables.

This is sheepish of me – the sanitized stalls are as ample as a monster home, and the exhibits therein are firmly focused on Diana as an apostle of charity and caring. There are about two dozen of her gowns and outfits on display, including the famous wedding dress with a train longer than the 8:23 from Euston, a notebook with a prayer written by Mother Teresa, and the manuscript of the reaction of her brother Charles – by then the 9th Earl Spencer – when he heard of the fatal Paris crash:

> I would say that I always believed the press would kill her in the end, but not even I could imagine that they would take such a direct hand in her death . . .

We are a crowd, but not a crushing one; about 15 coach-loads on an average day, fewer perhaps on English summer mornings like this one – sun plus rain plus chill plus gales. (Althorp is open to the public only in July and August.)

We gaze with humility on the handwritten score to "Candle in the Wind," and on the piled Books of Remembrance and children's simple tributes. And we see Diana as her family would have us remember her: embracing lepers, comforting AIDS patients, chatting with an Angolan amputee, with the actual outfit the benefactor is wearing in the photograph mounted on a mannequin, with a card that says:

> She needed a practical and low-key wardrobe for this work. It was her own idea to wear the "off-the-peg" Ralph Collection sleeveless denim shirt with stretch trousers from Armani Jeans and Connelly shoes . . .

What we do not see is Prince Charles – only a Christmas card from before their wedding signed "with much love, from your tap-dancing partner" – and no Dodi, of course, of course. Elizabeth, the Queen Mum, Andrew, Fergie, even William and Harry are subordinated to the shrine of the late Armani Princess.

To the grave, now, in drizzle and wind, a long path snaking from the mansion to a small pond in which ducks and moorhens dip and dabble, and lime trees curtsy in the breeze. There is a monument on the island in the pond's centre and Diana's cameo is set in a small Greek temple on the shore, before which today's pilgrims have laid a hundred small bouquets.

Fresh flowers, still – nearly three years after.

The weather is too foul to linger. I walk back to the stables and enter the gift shop and find Charles, the 9th Earl Spencer, at the check-out counter, autographing books and posing for snaps. He is Hugh Grant–handsome in a blue gingham shirt and Marlboro Classic khakis, gracious as befits the landed gentry to those who spend $36 for his *Althorp: The Story of an English House* – and as petulant as a princess when I sidle to his noble flank and beg for an interview.

"I'll buy your book," I wanly protest, but this gets me nowhere, either.

(Later, I find the Earl – in the same blue blouse – gracing the latest issue of the celebrity magazine *Hello!* He is escorting Elton John to the Final Resting Place, the singer having had a change of heart, according to the magazine, since complaining two years ago, "I just feel sad that she's on that island – it's as if she's all alone again.")

I take a tuna sub and an orange juice ($11) at the café in the stables and grab the double-decker back to town. I'm in London by three and soon am tramping through Hyde Park, just in time for another hurricane.

Tucked into the gilded gates of Kensington Palace, where once a mound of tear-blessed flowers lay, is a single bunch of red silk roses and a spray of purple blossoms that have wilted in the rain.

It costs $20 to visit an uninhabited wing of the parkside Alhambra where Diana dwelled as a blushing ingenue, a dazzling consort, and a single mum. We are warned straight off we will see neither Diana's living quarters, nor her relics. (The dresses that normally are on display at Kensington are absent until 2001; they may be the ones in the stables at Althorp.) Only one large chalk portrait – and postcards in the gift shop showing Diana dancing at the White House with John Travolta – give the game away. All the rest is history.

It is splendid history, though – the State Apartments of William and Mary and the Jameses and the Georges, their Chinese porcelain and Tintorettos, Queen Victoria's boudoir, and a collection of spectacularly dowdy gowns worn nowadays by our noble Sovereign.

"Nothing too short and nothing too tight!" says the audio-guide.

In a delightful exhibition of clothing imposed on royal offspring over the centuries, we see a white organdie dress trimmed with Valenciennes lace worn by HRH Prince Henry in the year 1902, back when kings were kings and their boys were dressed as girls.

Prince Henry died in 1974, but his widow, the Dowager Duchess of Gloucester, still lives at the other end of Kensington Palace at age 99, a runner-up to the Queen Mother in seniority, but, according to the London newspapers, well ahead in senility.

Amusing trifles, these, but off the mark. North of Hyde Park we gallop, across Bayswater Road, to the Café Diana in Notting Hill.

Here she is, at last, the way we knew her: Diana in court dress, in a Philadelphia Eagles sweatshirt, in a rubber raft, in red, in black, in blue, in sequins. Diana pensive, pouting, playful; romping with her babies, garlanded in Indian petals, perfect in tiaras and tennis shorts; everything too short and too tight.

This is the tiny Arab eatery where the Princess of Wales used to queue up with the commoners for cappuccino and bring her boys for gammon and eggs. Among the many photos of the celebrity consort are a few of her posing warmly with the Iraqis and Lebanese who run the café. I order my dinner, a $16 platter of falafel and hummus the Princess would never go near.

"This food too heavy," says a server named Fouad Abdel-Fatah. "She always eating the English way."

I sit in a straight-backed wooden chair and this was where she often perched, Fouad says. He beams with the memory and says, "In Britain is good, the royal family. It has nothing to do with the government. Is not good if it have hand in everything, like Saddam."

Fouad Abdel-Fatah says he still expects the Princess of Wales to walk through the café door at any moment. "I respect her so much and love her so much," he says.

He is a former reluctant warrior from Beirut, ten years in London, who has given his wife two English daughters and a pair of British twin baby boys.

"Maybe one of your girls will marry Prince William or Prince Harry," I suggest.

"Is nice dream, but I don't think will happen," the waiter says.

He smiles, and it's the first time I've seen one, doing Diana in a day.

– National Post

The Legend of Donnelly's Arm

——————— • ———————

Ah, cruel Death, why were you so unkind?
To take Sir Dan and leave such trash behind
                                    – Eulogy to Dan Donnelly, 1820

I am sitting at a bar in the green heart of Ireland, holding the champion's hand. For a boxing fan who has crossed the Atlantic to be here, it is an unforgettable moment – particularly since the champ whose hand I am holding has been dead for 174 years.

It is Saturday noon in County Kildare, and the Hideout Olde World Pub is filling with local families coming from the market and a brace of habited, elderly nuns drinking, I pray, straight tea. Outside, the April sun is shining, and the village of Kilcullen, on the River Liffey, 25 miles southwest of Dublin, basks contentedly, secure in the fame and commerce that flow here, thanks to my desiccated friend.

"Let me take a picture of you," my wife, Linda, says, brandishing her little camera. I hold up the morbid relic, which is not only the hand but the *entire petrified right arm and shoulder blade* of a 19th-century Irish sporting hero named Dan Donnelly, and manage a wan smile. The photo session done, I give Donnelly's Arm back to the publican and return to my Murphy's stout and my cod Mornay.

The Hideout, which has displayed the famous appendage since 1953, is a comprehensive museum of macabre Hibernian playfulness. Above my head is a knob-jawed Indian crocodile, 12 feet long with teeth like fenceposts, and on adjacent shelves are the propeller of the first aeroplane to cross the Irish Sea (it crashed on Irish soil), a harp carved from the shoulder blade of an ox, one Bengal tiger skin complete with head, a quiver of bona fide Congolese poison arrows, and a fine example of a Celtic cross painstakingly crafted from matchsticks and toothbrush handles. The dining tables rest on antique treadle sewing machines. But all of this pales, of course, beside the singularity of Donnelly's Arm.

Who was Dan Donnelly and why did his disciples think to save a hunk of him for Ireland to honour? Why did it take more than a century for his right arm to make its way to a display case in this exuberant rural restaurant? The answers lie enmeshed in the proud, painful histories of Donnelly's sport and of his country. And the search for them leads a traveller to obscure corners of this old and eloquent land.

A couple of miles north of the Hideout pub, on the rolling plain of close-clipped pasture known as the Curragh, a weathered grey obelisk rests plumply inside an iron fence. Squat clumps of yellow-blooming gorse bedot the hillside beyond the monument, and a father kicks a soccer ball to a pair of squealing daughters clad in jumpsuits of astonishing pink. There is no one else around. The inscription on the monument says:

DAN DONNELLY
BEAT
COOPER
ON THIS SPOT
13TH DEC 1815

It was not boxing as we would recognize it. The rules, codified in 1743 in the sport's first British flowering, were rudimentary: ". . . no person is to seize his Adversary by the ham or the breeches. . . ." A bout could last a minute, or an afternoon. There was as much wrestling as punching. A round ended when a man was knocked down, or simply knelt for a rest. Matches concluded in unconsciousness, death, dispute, or mass arrests. Shambling "champions" toured the countryside, taking on all comers. The entire enterprise – sparring, fighting, betting – was illegal almost everywhere. It was insanely popular.

The core of combat, then as now, was personal and national conceit. George Cooper was English, a bargeman from Staffordshire. Dan Donnelly was a son of the Dublin docks, the ninth child of his mother's 17, his native Ireland a restive fief of the old, mad George III. Britain had never been stronger, or Erin weaker. It was six months after Wellington's epochal victory at Waterloo, 17 years since Catholic Ireland's first abortive Rising. Twelve decades later Joe Louis and Max Schmeling would reprise the roles at Yankee Stadium, surrogates for freedom and the Reich.

In 1815, in the vague December daylight, there were 20,000 hoping, hating patriots here on the Curragh. The railroad had not been invented. They came by cart, by carriage, by towboat, by foot. Noblemen mingled with fishmongers and wheelwrights. The lust for blood leavened them. They called themselves the Fancy.

After hours of negotiations of stakes and side bets, the carnage began. The object was to render the opponent prostrate for half a minute or to otherwise so impair him that his managers surrendered. Donnelly, who had been discovered a couple of years earlier in the Dublin slums gallantly pummelling a neighbourhood bully, had as his Don King a prominent fancier of the art named Captain Kelly. Such "seconds" stood in the arena with their fighters and dragged them to their feet when the lights went out.

It was, by surviving accounts, a hell of a fight. In one telling the Dubliner was laid flat in the second round but was revived when Kelly's beauteous daughter kissed him and whispered that she had bet her father's entire estate on his success. An Irish folk song, "The Ballad of Donnelly & Cooper," remembers this. It may even be true. Another version of the tale holds that Miss Kelly shoved a stalk of sugarcane into the comatose Donnelly's maw, saying, "Now, me charmer, give 'im a warmer."

Revivified by whatever means, Donnelly rose before 30 seconds had passed and delivered his trademark blow, a cross-buttock hip throw that left him sitting atop the bloodied enemy. And so it went until the 11th round, when Dan Donnelly broke George Cooper's jaw and England was defeated. It had taken 22 minutes.

The Fancy exulted, collecting wagers from backers of the bargeman at odds of 10 to 1. The Irish conqueror was lifted from the field by the throng. And now, near the close of a subsequent century, in the yielding turf of the Curragh, I walk the same path, following a double row of shallow footprints, maintained with loving exactness, that lead from the low, grey monument to the hilltop far beyond.

Flush with celebrity and his £60 purse from the Cooper fight, Dan Donnelly decided to go on tour as Champion of Ireland. Soon after, in England, the Prince Regent purportedly knighted him one evening at a house of pleasure; probably they both were as drunk as lords. Intoxication was Sir Dan's habitual state of being. It was said that his training regimen involved five draughts of malt for every round of sparring. It was an age when a fighter could make do with as much anesthesia as he could get.

Back in Dublin the champion went into the hospitality trade, running a succession of pubs, pulling pints for the clamouring Fancy and one or two for himself. This would become the familiar path of many an ex-fighter. Jack Dempsey would do the same on Broadway. And the great Louis, his faculties nearly gone, would close his days sadly glad-handing in Las Vegas.

Some of Dan Donnelly's oases still stand. Kitty-corner from St. Patrick's Cathedral – where, like Donnelly's Arm, the skull of

Jonathan Swift was kept on display for decades – in the dreary
Dublin district called the Coombe, I take lunch at Fallon's Capstan
Bar, where Sir Dan held sway in 1818. The fare is plebeian (vegetable soup, cheddar on toast, Guinness by the ebony pint) and I
sit on a worn, tweed-covered bench in the snug by the front
window, jotting notes, immersed in Ireland. Behind me is a
ceramic Dalmatian missing a foreleg, and on the bare-brick walls
are old tobacco advertisements and the smoke-dulled red regalia
of the Manchester United football team.

At the Capstan, Dan Donnelly went broke, as he had in Capel
Street and Poolbeg. But he did not throw in the towel. He moved
on to the Four Courts and another pub on Greek Street. That
site is now the Dublin Motor Vehicle Office, the Oifig Cláraithe
Gluaisteán, but there is a plaque commemorating the fact that
just after midnight on February 18, 1820, Dan Donnelly dropped
dead in the Greek Street pub. He was 32. It might have been a scle-
rotic liver or venereal disease. But the popular opinion was that
Sir Dan had drunk too much iced water immediately following a
feverish game of racquets. The irony was unmistakable: It was the
water, not the whiskey, that killed the Champion of Ireland.
Succouring kisses and sugarcane could not avail him now.

The city wept and wailed. At the magnificent National Library
in Dublin, in a reading room as still and sanctified as a synagogue,
I pore through the newspapers of the day. For me it is an epiphany
– the confirmation, in fading ink on a printed page, that there was
such a man, in such a city, so long ago. Delighted with this
ratification, I copy the account of the funeral from *Carrick's
Morning Post* of February 23, 1820:

> An immense number of people, some in carriages, and some
> on horseback, moving in slow and measured pace, formed part
> of the procession . . . the GLOVES were carried on a cushion
> in front of the hearse, from which the horses had been
> unyoked by the crowd, and multitudes contended for the
> honor of assisting in drawing it. . . .

. . . whatever failings he might have had, he never was ashamed of his country; abroad or at home he stood up in its defence, and was always ready to give a milling to those who disputed its pre-eminence. . . .

Gazing around the gallery, half-dreaming, I wonder: A century from now, will anyone come upon my own scratchings, as I have delved into these?

The dead champion was interred on the grounds of the Royal Hospital in Kilmainham, while the magazines filled with elegiac verse:

Oh, Erin's daughters, come and shed your tears
On your Champion's grave, who loved you many years
To Erin's sons this day's a day of sorrow;
Who have we now that will defend our Curragh?

And:

What dire misfortune has our land o'er spread,
Our Irish Champion's numbered with the dead.

The trouble was, poor Donnelly wasn't numbered with the dead for very long. It was the heyday of the professional grave robber; in Dublin they were known as "Resurrectionists" or the "Sack 'em Ups." Their trade sprang from the prohibition (until 1832) of the use of human cadavers in medical education. As executed murderers were the only exception, and since in Ireland in the 1820s professors of surgery outnumbered the recently hanged by a ratio of about six to one, it was inevitable that a commerce in contraband corpses would spring up.

It became imperative, therefore, for the tombs of the freshly departed to be guarded day and night. But the Champion of

Ireland had had the bad judgement to die in the middle of winter. For a day or two a phalanx of bereaved boxing fans attended his burial place, but then, as *Carrick's* reported:

> Their naturally jovial disposition and the severity of the weather prompted them to make too frequent libations on the tomb of the departed champion and disabled them from perceiving or opposing those riflers of the House of Death.

So the sepulchre was opened and the reasonably uncorrupted body taken to the laboratory of a medico named Hall. But Dr. Hall was a member of the Fancy. Instead of thanking the slavering Sack 'em Ups, he recoiled in horror when he recognized the illustrious Beetlejuice they had just dragged in.

"Take him back!" the physician prescribed. But first he went for his hacksaw and detached Dan Donnelly's strong right arm. Thus was created one of Ireland's most ghoulish souvenirs.

All this was public knowledge 174 years ago. In a letter to *Carrick's* two days after the funeral procession, a man named Burrowes delineated the whole affair and added:

> I am conscious it will raise the tender feelings of the Fancy, to know that that arm, the object of their highest admiration, and the terror of England, is subject to scoffs, and flung ingloriously into a filthy sink.

According to the only biography of the champion written in the past 170 years – *Dan Donnelly: His Life and Legends*, by Patrick Myler – the arm soon found itself at the medical college of Edinburgh University, where it was disinfected and lacquered and used in anatomy lessons. It then played out the 19th century as an exhibit in a travelling circus.

In 1904 a Belfast bookmaker and barkeeper named "Texas" McAlevey purchased the limb and displayed it at a pub called (aptly) the Duncairn Arms. Later it was relegated to the attic of

McAlevey's betting shop on Winetavern Street, where it was dismissed as just another commonplace severed human body part. Then a wine merchant named Donnelly (no relation) bought it just for fun, and he gave it in 1953 to a man named James Byrne, who owned the Hideout in Kilcullen, the nearest village to the rolling Curragh where George Cooper's mandible had been shattered so many decades before. And there it has remained.

Most guidebooks to Ireland don't mention Donnelly's Arm or the fight with George Cooper or the Hideout Olde World Pub. However, the wonderful mummies in the crypt at the Anglican Church of St. Michan's in Dublin, just a block from Dan Donnelly's Greek Street deathbed, draw tourists by the busload. And the detached, yet still miraculously undecayed, head of St. Oliver Plunkett, who was executed in 1681, draws myriad supplicating pilgrims to the town of Drogheda, north of the capital. So it is not an aversion to the public display of whole or dismantled dead Irish people that is to blame for the arm's relative obscurity.

Neither, to be sure, is it the fault of Myler, a boxing columnist and assistant editor at the *Evening Herald* in Dublin. In fact, it is Myler who has laboured most diligently to keep the expired champion alive. Across the street from the offices of his newspaper is a small restaurant called, undeservedly, the Ritz, and it is here that Myler and I meet one afternoon to drink tea and talk about Dan Donnelly. The journalist seems alternately bewildered and delighted that a foreigner should be interested in such parochial arcana. His eyes ask, Why aren't you off driving the Ring of Kerry or kissing the Blarney Stone? But we've done that already.

"At the launching of my book in 1976," says Myler, a benign and bespectacled man (like me), "Jim Byrne brought the arm to Dublin. I wanted to take it home, lest it be stolen, but my wife refused. She said, 'I'm not letting that thing in my house. What if the rest of him comes looking for it?'"

"Has there been much written about Donnelly?" I ask.

"Yes," says Myler. "Mostly by me."

The burial ground at the Royal Hospital once was called Bully's Acre, but I don't know why. It is located at the northwest corner of the landscaped grounds of the magnificent old sanatorium, surrounded by a high stone wall and the roaring traffic of the South Circular Road. Somewhere in there, I presume, lie the remains of the remains of Dan Donnelly.

I am craning through the window of a hurtling city bus, crumpling my map in fevered anticipation. Beside me is my stoic wife, who already has endured the St. Michan's mummies and Oliver Plunkett's severed head and who now is being dragged off to hunt for a tomb that almost assuredly does not exist. And we are bound for further delights this morning: a tour of the Kilmainham Gaol, the hulking prison where many of the heroes of the 1916 Easter Rising were summarily shot. It's across the street from the cemetery.

The wall around the burial ground is seven feet in height. I try to stand at its base and jump as high as I can, but all I can see are trees. Dejectedly, I walk along the barrier for a while and come to a battered blue wooden door.

"There's no way that door isn't locked," I say.

"Why don't you try it," my wife, always the optimist, suggests.

"Why bother?" I shrug and then, playing with the handle just for effect, I find that (of course) the door is unbolted.

Myler says that 20 years ago he was informed by an elderly cemetery caretaker of the exact location of Dan Donnelly's (unmarked) vault. The old man's tale may have been true or it may have been invention, but either way, Myler, to his credit, wouldn't share the secret with me. So now my wife and I are through the blue door and crashing through the underbrush like David Attenborough in pursuit of orangutans.

After a few moments of this, we discover, nearly hidden in the rampant shrubbery, great stone angels and fractured cherubs in states of wonderful dilapidation. For accompaniment, there is birdsong and a small brown rabbit. We come across a couple of tombstones in this hauntingly tumbledown field, with their inscriptions legible. There is a Henry Walker from 1823 and a John Dinnham, interred one year later. We find no Donnelly, but it doesn't matter. The searching has been reward enough.

"Do you know what I'd love to do?" Desmond Byrne asks me. We're sitting at one of the antique treadle sewing machines, beneath the 12-foot Indian crocodile, at the Hideout Olde World Pub in County Kildare. Byrne, a slim, red-bearded, well-mannered man, inherited the Hideout from his father and grandfather, and with it, of course, Dan Donnelly's dead right arm.

"What?" I reply.

"I would like to take it to America and march with it in the St. Patrick's Day Parade."

We're looking up at the display case where the relic rests, along with a couple of contemporary portraits of the champion and a copy of Myler's book. The arm is fully extended, the fingers curled, with the exception of the index finger, which is pointing right at the ale taps, as Sir Dan himself undoubtedly would be were he still alive and attached. A couple of bus tours have arrived, and delegations of well-lubricated Britons are snapping photos of the hoary thing.

So far, insurance costs and fear of mishap have kept the arm from being paraded up Fifth Avenue. Once, when a visiting Welsh rugby team let slip that it planned to swipe the arm and hold it for ransom – probably beer – Byrne took it home for safekeeping. The next morning, upon opening the pub, he found a "bloody" joke-shop hand in the locked and alarmed display case. So he's skittish about transporting his meal ticket over the sea.

"How much do you think it's worth?" I ask.

"I can't value it," Byrne answers. "There's only one of it."

"Unless we dig him up and take his *left* arm," I interject, cleverly.

"I have this belief," Byrne goes on. "Things like this only have value when they're on the wall. Off the shelf, where people can't see it, it has no value. Look at all the Van Goghs disappearing into private hands. That's terrible."

I ask Byrne if I may take a photograph of him with Donnelly's Arm. He unlocks the display case and takes the arm out and sits on a barstool, holding it tenderly, around the wrist, like a father leading his child to school.

"I suppose it brings out the cannibal in us," my host says, pondering the remnant of humanity with which he is posing on a perfect Saturday noon in the green heart of Ireland.

"It's the reflection of our mortality," I ruminate. "It points to the unknown."

"Yes," the publican replies. "Why do we love horror? We haven't really left the caves, I guess."

– Sports Illusrated

ASIA

Previous page: Angkor Wat, Cambodia (Agata Motyczyńska)

At Christmas 1983, I had been posted in Beijing for the Globe and Mail *for about three months when a 16-year-old Chinese girl named Mei ("plum") with excellent English-language skills began to telephone my office, daily at first, then several times an hour. This was extraordinary – I had no other contact with "ordinary" Chinese citizens – and, I thought, innocent. We talked about literature and music and poetry, and a teenager's dream of love.*

She began to write to me, in letters I still possess:

In the phone, I can tell you everything secret that I can't tell any another, for you can't see me. I don't treat you as a strange foreigner. We are both human beings. You understand me, thank you.

Then it began to get crazy. She would call ten or 12 times in succession, giggling and screeching into the phone – "You are foreigner. You have S-E-X with monkeys. You will die, you will die, you will die, you will die, you will die . . . "

"Who are you?" I pleaded.

"My name is Jane Eyre! My name is Jane Eyre!" she wailed.

"Make her stop," I begged my government translator, but he just shrugged.

The calls ended in February, as suddenly as they had begun. I do not know why she chose me, or what became of her. For me, she represents all the sad mysteries of China, and how little I understood.

Mei would have been 22 the night the tanks rolled through Tiananmen Square. And it would be ten years after that before I would see our shining city again.

China 1999:
Aboard the MV Nan Hu

This is the last slow boat to China, a full-length liner with 600 berths and a dozen paying passengers, her decks splintered, her bows rusted, plying a slimy sea.

Once a week, she churns from recaptured Hong Kong to the revolutionary Motherland, a 16-hour, overnight cruise up the rocky Guangdong coast to the port of Shantou. Picture an ageing *Titanic* still afloat, tenanted by a handful of elderly Cantonese, crewed by their shirtless, spitting descendants, and you have the image. She is white below and vivid green above, but not long ago, *Nan Hu*, like People's China, was red all over.

She must be 400-feet long. Christened in Scandinavia, half a century ago, as the *King Olav v*, refitted in 1970 as MV *Taiwan*, and with signage still visible in Finnish, English, German, Danish, and Chinese, her history is as spotted as her carpets. Her current name means "south lake," but you could call her HMS *Metaphor*.

She is tied up, when we first see her, at the farthest end of the gleaming new China Ferry Terminal in Kowloon, on the mainland side of Hong Kong's breathtaking harbour. Beside her are moored the jet-propelled hydrofoils and hovercraft that hustle between the Special Economic Zones of the Pearl River Delta and the reverted British Crown colony. With our $60 first-class tickets in hand and in no particular hurry, I and my travelling companion – he is a former Communist Red Guard from Shanghai who wound up owning a tavern in Scarborough, Ontario – have no idea that such a charming old hulk as *Nan Hu* might still be in service. Boarding her, shown to VIP Stateroom No. 3 by a grinning steward with a flagon of steaming water, we laugh out loud in delighted surprise.

The compartment is large and commodious, with four big, filthy portholes and a private shower, starboard amidships. There are lounge chairs, air conditioning, a desk for the intrepid correspondent, and electric lights that actually work. Settling in amid such splendour, my friend, F.Y., says, "I feel like Chairman Mao," and he begins to sing an anthem of his crimson-coloured youth:

> *Sailing the seas depends on the helmsman.*
> *Making revolution depends on Mao Zedong Thought.*
> *Fish cannot leave the water.*
> *Melons cannot leave the vine.*

The revolutionary masses cannot leave the Communist Party . . .

In the 50th year of Mao's People's Republic, precisely ten years after the carnage of Tiananmen Square – the anniversary is on the weekend – we are bound, eventually, for Beijing by ship, train, and taxi, by luxury bus and three-wheeled pedicab. We have no agenda other than to heed the advice of the Portuguese cleric Gaspar da Cruz, who touched the Guangdong coast in 1556 and wrote:

> That whereas distant things often sound greater than they really are, this is clean contrary, because China is much more than it sounds and thus must be seen and not heard, because hearing it is nothing in comparison to seeing it.

"Dinner service ends at 5:20," a crewman barks, shattering our reverie. It is 5:10 and counting. He sells us meal coupons for $5 each and disappears. It is for us to find the proper mess. With increasing anxiety – this being Hong Kong, we haven't eaten a meal for nearly two hours – we scour the slatted decks. Trotting forward, then astern, we locate the karaoke bar, the video arcade, the duty-free boutique, corridors of empty cabins, and barracks with beds stacked three-high on iron frames and the wheelhouse itself, all of them dark and abandoned. The entire crew of 100 is squatting below decks, shovelling home their rice and fish from stainless-steel tiffins, then spewing the bare bones overboard as the skyscrapers slip silently by.

Through the display window of a padlocked sundries shop, above the stores of toothbrushes and playing cards and cans of Pabst Blue Ribbon, we spy two small, unframed portraits of Mao himself. They may have been left hanging here as sardonic kitsch, or even as sincere tribute. Or perhaps no one has been in this room to remove them since the Great Helmsman "went to see Marx" in 1976.

Finally, with the seconds to starvation ticking away, we chance upon the vast saloon. It holds dozens of battered mahogany tables, none of them occupied, and a service counter as long as a soccer field, on which are reposing two gigantic pots, one for rice, one for the potage du jour.

Seeing Overseas Compatriot (F.Y.) and Foreign Friend (me) in full flight, waving our meal coupons, a beaming waiter called Wang – the world's most common surname – shows us to our seats and fills our bowls.

To an old China hand, the first mouthful brings it all back – the thick, clotted grains, the clatter of chopsticks. And F.Y. slurps down a brick of bean curd – it is burnt, and the broth is thin and oily – and he turns to me and says, with deepest feeling after a decade in Canada, "It tastes like China."

Out of the world's most beautiful port, we sail the ocean green.

Thick and greasy, thronged with fishing boats, container barges, sampans, and petrol tankers, the waters wash the endless, formless suburbia of the Hong Kong "new towns." These are the refuge of millions of Chinese who fled Mao's mad dominions for a better life and found it, only to be ransomed to socialist sovereignty in exchange for Deng Xiaoping's promise of "one country, two systems."

Then, open water, and the peaks lost in the acid fog. No gulls follow us, no tenders sail abeam. I walk out on the open deck and watch the Chinese watching me. I have done my share of ferries, but this will be the first night of my life on the open sea.

I flew into Beijing 16 years ago, as green as a scallion, and was let loose to report on the Celestial Empire for 24 bewildering months. Back then, all China was a vast *Nan Hu* – tattered, shabby, tethered to central command, afloat on a sea of regurgitated rhetoric and the blood of the summarily purged. Stifled by Party minders, feeble in my grasp of Mandarin, I stared at the toilers in their blue coveralls and saw only sameness and slavery. "Even if you're a one-in-a-million guy," I was fond of saying back then, "in China, there's a thousand others just like you." Then little Deng opened the blinds and let in the light.

The giddiness that followed his *gaige kaifang* ("opening and reform") – a phrase we will hear cited by nearly everyone we meet on this journey – brought the benighted billion a sudden prosperity and economic liberties unknown in modern China. Sensing not a whiff of protest, we foreign correspondents of the mid-1980s filled our columns with millionaire peasants, Pierre Cardin, giant pandas, and Mickey Mouse. Then came Tiananmen Square.

Ten years later, awash in memories and questions, I stand on the deck of the *Nan Hu* and watch the bow wave slice me toward the centre of the world. I am back in the land where all is clean contrary.

On Deck Three, his feet propped up on the Main Service Desk, is a boy named Xu.

To be accurate, Mr. Xu is no youngster. He has been sailing the South China Sea aboard this tired scow for 20 years to feed his wife in Shantou and their three hungry children. Once upon a time, he says, *Nan Hu* often was stuffed to capacity with shoppers and tourists and bureaucrats given a weekend pass to the British-occupied entrepôt, but now 20 passengers is a sizable load and poor Xu earns – he points to his stubby choppers – barely $60 a month, "only enough to fill up my mouth."

I ask if he dreams of better times, and he answers:

"What's the use of dreaming?

"Shantou has a municipal port, and a port must have a ship, so the city government keeps it sailing," he explains. "The highway killed our business – why spend all night on a boat when you can get to Hong Kong on a bus in four or five hours?"

The Chinese government refers to such hopeless causes as the *Nan Hu* as "money-losing state enterprises" and, in most cases, salvages the furnishings and scuttles the wreck. Certainly, no one is profiting from tonight's sailing – the crewmen haven't received a bonus in years – but the propellers turn and the old barge lumbers sadly on.

Mr. Xu says he has seen James Cameron's *Titanic* twice – it sank both times. I ask him if we are in any danger of a similar fate this midnight.

"Don't worry," he reassures me. "Down here, we don't even get the fart of an iceberg."

"Has anyone ever jumped overboard?" I wonder.

"Maybe," Mr. Xu inscrutably replies.

At five o'clock in the morning, I shake F.Y. awake and announce, "The Great Helmsman was wrong – the East isn't Red."

It's a leaden grey, as pale as bean curd, as dawn lights the China coast. By seven, we are tiptoeing through the fishing fleet and men casting nets from frail rafts, into the port of Shantou – a smallish city, no more than a million or two – and finally nesting beside two naval frigates, bristling with cannons that have been hung with the gunners' laundry for want of war. I have slept like the dead with the growl of the engine just below my bunk.

In the Customs hall, where there are more agents and officials lolling about than disembarking passengers, the only hitch comes when F.Y. has his copy of a Hong Kong tabloid called *Apple Daily* seized as "pornographic." (One country, two systems.) He has been reading a story about a doctor who claims to be able to transplant cadavers' hands onto the arms of amputees. His next endeavour is to perform a similar procedure on the human penis.

In my day, arrival in a city would have meant a formal welcoming party – maybe even a band and garlands of paper flowers – a three-hour "brief introduction" by local Party functionaries replete with tributes to the gaige kaifang, and a fusillade of phony statistics. Now, we just hail a cab from a stand at a harbourfront park where, before eight in the morning, at least 200 women – no men – are line dancing in miniskirts to a Cantonese disco song.

"The Communist party has done a good job," the driver says as we hit the open road. He has the Toyota doing 80 miles an hour on a magnificent new four-lane freeway, he has a Marlboro alight in his lips, and his Nokia phone is ringing in his pocket with the "March of the Toreadors."

"They've solved the basic problems of food and clothing for 1.2 billion people. Now let's see if they can proceed to giving us a comfortable life."

We'll call the man Jade Victory. He is in his late 30s and he sports a flat-top haircut that the Chinese air force could use as an emergency landing field. He and his younger partner, a fellow named Golden River, have bought the Toyota outright for $80,000 after driving it for a Shantou livery company for six years.

It has 841,000 kilometres on the odometer and it runs as smooth as silk.

"I hear that, in Canada, you can get rich just selling vegetables or flowers or working on a farm," Golden River says, two hours or so into our land cruise northward to the province of Fujian. "But where are we going to get the money to get to Canada?"

"Do you have family planning in Canada?" he wonders a moment later.

"We have a natural form of population control," I tell him. "In Canada, it's too cold to take your clothes off to have sex."

"But you also have summertime!" the chauffeur replies.

"Do you guys consider yourself free in China?" I ask.

It would have been an unimaginable question to pose in 1983; as unthinkable as private taxis, miniskirts, or personal telephones.

"Yes!" both men immediately cry. "We are free. Freer than ever."

"It's not that we don't have the freedom to oppose the government," Jade Victory goes on. "It's just that you can't beat those guys. They act like they're our big brother. Their idea is, 'You can negotiate with us, but you'd better not oppose us.'

"Let's say us taxi drivers go on strike – they just arrest the leader and settle the problem somehow. Those kids in Tiananmen Square ten years ago – they made a huge demonstration and they couldn't beat the Communist party. You see – you can't beat those guys."

Along the freeway, the feverish mercantile districts of Guangdong give way, at last, to the Chinese countryside, little changed since Friar Gaspar da Cruz – the burning, unforgettable green of the paddies, the nuzzling buffaloes, the old women in their conical hats, bent to the backbreaking harvest.

We fill up with Mobil regular at 40 cents a litre. At a toll booth – there is one every few miles – a peasant sells us stalks of sugar cane and we chomp at them in the back seat, bathing in the luscious juice. We hurtle past tractors and swaying old trucks. A black Lexus leaves us in its wake.

The cellphone rings again. It's Jade Victory's better half.

"What if we asked you to take us all the way to Beijing?" I tease the husband. "What would your wife say?"

"As long as I'm making money," he replies, full throttle on the new China road, "she doesn't care where I go."

– *National Post*

China 1999:
The Ruins of St. Teresa's

FUJIAN PROVINCE

"Our hotel declines those who suffer from insanity," the notice reads, but they let me have a room anyway.

We have come up from Hong Kong by ghost ship and private taxi, and now a magnificent, modern, purple bus has brought my friend F.Y. and me to Fuzhou City, exactly on time.

It is the burgeoning, libertine capital of a bountiful province on the South China Sea. Yet it is this province that the men and women who wash and sweep and stir-fry in our Canadian Chinatowns pay a doleful ransom to smugglers to flee.

"After or before dinner, to drink something, you will have a taste of it inside," another flyer announces, irrefutably. "While you are enjoying the pure tea of south Fujian style with your friends, you can look at the distance as well as get drunk."

But the distance, from the ninth floor of the Mighty China Hotel, is a sobering vista of motorcycles, markets, and mist. Only at 4:30 in the morning, at the first slight hint of light, are the jagged peaks that ring the town existent. By 6 a.m., they are lost in the unfiltered filth of China's urban air.

The bus trip, a venture of a public company trading on the local stock exchange, has been another in a series of demonstrations of the country's recent progress that leave F.Y. and me gasping. The coach is filled with 42 well-dressed businessmen (and one woman) barking into cellphones that ring with "Auld Lang Syne" and "The Moonlight Sonata"; a tasty boxed breakfast is handed out, gratis; and a complaisant hostess fills our mugs with tea while a succession of ludicrous kung-fu flicks blares from the colour TV.

For 110 miles, as our driver hurtles at breakneck speed, weaving across all four lanes of traffic, Fujian displays an unbroken landscape of commerce and competition.

In every town and village, hundreds of red-brick houses stand half-built – or half-demolished; it is impossible to tell which are going up and which are coming down. The work is done entirely by hand from bamboo scaffolds, the bricks baked from roadside clay in mediaeval kilns.

There are Shell stations, Suzuki and Volvo dealerships, factories, vegetable farms, lichee plantations, terraces of tea bushes, hundreds of private shops and restaurants. Lofty mansions pierce the sky – turrets, gables, cornices, balconies, gazebos, pagodas, corbels, and eaves glued together in a pastiche of coherent architecture and a panoply of conspicuous wealth.

Then, walking the town, at the Fuzhou central market: meat, poultry, fish, frogs, snakes, oysters, noodles, roots, tubers, grains, spring onions, spinach, cauliflower, durians, paw-paws, New Zealand Royal Gala apples, Ecuadorian bananas, Ponds soap, Doublemint chewing gum, Martell cognac, Danone yogurt, Cadbury chocolates.

I remember the bare stalls of my years in Beijing in the 1980s – the indolent shop girls and their snarl of *meiyou* ("don't have"), the bitter persimmons and wormy apples, the hills of cabbages hoarded as winter's only greens – and marvel at the miracle of the intervening years.

We take a taxi along the frantic boulevards to Fuzhou Station to buy our tickets for the rail journey north.

The young driver, to my surprise, is encased within a fearsome iron cage. In my day, crime in China was unknown. Or so we were told.

"Are there many robberies?" I wonder. The cage has rattled my relaxation and made me think of hometown Brooklyn.

"Many, many," the driver says. "And killings, too. Many, many." He laughs it off.

"If you haven't been robbed, you're not a taxi driver."

An hour outside Fuzhou City, in the small town of Shou Zhang, 15 pigs are being hustled across the street by a man who kicks the stragglers in the head.

On Spadina Avenue in Toronto, F.Y. says, Shou Zhang – "first settlement" – is well known as the fount from which hundreds of Chinese emigrants make their furtive escape. And this, we soon learn, is true.

At the village seniors' hall, men are snoring in unpadded bamboo recliners and another group is playing cards for small cash. A television is showing a cooking program – octopus and venison are the featured dishes – and above our heads are photographs of overseas donors to the pavilion and a calligraphic inscription that reads, as if quoting the New Testament, "Ask and you shall receive."

It is the kind of building where – within the indelible memory of every Chinese over 30 – neighbour was turned against neighbour and child against parent in the "struggle sessions" of the Great Proletarian Cultural Revolution. Now the persecuted and their tormentors lounge in unforgiving proximity, under frescoes of Old Man Longevity and various Buddhas, fat and serene.

The first man we meet has a daughter in Washington and a son at school in Japan. How did they leave China, we inquire. And the familiar story begins:

"I had to borrow everything I could from loan sharks to pay the smugglers who helped my daughter get to America," he says.

He is a rice farmer whose crop has been transplanted from the flooded paddies for its summer growth, leaving him idle until the harvest.

Nearly every man in town has the same surname, Zhen. So we can call him Mr. Zhen No. 1.

"The interest is 2 per cent a month. But my daughter and her husband have only a small grocery shop and it is not doing very well. She has no status in America and cannot ever go back there if she leaves.

"So we are trapped. If she does not send me a cheque every month, I must go even deeper in debt."

The conversation turns to the question of liberty and Tiananmen Square; in new China, we find, the topic is welcomed, where once it was hushed and taboo.

The rice farmer says, "In this area, people don't care about democracy and freedom. But it is true, that those in power are better off than those not in power. And when those in power have a chance to get some bribery, there is nothing we can do."

He motions, as if by example, to the retired Communist Party overlord of the village, a certain Mr. Zhen No. 2.

Mr. Zhen No. 2, it turns out, is a lovely gentleman who does not have a child toiling in the West. He has five of them, four in the United States and one in Toronto's Chinatown.

"I would go also," he says, "but she does not pay enough tax to sponsor me." He walks us down a narrow alley to the brick row-house he calls home.

Five generations of Zhens have lived in this courtyard, he says, and he shows us the venerated tablets of their names. But there will be no more generations in Shou Zhang – his grandchildren are New Yorkers now, without papers or passports, or the heirs to Spadina's voiceless working poor.

The intricate mechanics of human smuggling he either does not ken or wisely wishes not to share. He tells us that local men – he doesn't know their names – arrange for a Chinese passport to be issued and a "tour group" or some such to be formed. The route to North America may twist through the Caribbean Islands, or some other country.

The night of departure, "we pray to the Buddha for them to reach America safely. And then we can only wait and worry until we get the telephone call that says they have reached their new land."

In Shou Zhang, we meet no one – not a soul – who does not have a child or sibling in North America. The dentist thinks of going; the young men at the video rental shop are scraping together the dough. The asking price, they say, is US$50,000. And this in the midst of Fujian's abundance, and in the face of what they know will be their fate overseas.

Overseas, they believe, eight or ten years in the basements and back rooms of Chinatown, paying off their indenture, will elide into a lifetime of wealth.

"We only care about making money," one of the video boys snorts.

"What about freedom?" I ask.

"There's no freedom if you have a wife," he answers.

And a giggling girl who looks to be in her middle teens gives her husband an elbow to the ribs.

"They do coolie work – wash dishes – the hardest labour," a Mr. Zhen No. 3 reports, amid the pungent incense of the local Buddhist shrine. (A new and bigger temple is being built next door.)

His own son, a kitchen hand at a restaurant in Scarborough, Ontario, has gained his landed immigrant status and is home in Fujian for a visit. Like many of his compatriots, he has convinced a Canadian refugee tribunal that, as a furtive emigrant, he would face imprisonment if he were sent home.

Whether or not this true, I cannot vouch.

Says yet another Mr. Zhen, "if you get sent back home and they catch you, do you know what they do to you? Nothing."

"Do you want a girlfriend tonight?" the voice on the telephone coos.

"Would you like a massage?"

"How many girls would you like?"

We are back at the Mighty China and my phone is ringing off the hook with hookers. Downstairs, the lobby and discotheque are stuffed with young women in platform shoes and thigh-high dresses, seeking trade.

"If you need more bed, please contact with the reception desk," the hotel service book helpfully advises.

But F.Y. and I resist the sirens' appeal and steadfastly head to the hotel restaurant, where the menu offers "cruel with sweet potato" and "New Zealand sirloin steak with vanilla sauce."

"You like massage?" the maitre d' inquires.

So near the sea, we ask to be driven to the beach before leaving the province.

A man from the Fuzhou tourist board steers us to a sandy strip where gaunt men, wringing wet, are hauling ashore weighty nets of wriggling fish, and even a giant brown ray. They lop the monster's tail off and heave it in a wicker bicycle basket, its gills still gasping.

This is flat, rice country, the very image of Asia, verdant, immemorial and wide. Yet higher than the distant hills, we see, in nearly every hamlet, a red crucifix atop a towering steeple. Christian missionaries here, it seems, have ploughed most fertile ground.

One tower is even more prominent than the others – a square, white-tiled turret that must be 100 feet tall. Through the claustrophobic streets of the surrounding ancient village, our driver navigates toward this goal.

It is a church, of course – the characters above the Gothic doorway spell out "Heavenly Lord Pavilion." The gate is locked, but soon a man emerges from a nearby home and takes out the key and bids us walk inside.

The next scene is almost incomprehensible. While the church tower is intact, the rest of the building has been hurriedly and crudely demolished. Tons of rubble – broken tiles, shattered glass, walls, floors, ceilings – lie in shambles where the vault and nave once stood.

"They would have blown up the tower, too," our guide says. "But they were afraid if they used explosives, it would fall on the village."

We learn more. This was a Roman Catholic church – St. Teresa's – and Communist China has always and steadfastly viewed the Church of Rome as anathema, and its adherents and priests as puppets of a foreign pope. The parishioners of this village, defying authority, had built this edifice by hand, brick by brick, with years of their own labour. Late last year, they began to worship here.

On May 4, a Tuesday, with no advance warning, about 300 police officers and other men began to bulldoze and sledgehammer the edifice into pulp.

"We were screaming, weeping, and praying," a man says. "Some people refused to leave and they were carried away by three or four men."

"Our religion teaches peace," another man offers. "We don't bother anybody. The Chinese constitution guarantees freedom of religion, and freedom of assembly.

"We think the truth is this – they believed that foreign countries were helping us build this church because they did not believe we in this small village could build it ourselves."

No one was arrested, we are told. Benches have been laid across the rubble beneath the tower, a brass crucifix and some candles have been placed on a small table, and Sunday services continue. So it was not the worship that was fatally offensive, it seems – it was the building itself.

One man claims that 17 other Roman Catholic churches have been torn down in this county, and offers a possible, though bizarre, explanation. The lofty spires, he says, irritated the local spirits, violating the harmonious feng shui of some commissar's home or family tomb. So he commanded that they be obliterated.

It is a plausible theory to explain a campaign that seems to have been purely local.

Back in the taxi, we are stunned into silence. All that we had seen so far on the northward journey – the prosperity, the abundance, the mobility, the frank conversations with strangers – pointed to a China impressively self-sure. And then St. Teresa's.

To lull us to sleep and renew our spirits, the Mighty China Hotel offers a folded card on each bedside table.

"One of the greatest pleasures in life," it says in English, "is simply to be treated as an individual."

In Chinese, my friend teaches me, there is no character for "individual." In Chinese, the card in the hotel reads, "One of life's great pleasures is to be treated with respect."

– *National Post*

China 1999:
The Reluctant Emigrant

SHANGHAI

Ten-pin bowling with a Communist congressman is not a sport I ever thought I'd play.

But here we are in the alleys of a grungy little hotel in the suburbs of the Paris of the Orient, urging our shots with body English, or, in his case, body Chinese.

The dive where my travelling companion, F.Y., a Toronto Chinese-Canadian, and I are staying along our trek to Beijing is less than three years old. But already the shower curtains are as mildewed as a Rangoon tenement, there are hundreds of deep, black carpet burns in my room, where ignorant travellers have flicked their cigarettes, and the flies are so big that the room gets too dark to read whenever one lands on my lampshade.

This, too, is the new China. The man against whom I am kegling with increasingly competitive fervency is a member of the Shanghai People's Political Consultative Conference, a rubber-stamp imitation parliament. We are strenuously arguing about human rights, Tiananmen Square, and the bombing of the Chinese embassy in Belgrade as we play.

"What do you do at those meetings?" I wonder.

"We just shake hands, clap hands, and raise hands," the (unelected) congressman admits. "But some dissent is now being introduced."

My adversary is no fool. He expertly plays both sides of the political and economic fence. He owns this hotel and other assets worth millions in hard currency. And, taking no chances on a return to the Ten Years of Chaos, he has applied for an entrepreneur's visa to Canada, and is days away from getting it.

"Why do you want to live in Canada," I ask him between frames.

"Oh, I could never live there," he sniffs. "I am Chinese. I will become a citizen of Canada and make money there, and send it back to China. I will still live in China. Maybe, in my old age, I will retire in Canada."

"Why the hell should Canada give you a visa if you don't want to live there?" I demand, becoming uncharacteristically unsettled.

"Because I am going to make investments and do business that will make both me and Canada wealthy."

Let us call our chum Mr. Yang. The hotel, the bowling alley, and a small restaurant nearby are merely his sidelines, and unprofitable ones at that. His fiduciary interests are manifold; among them, the importation into the People's Republic of capsules of Omega-3 fatty acids extracted from the blubber of Newfoundland seals.

These are sold in the sundries shop at Mr. Yang's hotel, in a blue box with a Canadian flag, as an alleged coronary tonic. Beside them are dozens of packets of condoms, aphrodisiacs, penis enlargers, elephantine dildos, and a battery-powered, high-suction, vibrating, pink plastic artificial vagina, all of them domestically produced. As the Celestial Emperor informed an English ambassador who was seeking trade 200 years ago: "We have no need of foreign manufactures."

A corridor leads to an elaborate health spa with plunge pools and wet and dry saunas. Outside the hotel banquet hall – a plaque designates it as The Toronto Room – as at most restaurants in burgeoning coastal China, are aquariums proffering dozens of sea creatures from slugs to sharks and cages holding eight different species of (apparently) edible snakes. Down in the bowling alley, meanwhile, we are going at it hammer and tong, with F.Y. translating the intercourse with increasing discomfiture.

"The Chinese people hate the United States and all of NATO," Mr. Wang announces, launching another exchange.

"Then why are you becoming the citizen of a NATO country?" I ask.

"That is business," he says. "That has nothing to do with politics."

Vainly, I try to explain that it is precisely because of Canada's political system – the rule of law; the independence of the courts; the accountability of Parliament to the voters – that the country has become so trustworthy and bountiful that even Mr. Yang himself seeks to join it, or at least to show up late in life to collect his Old Age pension. But these concepts are as alien to him as knives and forks. "Democracy brings only chaos and turmoil," he deposes, flatly.

"We are standing on a mountain and he is standing on another mountain and he cannot see the whole scene," F.Y. whispers. "He is resisting you. But, in his heart, he knows the truth."

Bitterly, we bowl on. "Do you agree with me or not?" Yang demands.

"We're talking about the right to *dis*-agree," I announce, closing the subject. Then I rattle off strike; spare; spare; spare; spare; spare; strike; and beat our next Canadian by 45 pins.

We have come the last thousand miles by train, crammed in a second-class sleeper. Here, the antagonists included a young sculptor whose classmates, ten years ago in Beijing, helped erect the statue of the "Goddess of Democracy" that taunted the Communists to their very nucleus, just before the bloody end. Yet now, even this educated artist grew fiercely angry and shouted, "The students were wrong! Turmoil must not be permitted!"

And a young manufacturer of fashionable eyeglass frames: "The students' slogans were correct, but their methods were wrong. They had to be stopped, or they would have destroyed the reforms."

And another Communist Party member (and millionaire) at dinner: "The demonstrators had to be suppressed."

"Did they have to use live ammunition?" I asked.

"No, of course not," he replied, softly. "Mistakes were made on both sides."

We were rolling through the dark hills of Fujian and Anhui provinces, sucking oranges and peeling lichees. It might have been lovely, but rain washed the scenery away.

The sculptor showed us photographs of his masterpieces. He said that a commission for a single work – eight giant snorting, rearing, concrete horses for a public building – had brought him 400,000 yuan – about $80,000 Canadian.

"I do allow that I am a beneficiary of the reforms," he said. (The good old *gaige kaifang* again.) "But we do not need your so-called democracy."

I recited a bill of civil rights and said I thought all human beings deserved them – even the Chinese. This would have been unthinkable when I lived in this country, 15 years ago. We would have talked only of the dismal weather, and Dr. Norman Bethune. I said, "Look what you have been granted in the past 20 years – the freedom to create, to travel, to earn as much as you can. Then look at the freedoms you have not been given – freedom of the press; freedom of opposition; freedom of the people to choose their government. These freedoms must be very powerful, because the party is holding on to them so tightly."

"The common people are stupid and uneducated," the sculptor snarled. He used the term "old hundred names" to describe the peasantry. He said, "They should never be allowed to decide such vital things."

"The great misunderstanding that prevails concerning the rites of the Chinese, arose from our judging their customs by our own," wrote Voltaire, who never rode a Chinese sleeper. "For we carry our prejudices, and spirit of contention along with us, even to the extremities of the Earth."

But the Chinese hold themselves to live at the Earth's centre, not its edge. It is they who are eternal; it is we who blow like chaff.

We are in a tiny settlement called Peace Village, far from the view of Shanghai's piercing towers. The summer's new wheat ripples in the fields, and women – it is always the women – bend to their vegetables, pulling weeds. Old hundred names.

An aged woman, grinning, nearly deaf, leads us up the staircase of a stone-floored home to show us her bridal chests. She was not born of this place, she said – she came from nearly two miles away. She was carried here in a palanquin on her wedding day, to marry a man she hardly knew.

That man is with her, taking her arm, steadying her as we climb the stairs to see her faded antique cabinets. He uncovers the treadle sewing machine that earned his tailor's living and fed his four heirs. These are F.Y.'s parents. Their eldest son has come home.

We go to the kitchen and there is an ancient stove with bamboo steamers fuelled by dry wheat stalks.

"I remember kneeling here, feeding in straw, blowing to kindle the flames," the son says. He is 53; his parents nearly 80. Their life history is the episodic torment of China in the 20th century – the flight from the Japanese, who burned Peace Village to ashes; the Cultural Revolution that obliterated the tombs of their ancestors; the famines and the fanaticism; and, finally, the latter-day enlightenment that freed them from politics and hunger, forever, they believe.

We drink tea from the Fujian terraces we have just passed on the train. I am deeply honoured, I say, to share their table. And proud that their son would bring me to this humble place, that I might gauge the length of his life's journey.

"I must ask you something," my friend begins now, in his mother's fading ear. It is the question that, I know, has weighed on him since we embarked on this homeward road. Yet, as eldest son, it is his duty.

"Mama, when you – when you are gone – do you wish to be cremated or buried?"

"If I am buried," she replies, "you are so far away. When all the other families come to sweep their graves, you will not be there. You are so far away."

The mother smiles.

"And I will be so lonely."

– National Post

China 1999: The Homecoming

•

HEBEI PROVINCE

There are 930,000 villages in China. This is mine.

In the summer of 1985, still as overwhelmed by the enormity of the Middle Kingdom as I had been on arrival two years earlier, I applied to the Information Department to be permitted to dwell a while in an ordinary rural hamlet.

My goal was to perform "the Three Togethers" with Old Hundred Names, as the peasants are called – "Live together, eat together, work together" – a slogan that, during the Cultural Revolution, whitewashed the forced expulsion of millions of intellectuals to oblivion in the archaic countryside.

Hence my delight when I was told I could pass a week in the cotton fields of Hebei province, that I might learn from the farmers how lucky I was not to be one of them.

The destination was this unremarkable – in fact, hideous – little town on the North China Plain, whose name is translated as Zhou Family Village, although no family there was named Zhou.

My hosts were a clan called Lei ("thunder") – a patriarch dubbed Peaceful China, his wife, her ancient granny with tiny bound feet, three sons, and a daughter.

They gave me a room of my own, overfed me with pork and watermelon and sticky-rice buns, walked me around the town, let me pick cotton until my fingers bled (it didn't take long), and graciously shared their backyard latrine, festive with squirming maggots.

"Come back and see us!" the Leis cried out (sincerely, I thought) when we parted. And I always hoped I would.

Now it is 14 summers later, and my friend F.Y. and I are on an overnight train, rocketing northward out of his native Shanghai, trying to find my little Zhou Family Village on a map.

Overnight, we have changed climates and centuries. We had gone to our berths in the coastal subtropics and risen as the long, green express crossed the trickling Yellow River, half its kilometres-wide channel bone-dry and weedy in this waterless season.

Up here, the land is sere where the south had been sodden; flat as a plate where the south was lumpy and folded. On the highways paralleling the tracks, not a single private car; only donkey carts, tractors, bicycles, and even lumbering bullocks, towing creaking wagons of coal.

Everywhere I look, there are heaps and hills of garbage, heaved from the trains, dumped from homes and foundries. The Chinese call it "white pollution" – plastic bags, instant-noodle containers, cigarette wrappers, an indissoluble blight.

The quantity of trash cannot adequately be described. It fills every gully and watercourse, even where sun-kissed, naked boys are splashing and swimming and netting fish and frogs. It lines every pathway, surrounds every courtyard and house and village and factory fence. A Great Wall of Garbage.

Once, the Yellow River in flood was known as "China's Sorrow." The misery of the new material dynasty is man-made. No one has taught Old Hundred Names or his urban cousins that today's refuse does not melt into the soil like nature's wastes.

Now, emulating the fastidious Japanese, they are even using disposable chopsticks. How many forests will be sacrificed to this fetish?

On board the train, tossing in my upper bunk, squinting at the map, seeking to locate my village, my recollections are as hazy as the helpless, befouled sky. (In 1985, I was taken from the railhead in a government limousine.) Luckily, we meet a few Hebei natives and from them we get the general directions.

These have us disembarking in a county seat called Hardship Market, which seems to be a rather dull and dusty little burg, until our taxi turns a corner and suddenly enters "China Leather City" – hundreds and hundreds of modern shops and factories and warehouses stocked with fashionable coats, bags, and shoes. Towering hotels and a convention centre for foreign buyers have just gone up, here in the middle of nowhere.

As always, the Celestial Empire is a labyrinth of surprises. Unlike before, it is the sudden pulsar of prosperity that startles, not the overweening woe.

The first thing we learn in Zhou Family Village is that Peaceful China Lei is dead.

We are crawling through a narrow alleyway and nothing has changed at all. One paved street, the same brick houses, the same dimly lit shops and pushcarts and vendors. So much for China's miracle.

"He's dead," says the first woman we approach. "Dead a long time."

Back to the main street. A chubby woman, grey-haired, still in her padded winter coat and thick long underwear, though it is sunny and 30°C, is just turning from a fruit seller with a plastic bag of yellow plums.

Seeking to locate the remnants of Peaceful China's family, we are about to show her a photograph I took 14 years ago, when everything clicks and the woman yelps, "It's the foreigner! He used to live with us!"

Glowing, we embrace in the middle of the street and Mrs. Lei leads me home. Number Three Son is there, as it happens, and Only Daughter and the wife of Number One.

Trays of melon and plums and cherries are brought out, mounds of rice wrapped in bamboo leaves, flowery tea and fading pictures. The news bubbles from all of them, all at once.

Peaceful China, dead of stomach cancer a decade ago at the age of 63, close to the national life expectancy. Granny with her tiny feet, gone to her rest at 90, her ashes in a buried urn. And Mrs. Lei, surrounded by her children, beaming, abundant in her blessings: "All I have to do these days is sit around and enjoy myself."

The house is unaltered. The floors are still bare concrete, the walls mostly unadorned. There still is no indoor plumbing and the reeking old latrine still serves. Lilies grow in the central courtyard where the sons' motorbikes are parked. Upstairs, my room has been rented to a student from another town.

All I sought in Hebei in 1985 was to glimpse the unremarkable. Although Peaceful China Lei was a Communist Party member and his home certainly was not chosen for me by chance, I believed I had come as near to core as a resident correspondent might be allowed. Now, with this surprise return, my faith is ratified.

But Zhou Family Village, in its way, holds its own surprises. As the wife of Number One Son explains, this is the only hamlet in the region – perhaps in all China – that has chosen not to abandon collectivization.

Twenty years ago, Deng Xiao-ping liberated the Chinese farmers; here, uniquely, they declined. Finally given a choice by the Communists, they chose communism.

The laborious cotton crop has been abandoned in favour of more profitable wheat and corn, but the land remains in communal hands. So, too, does the local factory, which turns out "Evergush" brand water valves.

While the free-thinkers of other villages are scrambling to get rich – or growing dangerously desperate in their failure – the comrades here are pulling down a handsome $2,000 a year as their slice of the mutual pie. (In 1985, their average income was $350.)

Number Two Son arrives, summoned on his mobile phone. Like his father, he has joined the party and he serves the Motherland as the commissar of a neighbouring town.

In his bedroom is a 1999 calendar featuring a different photograph each month of Chairman Mao Zedong, whom the disciple closely resembles, with his round, tanned face and black halo of hair and constant cigarette.

"Chairman Mao is my hero," the son proclaims.

But there is a difference – Number Two Son was not appointed to his current post by Maoist decree. He was elected to a three-year term by his constituents in an honest, secret, competitive poll. This is as far as the central government has permitted direct democracy to rise – the election of officials, Communist or non-Communist, at the village level, in every one of the 930,000 villages.

Ten years after Tiananmen Square, foreign observers question whether these ballots are the first saplings of genuine democracy or merely a pretence of pluralism by a totalitarian regime.

The Carter Center of Atlanta, which has monitored several of these votes, maintains "the villages we observed were not 'Potemkin villages,'" but cautions "Jeffersonian optimists fail to understand that the soil in which 'grass-roots' elections have been planted in China is very different from the soil in the West."

At Zhou Family Village, the soil is as dry as flour, the sky as parched as sand. A Canadian, transplanted here, might feel relegated to the Middle Ages; yet a rural Chinese toiler sees a new epoch of relative bounty and ease.

One by one, I ask the Lei family to tell me their dreams, their ambitions. One by one, women and men, they answer, "I am content. Life is good."

As the Tao Te Ching, the basis of Taoism, says, "Let people return to simplicity, working with their own hands. Then they will find joy in their food, beauty in their simple clothes, peace in their living, fulfilment in their traditions."

It is time to depart. The taxi driver has heard on his cellphone there has been a mishap at home in Hardship Market.

His young son, playing with other boys, has been struck in the eye by a needle fired from the water pistol of some sick prankster. They need the vehicle to take the boy to hospital. So we must go.

He will drop us and our luggage at the side of the road to flag down a passing bus. Beijing is six hours away.

"Promise you will come back," says Mrs. Lei as she walks us through the door. Her three sons are with her now and their wives, all touching me, shaking hands, waving farewell.

"I promise," I reply.

"Heaven doesn't choose sides," says the Tao. "It is always with the good people."

– National Post

China 1999:
Tiananmen, Ten Years After

China is a despotic state whose principle is fear. In the first dynasties, when the empire was not so extensive, perhaps the government deviated a little from that spirit. But that is not so today.
– Charles Louis de Montesquieu, 1748

The sufferer sits at a low, polished table, picking at snacks, not touching his tea.

Ten years ago tonight, resisting the murderous advance of his own generation in green fatigues on the Boulevard of Eternal Peace, he committed an act the authorities labelled "hooliganism" at his semblance of a trial.

Then they sent him to prison.

"They took the best years of my life," he says softly.

"I could have had a wife by now – maybe a child. By now, I would have had a good job and been promoted to a better salary.

"They took my best years away."

My journey across China by land and sea has come to this – a small, modern hotel in the capital and a heart-wrenching hour with one of the invisible victims of Tiananmen Square.

Outside, there is thunder and lightning, and the rain comes in curtains of mist.

I remember a May afternoon ten years ago, when a fierce and sudden hurricane washed away the tents of the poets and the hunger strikers at Tiananmen, just as the tanks would shred their splendid fantasies, after midnight on June 4.

The man sitting before me is no radical, no Jefferson, no firebrand. Along with the other workers of his unit, he joined the million-man and woman marches of May 1989, when a crusade against corruption and nepotism within the Communist dynasty was being tolerated, if not encouraged, by some faction in the ruling class itself.

These merry protests were no crime, far from it; even policemen joined the parades. For the first time in People's China, there seemed to be an instant without fear.

That instant has passed. No one in this city expects a single act of public commemoration tonight. Known dissidents are under house arrest. Tiananmen itself is a walled-off work zone.

On the tenth anniversary of one of the most indelible events of China's incredible century – a century that began in imperial vassalage and concludes in McDonald's and microchips – the rebels of 1989 are scattered and defeated.

Most have evaporated into careers and families. A few fight the fight from the frustrating comfort of Princeton, Toronto, Taiwan.

The unyielding men whose "liberation" army obliterated their movement remain in secure command. (Though we can never know the depth of infighting and rivalries within the party itself.)

More than 200 patriots, bystanders, and "hooligans," by foreign estimate, remain in jail.

These are the men and women who – like my friend with his untouched teacup – threw rocks and flaming torches at the oncoming tanks on that warm June night, smashed barricades, destroyed weaponry, went wild in their rage.

Sentenced for arson, sabotage, looting, and "counter-revolutionary incitement," most will be released within the next five years, into a remade, competitive society for which they are completely unprepared.

"I don't care about politics" will be the mantra they hear when they are turned loose. "I just want to make money."

Yet this attitude is, in itself, powerfully political – a clue, perhaps, to the sort of government this generation will build, when its turn arrives.

From the sanctuary of a Western democracy, it is painless to judge that China in the spring of 1989 suffered from an oversupply of innocence.

Foreign reporters were made to feel we were the torchbearers of liberation. Posers like me squatted in tents and rattled off quotes from Winston Churchill and the U.S. Bill of Rights. A medical student in a dusty smock held up a sheet of paper and a pen, and sighed, "May I have your atmosphere?"

"We demand freedom!" a young woman told Patrick Brown of the CBC.

"We demand democracy! We demand free electricians!"

Now the former prisoner sitting before me is exactly that – a free electrician. He has no job, no cash, a criminal record, no wife or parents, few prospects, no passport, and little hope.

"I'm still not reconciled," he says. "I came out into a new world, but the corruption is even worse than before."

He speaks bitterly of his years of incarceration. The unsalted cornmeal mush that "even a pig would not eat." The threats and beatings and labour. The monthly visit by a faithful sibling who was his only reminder that the fabric of human life and love endured beyond the walls.

"I could write a book this thick," he says, holding his fingers an inch apart. "I could write three books about that prison."

When he emerged, neighbours and old friends consoled him. "You were wronged," they said. But then they resumed their own scramble for sustenance in this mad free-for-all of a capitalist capital and he is utterly alone.

"I have nothing to lose now but my life," the sufferer says.

The rendezvous concludes and I wander into a bookstore near Beijing University, where so much of the soul of Tiananmen ten years ago was born. On display are: Sartre, Barthes, Borges, Dilbert, the Holy Bible, Bill Gates, *Long Walk to Freedom*, *One Hundred Years of Solitude*, biographies of Washington, Edison, Kissinger, Patton, de Gaulle.

I meet the bookseller. He has recently returned after four years at a North American college. He says, "Change will not come to China by shouting political slogans in Tiananmen Square. It must come through social change." This transformation, he says, unalterably and irreversibly, has already begun.

To see Beijing in astonishing time-lapse after a decade away is proof. Tonight, the square will be quiet; there have been martyrs enough. This is only temporary. Ten years from now, all the libraries of China will offer the sufferers' tales.

– National Post

Climbing Mount Kinabalu

•

BORNEO

F our hours before sunrise on the shortest night of my life, I am squirming in the upper berth of an alpine dormitory when Jimmy the Malaysian Mountaineer comes pounding at the bolted door. I fumble for my glasses and my flashlight and illuminate my McDonald's Olympic wristwatch. It is 1:53 a.m.

"Good morning!" Jimmy announces with sadistic bonhomie. Departure for the summit of the highest mountain in Southeast Asia has been fixed for two-thirty. The final ascent will require at least three hours, so it is time to get up.

We are going to follow a breathtaking gradient of mud, roots, and tumbled granite slabs, then a ribbon of anchored ropes on a naked rock face – by torchlight, through the utter darkness. This will allow us to greet the rosy dawn from Low's Peak at the pinnacle of Mount Kinabalu, 13,455 feet above the glint of the South China Sea and the jungles of fabled Borneo. Then we will swagger back down to the horizontal world with the lightheartedness of heroes.

Four fellow adventurers who have been snoring like lawnmowers in adjacent bunks are roused by Jimmy's announcement. We proceed downstairs to the commissary for a slice of Styrofoam

toast. About 40 other climbers, younger and fitter, are feasting on
the loathsome grub.

"I want to go home," I am thinking as I sprinkle teaspoon after
teaspoon of sugar into my tea. Then I remember that home is
11,000 feet straight down, plus 26 hours by air. There is a gravel
helicopter pad adjacent to the rest house, but the Kinabalu fog, as
thick as cotton wool, rules out aerial rescue. The only route back
to Canada will be one cautious step at a time, down the same trail
I crawled up yesterday. Jimmy and his brother Borneans chat and
sip coffee and shoulder their packs for the assault. What he
chooses not to tell us is that, in his native language, the name for
this jagged little hill translates as the Place of Death.

I am no stranger to dizzying heights. My catalogue of previous
conquests includes Pikes Peak in Colorado (in a '66 Mustang),
Huangshan in central China (by cable car), and a ski run at
Centennial Park in Toronto (after falling off the T-bar numerous times).

Compared to these feats of courage and endurance, the ascent of
Kinabalu – the tallest mountain between the Himalayas and New
Guinea – is a mere scamper through a gentle dell. Children as young
as six have done it, tour guide Charlie Chan (his real name) assured
me as we barrelled toward the park; so have countless old women
and vast legions of the blind. But I am none of these.

"The mountain is a joy," the *Rough Guide to Malaysia* told me,
"seemingly tailor-made for amateur climbers." A pamphlet produced by the Malaysian state of Sabah promised "cool serenity"
and "ever-changing grandeur." The view of the mountain from
the Shangri-La Tanjung Aru Resort in Kota Kinabalu, Sabah's state
capital, was magnificent. All that remained was the climb itself.

Certainly, pink-skinned surface-dwellers had done it before. A
British colonial official named Hugh Low had hacked his way
through the rhododendrons and carnivorous pitcher plants to
nearly reach the summit in 1851. (He declared the ultimate pinnacle that now bears his name to be "inaccessible to any but winged
animals.") By 1878, when the horticulturist Frederick William

Burbridge arrived to gather pitcher plants for transplantation in England, Kinabalu had ceased to be viewed by Europeans with mortal terror.

But the Dusuns' awe of the mountain's majesty never abated. In 1888, John Whitehead, a butterfly collector, was nearly to the summit when his guides bade him halt while the ghosts of the Place of Death were appeased. One man baptized Whitehead with lashings of spring water while another carefully tended a sacred fowl:

> Kuro has brought a chicken with him from Kiau; the bird seems half dead with cold; as yet I do not understand his reasons for doing this. Tonight he has remained in a kneeling position muttering Dusun prayers to the spirits and dragons of the mountain. I hear my name mentioned occasionally, and my men, who understand a little Dusun, say that he is telling these mythical worthies that we have only come to see their home, and do not intend doing any harm.

The Dusuns' need for elaborate ceremony increased as more and more intrusions were made into the aerie of their ancestors. When Major Colin Enriquez and a platoon of the Burma Rifles climbed Kinabalu in 1926, they were required to furnish seven white chickens and seven eggs and to fire off rifle blasts at sacred locations.

Neither Charlie Chan nor Jimmy the Mountaineer has mentioned animal or human sacrifice, leaving us to trespass in the Place of Death without benefit of clergy. As we begin the climb from the dormitory at a quarter to three in the morning, the only white chicken is me.

Step by robotic step, I pick my way up the slope. Sometimes the trail follows a stairway chiselled into the mountainside. More often, it is a muddy, rocky slog.

It has been this way since yesterday morning, when we passed through the wooden archway that marks the beginning of the mountain trail. (Starting from base camp, the trail gains 8,000 feet of altitude in a linear distance of six miles.) The vegetation changed from rain forest to sub-arctic. Birdsong fell away. Finally, in late afternoon, the dormitory appeared overhead, only 2,300 vertical feet from the top. But there was little glory in getting this far.

Now, at 4:45 a.m., the guide informs me that we have made it past the tree line, though it is still too dark to see. It is here that the rocky staircase ends and the ropes to the summit begin. Clutching the thick white strands with both gloved hands, I haul myself about 20 paces, then lose my footing on the dewy granite and start sliding down toward oblivion. For one terrifying moment, I hang from the rope in the blackness, then somehow yank myself back to solid ground. I sit on a log and stare out into the dark. I will go no higher.

A few minutes later, as the sun turns the cloud tops crimson, my five-hour, knee-crippling, downhill jounce to the waiting world begins. Soon, my giddy companions bound past me, drunk on the thickening oxygen.

At base camp, Jimmy the Mountaineer presents me with a certificate affirming that I have reached an altitude of 12,500 feet without a Mustang or a cable car. Back in the van, with one eye on the twisting road, Charlie Chan passes out devilled-egg sandwiches. Behind us, above us, the sacred mountain of Borneo evaporates in fog. We eat like tigers. The conquerors of Kinabalu have returned.

– Canadian Airlines Inflight

Sailing Through Cambodia

·

Siem Reap

The limo was a Nissan Sunny with a quarter-million clicks behind it and a kid named Khun at the wheel. He leapt from the driver's seat when he saw us coming out of the guest house and grabbed our bags, then made a grand show of opening the doors. It was twenty to six in the morning and the concierge was laid out on the lobby couch.

We hustled off to catch the ship that would convey us to the capital. Khun steered us down toward the harbour on a muddied highway with craters the size of cows. Beside the stilt-houses on either side of the boulevard the first baguettes of the day were being scorched on charcoal braziers. The world was lightening through smoke and haze. It was coolish for Cambodia.

We passed the crocodile farm and the heart-breaking zoo we had visited the day before. The monkey that had snatched and eaten my companion's ticket screamed in greeting as we motored by. I remembered the giant, indolent reptiles and the lone wolf pacing half-starved in his cell. We were almost out of the city now, the royal city of Siem Reap.

There was a canal to our left and a man was bathing, though the listless, tea-stained water could not have been a yard deep.

Coconut palms angled over the stream and the tin-roofed houses like toothbrushes in a bathroom cup. A footbridge led to a monastery of the resurgent Buddhist faith. We spied acolytes in saffron through the brush and the banana trees.

Hunger stirred. We had departed the guest house too early to take our breakfast and the restaurant where we had feasted on steamed frog with mushrooms was dark and devoid of life. We asked Khun to stop at a row of stalls and we bought some bread for 100 riels. The loaves still were warm and the undersides were blackened by ashes and they tasted oddly, but not foully, of fish.

This was the pure distillation of travel: a quick ad lib vault into Cambodia to see – finally after a lifetime of hastening to far lesser marvels – the ancient Angkor temples, and then to get down, some-how, to Phnom Penh, then Kuala Lumpur. We could have flown to the capital – there were seven flights a day – but Siem Reap was full of hoardings promoting the speedboat service. Hand-painted signs showed a streaking craft, its nose in the air, cutting the waves of the great Tonle Sap.

The romance was irresistible: Cambodia by sea. There was a complication. Our guidebook mentioned that the boats were occasionally fired upon by aggrieved Great Lake maritimers as they rocketed through sacred fishing grounds. (Slower ferries also plied the route but they took 24 hours to the speedboats' five.) Khun avowed that shootings had not occurred for months. "Yes, yes, sir-madame," he swore, it was safe, it was perfectly safe. We trusted him. We had to. He was the only Cambodian we knew.

He had driven us for three days through Angkor, to the haunt-ing alien face-towers of the Bayon and the endless vaulted corri-dors of carvings that seemed, in the heat and the rain and the all-too-recent horror of the country, impossible perfect and pre-served, a last cruel taunt that millions could be martyred while smiling angels danced in stone.

The legless beggars gave the game away. They waited for us at the gates as we descended from the ruins, still drunk on wonder, our heads full of monkey-kings and apsaras and godly Hindu myths. We gave them 500-riel notes (about 20 cents) weathered almost to dissolution, with eternal Angkor imprinted on the money, and on our minds. This was still Cambodia. The glories of the tenth century cannot be divorced from the hell of the 20th.

Now the next morning, the port was still miles away. The countryside opened and the shrubbery thinned and we could sense, but not yet see, the inland ocean that lay impassively in the womb of Cambodia. Soon there was water on both sides and the road, which straddled a dike between the channels, became even more pitted. We were being tailgated by a van from the HALO Trust, which clears land mines from the wounded nations of the world. Khun tried to outrun it. "Let them pass," I commanded. He slowed the Sunny down.

The district grew, as if it were possible, poorer. The permanent houses of Siem Reap gave way to huts of palm-thatch and bamboo, open to the road and the water. Some were on stilts above the jetties and others were erected on barges, to be towed to wherever the fish were running. Children toddled among the slats and chickens pecked for scraps and leavings.

Sixty years ago, a British author named Alan Houghton Brodrick came to this place and found

The banks of the lake are dotted with the floating villages of raft-and-pile dwellings, where live the Cambodians and many Annamese who have been for generations fishers in the Great Lake. . . . Here is the easiest fishing in the world. When the flood waters slip and slither inwards towards the lake itself, the fish drop down from the forest aquarium into the rattan traps. They jump and flap and flounder and smack against the slats and you can fill a whole sampan with them in half an hour.

It was still that way. Already – it was not yet 6:30 a.m. – flatboats were coming ashore and people were squatting in the infant sunlight and woven baskets were being emptied of glittering, thrashing, dying silver fish.

Suddenly, the road concluded in a mess of trucks and motor-bikes and men. We had come to the harbour. Khun made his grand gestures at the doors again. Freelance porters wrestled each other, and us, for our bags. I led Khun from the jostlers and paid him what we owed – US$45 for three days at Angkor and this pre-dawn shuttle to the port. This sufficed for our farewell, I thought.

Our ship was lying as heavy in the water as a hippo at high tide. It was just as in the placards – a wingless jet plane, red and blue at the waterline, white above, as long as a DC-9 and as narrow as a streetcar. On our tickets, in Chinese characters, it was called *Soon Lee* – "smoothly; successfully; without a hitch."

A narrow board and a length of twine connected the *Soon Lee* to land. Stevedores in fatigue pants and checkered scarves were hauling bales and bundles aboard. We flung up our duffel bags. Someone manhandled a motorbike up the groaning plank and they leaned it on our luggage on the roof.

Passengers were climbing aboard with briefcases, baggage, and children. We scrambled up the gangplank and took two seats at the port bow, nearest the hatch. (Sit on the roof, the guidebook had advised. In case of sinking there could be no escape from below. This seemed unduly paranoid.) A woman challenged us for the seats; she had probably and rightfully reserved them. We played dumb and stayed put. She gave up and went aft.

At 7 a.m., precisely on schedule, the *Soon Lee* pulled away. It eased southward down the narrow channel, with more stilt-dwellings and house-rafts and sampans and pirogues and flatboats on either side. A family of five sat across the aisle, sipping lichee juice and munching Pringles chips. There were 96 numbered seats. All were taken. Dozens more were encamped on the roof.

A television above our heads played chaste but screeching Asian music videos. We were out into the open water now, braving a light chop, but the jet-boat cut through the whitecaps like a sword.

Pelicans floated by, and a pink-winged, white-headed eagle such as I had never seen, or dreamt. There were mats of vegetation, and flapping flags where fish-traps had been laid. Men were rowing or motoring out to their catch in bobbing wooden tubs. No one shot at us.

A full-length feature began on the television screen. It opened with a jungle scene, gunfire, war. A subtitle said, in English: "Cambodia 1982."

The film was called *War Without End*. A team of American agents had been air-dropped into the nightmare. They blew up bridges, Communists, and each other. The air conditioning drowned out the soundtrack. No one else seemed to be watching.

For nearly three hours, we were out of sight of land. The lake grew heavy and flat. Then it funnelled into a river and life began – towns, villages, storefronts, trucks, bamboo houses with TV aerials. The *Soon Lee* slowed and the men from HALO climbed through the hatch, jumped onto a long-tailed dragon boat that came alongside, and were gone.

At half-past noon, we docked at a bend in the Tonle Sap River where it merges with the mile-wide Mekong. This was Phnom Penh. We hurried up the gangway lest someone steal our bags. Nobody did. Ashore, a young man held up a handmade sign with my name and the words, "I am friend of Khun." Khun had checked the guest-house registry and phoned ahead.

We needed a hotel. The kidnapper drove us to a relic from the Parisian raj that was redolent of elegance and must. We seemed to be the only guests and soon found out why. A block away, 10,000 students – the children of a blighted generation – were encamped in a public square, alleging election fraud. Loudspeakers bellowed and crackled into our bedroom. But politics was not our purpose here.

This was the voyager's liberty: to take from a journey what he chose to take; and his duty, to hold this freedom dear. We left the hotel and walked through the marketplace to the colonial Bureau de Poste and mailed the postcards we had written at Angkor Wat. Slowly, savouring the essences of this unknown city, we walked home along the littered avenues. We went out for beers on the riverbank. The postcards never arrived.

– National Post

This Night Will
Never Come Again

HONG KONG

Once awaked and started we shall go fast and far – farther than
you think – much farther than you want!
       – Wen Xiang, Prime Minister, Qing Dynasty

Patu is packing. Nineteen-ninety-six is running out on her and
she is running out on Hong Kong. She is going to Bangkok for
New Year's Eve, and a new life. "I'm passée," she says with finality,
flicking my protests like fleas.

She is 81. Picture her enthroned on her sofa, white-haired, long-
necked, unlined. We are in her flat in Causeway Bay. The suitcases
are on the floor, under the Northern Song celadon and the early
Ming Dynasty scroll. They are propped open against the small
dining table where Patu and I have sat until three in the morning,
drinking champagne and dreaming of Thailand.

I wander onto her balcony to survey the cluttered harbourside
of the most fascinating city on earth. It is nearly 1997, when Britain
will return (or forfeit, or abandon, or whatever verb suits your
feeling or your fear) the Crown Colony of Hong Kong to the successors of the Celestial sovereigns who lost and leased her in the

19th century – the same Communist warlords who shot down their own children in Tiananmen Square. The "handover," as the *South China Morning Post* calls it, will take place at midnight on the 30th of June. But Patu is getting out with plenty of time to spare.

She is hardly Chinese, though she has lived her life in China. Born in the British concession in the port of Tianjin, subject to the Crown but not to Chinese law, raised in a fantasy world of ginger snaps and racing ponies and almond-eyed servant girls, Patricia Borrows Will escaped to Hong Kong in 1949 as Mao Zedong's People's Liberation Army overran North China, with her baby boy lashed to the rail of a storm-tossed ship. Now her son is in California, her confiscated properties in China belong to the People's Armed Police, the combustible Italian for whom she left her loveless marriage is gone, and Patu is fleeing her history, and her empire's.

"I'm the last one left," she says, marooned in this mood of dissolution. "I'm the end of an era. I don't like what's happening here. I don't like it one bit. You can see it already – the nastiness from the taxi drivers, the looks . . ."

"It's their country, Patu," I upbraid her.

"Yes," the Englishwoman says. "But I don't have to live in it."

It is the third and final night of the Ms. Lan Kwai Fong beauty contest in the jazz-bar district where 21 people were crushed to death in a New Year's Eve stampede six years ago. Five contestants – four Chinese, one *gweilo* ("foreign ghost") – are lined up on a stage in a *boîte* called The Milk Bar & Café. They are wearing black micro-dresses and the insane three-inch Olive Oyl platform shoes that are all the rage here in Orchid Lane this last colonial Christmas.

The judges are to select the young woman who, according to the printed rules, best demonstrates "a combination of brains, looks, trendiness, social awareness, bar know-how, and physical agility (dancing)."

Tonight is the "brains" competition.

"You come home from work," one of the finalists is asked. "When you get to the bedroom, you find your boyfriend having sex . . . with another man! What would you do?"

"I'd tell him to have fun," Number Three replies.

Uproar and approbation.

A Chinese named Christy closes her eyes and draws the next question from the snifter. One of the judges has dared to throw what the English call a spanner in the works. It is the ugly head of politics, which all of us have come to Orchid Lane to escape.

"Christy – what changes do you think the change in sovereignty will bring to Lan Kwai Fong?"

There is a slight diminution in the atom-bomb noise level of the club. In Hong Kong, this passes for a hush.

The contestant thinks for a moment.

"More fun, more prosperous, more beauty pageants, and more night life!" she proclaims.

The worst of the Chinese is that there are so many of them. They get on your nerves.
            – Rev. E. J. Hardy, MA, *John Chinaman at Home*, 1905

Simon Chow is thumbing through a field guide to the poisonous snakes of Southeast Asia.

"Which one are we eating now?" I ask him, setting aside my bowl.

"This one," he says, pointing to a photo of a serpent with red and buff bands on its coiled green tail. "If it bites you, fifteen minutes, maybe you die."

Simon puts down the catalogue and recommences counting wads of paper money and stuffing them into bank-deposit bags. We are in his little shop in a district of Kowloon called Sham Shui Po, sitting under stacks of wooden crates, each marked according to regulations with the characters for "venomous serpent," although most of the reptiles that go into the cauldron here are as harmless as kittycats. A couple of other customers drift in for a bowl of five-snake soup – it is a favourite winter tonic of the Cantonese – and then drift out again, leaving me with Simon Chow.

"It tastes like chicken," I offer.

"That *is* chicken," the young man replies. "We use it to fill out the soup."

"Half of my classmates are in Canada," Simon is saying. He is an electrical engineer who moonlights as a book-keeper at the snake-soup stall established by his father. (Simon's sister supervises the daily uncaging, beheading, skinning, filleting, seasoning, and boiling.)

"Why aren't you in Canada?" I ask him.

"You lose a million dollars if you go to Canada," he announces. "First, you have to sell your house over here. You lose money. Then you get a job over there and you have to give all your money to the Canadian government as taxes. You are Chinese in Canada – you are second-class citizen and suffer racial discrimination. Then you come back here and you have to buy a house again and the price has gone up so much you can't afford it. You lose one million dollars."

"What about the Communists?" I persist. "Isn't one million dollars a small price to pay for freedom?"

"China won't change Hong Kong," he says. "Hong Kong will change China. Hong Kong is a test for China. Economics is more important than politics. China will never go back to the way it was before. If you had it bad before, and now it is good, you don't go back to bad."

No one guessed that British rule would end in as orderly a way as this – the stock market and property values zooming, the dollar (with the Queen's portrait replaced by a grinning lion) firm and stable, 200,000 Hong Kong Chinese with Canadian passports (a

Canadian diplomat's estimate) coming *back* to Hong Kong to wring still more profit from the bubbling entrepôt.

"Hong Kong is to revert to China fourteen years from now, though there are those who doubt that public order can be maintained that long," an Old China Hand had written in the *Globe and Mail* back in 1983, but I was just reporting what people told me on the streets. And people back then talked of swimming to Singapore.

That fall, Margaret Thatcher's government had made it clear that it would not try to hold the colony by military or moral force when the 99-year lease on the New Territories expired. (It was a few months after the Falklands War. Some patriots ventured that Britain should make a gallant stand at the Shum Chum River, led by Prince Andrew and a frigate or two.) All the early signals pointed to panic – the currency suddenly collapsing by 20 per cent; fistfights in the bus queues; a run on rice and a comic-opera scramble for visas to anywhere: Panama, Markham, Nauru.

Then came the negotiations (with no Chinese from Hong Kong included), the tide of exiles (half of them to Canada), the surrender document with its glib acceptance by the totalitarians of "one country, two systems," and their vows of no changes to Hong Kong's *laissez-faire* freedoms until 2047, when we'd all be dead.

Time passed. China abandoned socialist economics, freed its markets, untethered 100 million men and women to seek work in the coastal cities, the greatest migration in human history. Tiananmen happened. Heedless, we still shopped China for our toys, our clothes, our running shoes. Only a few expendable dissidents persisted in niggling with the iron fist.

Meanwhile, Hong Kong prepared for the inevitable. In 1983, an autumn typhoon seemed to presage the shift of the Mandate of Heaven, but at Christmas, 1996, it is sunny for 15 straight days.

I am here to watch the calendar turn and the Asian sun set on the Union Jack. It is my first visit to Hong Kong in seven years – the frenzy is familiar but the prices are astonishing. Six Canadian dollars for a can of Sprite; nine bucks for a cup of tea. The Christmas lights are the most magnificent in the galaxy – great green and red and white festoonery cascading down the commercial towers and tourist hotels; an Asian-looking Santa (this is new) on the Shing Mun riverfront; Fred and Wilma Flintstone ablaze in Bedrock at the New World Centre.

Night after night, the streets and the waterfront promenades are barricaded to motor traffic, squeezed solid with gawkers, revellers, families, pickpockets, Americans. At the Star Ferry pier, a squatting hunchback plays the two-string *erhu* and the melody makes me cry.

We are insects. We squirm down Nathan Road, are compressed by "platform assistants" onto the Kowloon-Canton Railway, are herded toward the inter-island docks by blue-suited bobbies with the crown of Our Most Gracious Sovereign on their hats. We infest the malls, the arcades, the ladder streets – sniffing fish, peeling lichees, fingering dry goods. We pause for ginseng broth, swill Guinness at twelve dollars a pint, piss in the alleys. There are millions upon millions of us. We are in Hong Kong, where the misery of China meets the majesty of kings.

In the 1950s, as Chairman Mao's insane Great Leap Forward spread starvation across China, a young woman named Ching Po left her infant son with relatives in Guangdong Province and commenced to run and walk and crawl toward liberty.

At about the same time, a teenage boy named Yen Hanwu fled Shanghai with an uncle and headed for Hong Kong by train. Ching Po was a stranger to comfort; Yen Hanwu, named for a learned emperor of an ancient dynasty, had grown up wealthy, attended by drivers and servants, the second son of jewellery merchants in the Paris of the Orient. But he had seen the Communists assign his parents for "re-education" in the wheat fields of Manchuria, and in the snows of Manchuria his parents had died.

Somehow, Ching Po reached the microscopic foreign enclave

of Macao, which already had been Portuguese for nearly 300 years by the time the British opium traders wrested Hong Kong – that "barren island," as one Sea Lord dismissed it, "with hardly a house upon it" – from the impotent armies of the Qing. From there, she was smuggled in a sampan to the British territory, part of a tidal wave of emigrants who would risk all they had to flee China for Hong Kong and who, even in 1996, were fleeing still, to be accepted in the colony at a fixed quota of 105 Celestials a day.

The policy of Her Majesty's Government in those early years was that any Chinese who reached Hong Kong could remain, and so Ching Po and Yen Hanwu stayed. Emaciated and exhausted, she found clan-mates to take her in; penniless, he worked in a cotton-matting factory, then an unlicensed food stall. At night, he tried to study English because the locals couldn't understand his Shanghainese.

Eventually, Yen Hanwu gathered a small savings and opened a cooked-food stand with a man he thought a friend. But his partner swindled and bankrupted him and left him easy prey for an organized criminal gang – the Kwan Lok Triad – who put him to work as a small-time warehouser and courier of illegal drugs.

"One day," Yen tells me, a broken, weeping man now in his sixties, "my boss put some heroin in my cigarette. They made me addicted, so I would do anything they wanted. I had to go to work for the triad. I was only a third- or fourth-class pusher – but four times I had to go to jail to protect my boss."

"He's telling the truth," a young social worker named Eddy Ip assures me. We are in Eddy's office at a Hong Kong government health centre. Above us, giant jets are making their terrifying forty-five-degree nose-dive to land at the Kai Tak airport. This is where the jeweller's son, still addicted, comes each morning for his methadone.

"I am so old," Yen Hanwu says. "I want to die soon. The sooner, the better. I have been suffering so long."

He complains of asthma and liver disease. Whatever English he learned at night school in 1950 is long forgotten. He lives in public housing on a few hundred dollars a month. He has never married. His older brother – named for yet another benevolent emperor from China's vast storehouse of history – has been lost to him for nearly 50 years.

"So much suffering," he says, and begins to cry again.

"What will happen to people like him when the handover comes?" I ask Eddy Ip.

"I think it will change gradually – less and less welfare for underprivileged people," the social worker answers.

"I have no plan," Yen Hanwu says. "Wait and see."

The methadone, which costs each addict one Hong Kong dollar – about eighteen Canadian cents – per day, seems effective. Yen Hanwu is grateful to the Queen for the treatment her mandarins provide in a colony that was established to turn China into an empire of dopeheads. He says, "If I were still taking heroin, I wouldn't be as good-looking as I am now." And he tries to smile.

Not long after her alighting in Hong Kong, Ching Po was introduced to an Englishwoman, herself an immigrant from North China, who was in the market for a servant girl. Patricia Borrows Will was then living – as she would for two decades – in a wing of the Repulse Bay Hotel, a tasteful beachfront manor on the far side of Hong Kong Island. In another wing of the same hotel lived Piero Calcina, the Italian businessman with whom Mrs. Will was passionately and permanently in love.

Life at Repulse Bay was sublime – cruises in Piero's converted naval vessel, angling for gamefish with silver spoons as lures, dinner and dancing at the swankiest nightclubs east of Rangoon. Mrs. Will and Mr. Calcina were partners in a trading company that secured the concession for shipping bullion in and out of the colony. She describes planeloads of pure gold.

Patu gave Ching Po one month to rest and fatten up, dubbed her Ah Po (a prefix denoting a junior), and set her to work at cookery and other daily chores. At these tasks, decades later, Ah

Po is working still. Such has been the human epic of Hong Kong –
the jeweller's son defeated, the servant girl preserved.

Patricia Borrows Will and Ching Po live together in the little
flat with the Song Dynasty porcelain above the harbour at
Causeway Bay. It is a complex of hundreds of apartments; Patu is
the only European in the block. Their relationship is Britain and
China, mistress and maid. It is also, I suspect, sister and sister. Ah
Po is going to Bangkok, too. In fact, it is she, not Patricia, who is
packing the suitcases, smoothing the dresses, closing the bags.

"I have forbidden Ah Po to die before I do," Patu says. Now we
are at dinner. The servant shuffles out of the kitchen, bent and giggling, with a crisp-skinned roast chicken, mashed potatoes, and
tiny, tender *bok choy*. The common language of the house is a pidgin
that I thought had disappeared with the opium trade – "Missy likee
finish?" I attempt to elevate the conversation, but of my tortured
Mandarin, the Cantonese housemaid catchee not a word.

The baby whom Ah Po left behind in China is now cook and
part owner of a Chinese restaurant in San Jose, California. His
children, and Patu's grandchildren in San Francisco, consider
themselves cousins. But it cannot be like that for the two older
women in the flat at Causeway Bay – their history disunites them.
While we feast on the chicken, Ah Po shuffles back to the kitchen
and sits at her rice bowl, alone.

A few years ago, not long after Patu and Ah Po moved from
Repulse Bay to this ordinary high-rise across the island, a Chinese
woman left her husband and her two children in another tower of
the complex, took the elevator to the 35th storey, and jumped. She
landed, "like the pulp of a tomato," on Patu's balcony.

Now, each day, Ah Po lights a stick of incense to honour the
spot where the poor woman's soul departed her body. Pots of
greenery adorn the scene. Patu calls it "a Buddhist ritual," but I
think I would do the same. Walking outside, I think of Yen Hanwu
and pray he lives on a lower floor.

The squabbling between Britain and China enervates Patu – if
only things could be as they used to be, with Piero, always Piero,

beautiful Piero. She retreats into her bedroom and emerges with a black-and-white photograph. It is she and her lover, at a Hong Kong nightclub, the lady slender and elegant, the gentleman distinguished and alive.

"The way we were," Patu exhales. She slumps down.

"It will never be like this again. I'm passée."

Piero died in 1970.

"What in the world were we doing in India?" she asks, suddenly. "And China? I'll tell you, we *bettered* those places."

"And when the flag comes down at the end of June?" I ask.

"I suppose I'll cry," Patu says.

Some day, no doubt, the people will select their own governor; and, even now, if they should be dissatisfied, he would probably be recalled. Such a thing as this rarely happens, nowadays. Good men, generally, are sent, and they are much respected by the people.

          – Mary H. Krout, *Two Girls in China*, 1903

In the ancestral hall of the Tang clan in the village of Ping Shan in the New Territories, there is a photograph taken in 1899 of the 14th British governor of Hong Kong. Sir Henry Blake has come to the hinterlands in the first months of their 99-year rental to Britain to pay his respects to the Tangs. The photo shows Sir Henry suited and stiffly collared, flanked by the long-robed male elders of a family that by 1899 had called Ping Shan home for at least 21 recorded generations, dating back to the Northern Song dynasty of Patu's porcelain, more than 700 years before.

Below Sir Henry is a photograph of the 28th governor, Christopher Patten, in the same location in 1993. Again, he is enveloped in Ping Shan Tangs – the 24th generation, I presume, now displaying a woman or two and dressed in coats and ties but with their Celestial dignity otherwise undiminished. Thus does a Chinese century pass – barbarians arrive, barbarians depart, but the Tangs endure forever.

Leaving the ancestral hall, wandering among the well-conserved temples and walled-in alleys of Ping Shan, I stand over a four-some at a mahjong table and ask one Tang if he supposes he will cry when the British flag comes down. "I am Chinese," he laughs dismissively, and returns to his clattering tiles.

Now it is the eve of Christmas Eve, 1996, and the 28th governor is standing under the grand staircase at Government House and lustily singing "We Three Kings of Orient Are." He is immersed, this night, in Pattens – wife Lavender, daughters Kate and Laura and Alice. The dogs Whisky and Soda are somewhere upstairs.

Government House is stuffed to the balustrades with invited carollers, colonial retainers, and the choir of the Cathedral Church of St. John the Evangelist. In my best blue blazer, I pad about the ground-floor salons and study the signed photographs of Elizabeth and Philip, Anne and Edward, Andrew (solo) and Charles (the same), Diana with her smiling boys. A sublime por-trait of a radiant queen looks down at me. Enchanted, I gorge on warm *dim sum* from silver trays and relieve myself in the Twyfords urinals. I swipe a matchbook, cherry-red with a crown embossed in gold. This night, I know, will never come again.

On an antique sideboard in a wide hallway, there is a framed photograph of Chris Patten and John Major at the steps of 10 Downing Street. The men are smiling and waving. (Perhaps it is the day of Patten's appointment.) Above them, on the wall, is an oil painting of a bearded emperor – the Son of Heaven – in saffron silks, enthroned in a pavilion of the Forbidden City while three supplicants kneel before him. It was the refusal of British emis-saries to similarly kowtow, I am instantly reminded, that led to so much strife in the 1830s; that led to the Opium Wars and the con-cession of Hong Kong; that created this amazing, impossible place, that brought West and East together, for a time.

The Order of Carols is handed around: "Once in Royal David's City"; "O Leave Your Sheep"; "Midnight Stars Make Bright the Skies" (in Cantonese). The choir – half its members Caucasian, half Chinese – is arranged in the foyer behind a towering silver crucifix.

There is a handsome tree, and mistletoe right above me. Children are gambolling uncollected, and grown men are singing unashamed.

O star of wonder, star of night, Star with royal beauty bright . . .

Once, it must have been like this in Zanzibar and the Gold Coast, in Port of Spain and Sabah and Calcutta, the colonial gentry mixing at Yuletide with their loyal native panjandrums. I am not British, but the audacity of their imperial accomplishment astounds me. *We bettered those places*, I hear Patu say, above the music and the voices. And now it is over, save for Gibraltar, Bermuda, St. Helena, a few scattered rocks in the sea.

The governor steps forward to present flowers and certificates of long and meritorious service to three Chinese members of his household staff, a gesture of farewell that, with the music and the warm mulled wine, rings heartfelt, Christmas at its truest. And the governor removes his glasses and tells us, "I have no idea what will happen in this house at Christmas, next year." Then he brightens and adds, "But I am certain that, if we were to return 50 years from now, the choir of St. John's would be here, singing." And he thanks us all and we step into the moonlight and down the steps to China.

Chris Patten had attempted to instil an enthusiasm for participatory democracy in the Hong Kong Chinese. He created an elected legislature, an institution London had not deemed necessary to the territory's governance for the previous 150 years, and dared the Communists to abolish it. For this, Patten was vilified as a venomous serpent by Beijing and as a meddlesome boat-rocker by many in the colony itself.

He should have known better. Economics is more important than politics, Simon Chow had lectured me at the snake-soup restaurant in Sham Shui Po. In Hong Kong, only a few diehard Jeffersonians hold out for a genuine parliament. Everyone else is at the horse races.

In the Celestial scheme of things, the tenure of the 28th governor – indeed, of all the governors – has been a fleck, an annoyance, a mere mosquito bite. The legitimate legislature is to be summarily liquidated on July 1, to be replaced by an appointed body whose members include several candidates who had run for seats in Patten's folly and who had been rejected by the voters. By then, of course, the royal portraits will have been crated and shipped, Governor Patten will have steamed out to France – *westward leading, still proceeding* – to write his memoirs, and Whisky and Soda will be festering in British quarantine.

Alfred Tropp saw three ships come sailing in, on Christmas Day in the morning. This alarmed him. It was 1941. They were the Japanese Navy.

Sapper Tropp of the Royal Engineers was on guard duty at the Murray Barracks. Across the harbour in Kowloon, the Japanese, who had violated the colony's frontier two weeks earlier, were broadcasting Deanna Durbin singing "Home Sweet Home," and the harrowing cry: "Give up the fight, British soldiers."

"It is all so clear," Sapper Tropp is saying. He has come back to Hong Kong, along with two dozen other veterans, on a Christmas pilgrimage to visit the graves of the comrades – British and Canadian – whom the Japanese shot, or captured and then bayoneted. We are in the penthouse of the Park Lane Hotel in Causeway Bay. There are tables of hors d'oeuvre and pastries. Governor Patten is going around the room, shaking hands.

I ask about Hong Kong in the weeks before the Japanese arrived.

"It was all rather strange and wonderful," Alfred Tropp says. He is a big, oval man, bald, 78, a wholesale leather-goods dealer in London before he retired. "Here I was, leaving all my friends and loved ones back home to come to this distant outpost, and it really wasn't that bad at all. Being good at cricket didn't hurt either. In fact, we were supposed to play a two-day match on Christmas and Boxing Day and the governor was to present us with spoons. It never happened, and the Japs got my cricket bat.

"I didn't know a place like this existed. We found the Chinese people so strange. *We* were ordinary; *they* were strange. They would go into the road when we walked by on the pavement. They were fearful of white people then. The regulars would sit in bed and be shaved by a Chinese servant while they smoked a cigarette. It *was* unreal. The white people here were *lords*. They lived a wonderful life."

Our talk is interrupted while the governor delivers a lovely speech: "This city has succeeded by holding fast to the values that we defended then." He says that Hong Kong "has provided an opportunity to escape from fear for millions of people." I think of Ah Po and Yen Hanwu. There are no Chinese in the room except the waiters.

"Would you fight the Chinese to defend Hong Kong again?" I ask Sapper Tropp, jokingly. He shakes his head.

"I feel it's inevitable that we leave," he replies. "The Chinese are well able to look after themselves now. They're quite capable of manufacturing everything they need."

In the lobby of the Park Lane, waiting for our bus tour of the battlefield of Hong Kong, I meet Graham Downing, National Chairman of the Royal British Legion, Pall Mall, London. I ask, of course, about the handover.

"If it's like it was in Nigeria," the chairman replies, "they'll be asking us, 'Why are you leaving?'"

I nod in sad agreement, though I've never been to Nigeria.

"We had a pilgrimage to Aden," Mr. Downing adds. "And they all asked, 'Why did you leave?'"

The tour is to be led by the indomitable Jack Edwards, MBE, FCIH, FHKIH, FRSH, champion of the Hong Kong's British, Canadian, and Chinese war heroes and author of the meticulously researched indictment of Japanese atrocity, now in its sixth printing, entitled *Banzai, You Bastards!*

Jack Edwards, who was born on May 24 – Empire Day – is the chairman and secretary of the Royal British Legion, Hong Kong and China Branch, an appellation from which he intends to remove the word "Royal," he vows, "only when I'm *told* to remove it."

The chairman leads our group to the Lei Mun Fortress, to the Hong Kong Cricket Club where the Winnipeg Grenadiers were ambushed and shredded, to the Silesian Mission where the invaders massacred their captives, to the former site of Patu's beloved Repulse Bay Hotel. The inn has been replaced by a huge condominium tower through which a five-storey gap has been left, allowing the dragon spirit who lives on Violet Hill to bathe in the bay in peace.

Of the old hotel, only the garage remains. In it, at Christmas, 1941, the Japanese murdered prisoners. The building is now a filling station and body shop with a Toyota sign on its flank.

I walk around the grounds with a woman named Wendy Reynolds, an English nurse who grew up in Hong Kong and was interned by the Japanese. Her husband, Peter, is with her on the tour. The Reynoldses were in Northern Rhodesia when it was granted independence as the Republic of Zambia.

"If you look at our colonies in Africa," Peter says, "ninety-nine per cent of the people are worse off now than when we were there."

"What about Hong Kong?" I ask him.

"Do you know the La Fontaine fable?" he replies. Mr. Reynolds begins to tell the story of two dogs – one scruffy and hungry, the other gleaming and fit.

"How do you live in such perfect condition?" the underfed dog wonders.

"I eat chicken every day and live in my own little house."

"And what need you do?"

"I bark at strangers. That's all I have to do."

"That's all? It sounds so easy. But – what's that around your neck?"

"This? Oh, that's the collar my master ties me up with."

At nine in the evening on Christmas Eve I haul up in a taxi to take Patu to Midnight Mass. In a day or two Patu will be gone to

Thailand, where she's been invited to work as a consultant to the nouveaux riches, setting up a school to train domestic servants. We set off, arm in arm, for the devotions. But the driver errs – he delivers us to St. Joseph's, not St. John's.

"This Catholic Church," Patu reproves him. "Wrong! No good!"

We end up on a cement bench in the garden beside the Anglican cathedral where Patu's grandparents were married, somewhere around 1880. (Her great-grandfather, William Henry King, had come out to Hong Kong as a constable in 1860, the same year the British and French torched the magnificent Yuan Ming Yuan Palace, up in Beijing.)

We are 90 minutes early for the service, but while we repose on the bench, the entire churchyard fills with Filipina housemaids – the Ah Pos of the new Hong Kong – and a few dozen bona fide Englishmen, and when the heavy doors of the church finally open, we find ourselves without hope of beating the throng to an empty pew. Scrumming like a rugby fullback, I grab a folding chair for Patu, plop her in it halfway down the nave, and repair to the very back of the church as the processional hymn begins and the same choir I had seen at Government House the previous evening comes in, singing "O Little Town of Bethlehem," following the same high silver cross.

Behind me, as the singing and the solemnity proceed, are the coats of arms of English dioceses and before me are the Pattens in the front pew decorated with the royal arms. I can't see Patu – she is awash in an ocean of kneeling, fervid Filipinas – but I can hear the choir and the intercession: "Let us pray, at this Christmas, for Hong Kong . . ."

"Amen," I breathe to myself, thinking of Han Dongfang.

I told the policeman who arrested me I would keep trying to enter China and that if after the tenth or the fiftieth time they decided to shoot me, I wanted them to remember that I was a good man.
                                                            – Han Dongfang, 1993

Late for their Christmas party, Jonathan and Nathan Han squibble down the bare dirt back street of a little town called Banyan Bay. Already, the dancing has started and there are platters of cookies and candies set out in the warm midwinter sunshine and a cotton-wool snowman has been tacked to the back wall of the village school. But Jonathan, who is two and a half, has lost a shoe, and his father goes trotting back to search for it.

Han Dongfang shouldn't run at all – he has only his left lung to sustain him. But there are many in the Crown Colony who are urging him to flee as fast as he can before the 1st of July, when the People's Republic that once branded him one of its Most Wanted Criminals takes ultimate control of Hong Kong, and its courts, and its laws, and its jails.

Han Dongfang's crime was self-confessed – he preached, in the drunken days before the tanks came to Tiananmen Square, that Chinese workers might be rescued from enslavement to the state only if they organized themselves into independent trade unions. For this, Han was labelled "China's Lech Walesa." For this, turning himself in after Tiananmen, he served 22 months for "counter-revolution," part of it in an unheated cell full of sick men, where he caught the tuberculosis that cost him his breath.

Now, at 33, deeply handsome, dark-haired, Han Dongfang waits in British Hong Kong for China to reclaim him, for the People's Republic to make of him what they will.

"I hate heroes," he says, when I meet him on Lamma Island, a quiet fishing outpost favoured by Chinese intellectuals and German hippies, 40 minutes by ferry from central Hong Kong. "I grew up with a Communist education – all those heroes from before 1949 who died for the New China. Now I hate heroes.

"Usually, heroes forget ordinary people's lives. They forget ordinary people's needs. They really want and love the feeling of being a hero."

Han Dongfang is the one aspect of the handover that the snake-soup vendors and Ms. Lan Kwai Fong and the property speculators find it convenient not to notice as the Union Jack is pulled down – the crusader who dares to look beyond "one country, two systems" to stare down the old men who murdered the soul of a generation. Hong Kong's overweening miracle may be the white heat of its economy, but for a century, it also has been the only place in China where a Chinese man might freely speak his mind. And this is ending.

Four years ago, his prison sentence served, the Chinese government expelled Han Dongfang. Free-world trade unions and human-rights groups brought him to the United States, where his dead lung was removed, where Nathan and Jonathan were born, where Han Dongfang became a Christian. Later, when he tried to re-enter his socialist Motherland, the Motherland refused.

"Last Saturday," the *Sunday Times* reported in August 1993, "he got as far as Canton before police dragged him from a hotel and beat him up. They deposited him in neighbouring Hong Kong after just seventeen hours, buying him an air ticket to Switzerland. Two days later, he tried to enter China again, but was turned back by border police." That was when he asked the militiamen to remember his goodness should they find themselves commanded to shoot him dead.

"Issues like this will come back to haunt Hong Kong," Chris Patten said at the time.

"Are you afraid?" I ask Han now.

"If you had asked me that question a year ago," Han says, in his elegant, self-taught English, "I would have answered immediately: no. But now I am getting a little bit nervous. After Wei Jingsheng and Wang Dan received very heavy sentences, that means the Chinese government doesn't care about international opinion about human rights."

Wei Jingsheng was hailed as "China's Shcharansky" before he vanished into the gulag for a decade and a half. Out of prison for a few months, constantly hounded and shadowed by Beijing's clumsy "secret" police, he was recharged with "subversion" and thrown away for another 14 years. Wang Dan was a student leader at Tiananmen. He will be in prison until the regime finds it useful to release him, or until the Mandate of Heaven overthrows the old, old men.

"Before 1994, they used political prisoners like cards, especially with the United States," Han says. "Every year, before Congress had to vote on Most Favored Nation trading status for China, they would release some political prisoners. But they haven't released anybody since 1994. That's why I say they don't care what the world thinks.

"In Hong Kong, after the democratic election of the Legislative Council in 1994, they said 'Okay – in '97, it's gone.' What did the international community say about the future of democratic Hong Kong? They didn't care either. From these two points I see the future of Hong Kong, and the future of myself."

In Hong Kong, Han Dongfang coordinates the collection and publication of the *China Labour Bulletin*, a derailing of the wretched working conditions that have underpinned China's furious economic growth. All the evidence the Chinese need to put him away he gives them, in black and white, once a month.

"I have published a monthly bulletin 30 times," Han Dongfang says. "My friends say, 'Each issue is enough for 20 years.' That makes me nervous.

"I get in taxis and the taxi drivers won't let me pay. They say, 'We want to go, too, but we can't afford to. You are famous. You can go. Go!'

"Almost all of my friends say to go. They say, 'If you are sent to prison for another ten or 20 years, it is not useful for anybody. What can you do in jail for the Chinese worker? For your family?' That's why they say I must go. But what holds me here is, I have to keep my principle. As a Chinese citizen I have the right to stay in my own country."

Han Dongfang came from a household as poor as Ah Po's. His parents – a peasant farmer and a construction worker – separated when he was three, then reunited in his teenage years. Between those times, he and two siblings subsisted on their mother's 30 yuan – less than ten dollars – each month. Han Dongfang grew up hungry. Now he'll eat anything – butter, blue cheese – food-stuffs that most Chinese consider as repugnant as unrefined Canadians deem snake soup.

"When you look at Hong Kong," I ask Han Dongfang, "what do you see?"

"An unfair society," he answers without pausing. "During the past twenty or thirty years, the development of Hong Kong has been very fast, but the social welfare for old people and children in Hong Kong is very far from fair. Of course, if you compare it to China, Hong Kong is much, much better."

"And when the British flag comes down?"

"For the Hong Kong people, I have only sadness. For 150 years, they were ruled by the British government. They had no democracy – they were second-class citizens in a colonial culture.

"People felt, 'We *do* have freedom – we can work hard and jump up in class.' But after 1989, after Tiananmen Square, Hong Kong people woke up. The majority had been very happy to go back to China, to feel like a real *citizen* and not just a *resident*. But when they saw the machine guns and tanks, the Hong Kong people understood immediately their future."

The man who hates heroes finds his baby son's shoe in a curve of the brown-sand lane. We walk back to join the party at the English-language nursery of Banyan Bay and find children of all colours, the two Han boys among them, dancing together in the sunshine. We have wished our Merry Christmases, and I am heading back to catch my ferry to the mania of Kowloon.

"The boys were safe in America," I venture in parting. "Why didn't you leave them and your wife there?"

"When a family stays together in times of difficulty," Han Dongfang replies, "it makes one more confident."

"The world is something like an egg,"
Said Mr. Gak to me;
"The yellow, that is China,

And the white, that is the sea.
The other little countries,
Like America and France,
Are tiny specks out in the sea –
You know that at a glance."
  – Evelyn Worthley Sites, *The True Tale of Jade Flower,* 1922

By New Year's Eve, Patu is in Bangkok with Ah Po, Governor Patten is said to be "celebrating privately," Sapper Tropp is back in London, Han Dongfang is preparing for a protest march to the New China News Agency, and the police are roping off Lan Kwai Fong to try to prevent another deadly stampede.

I am wandering around Causeway Bay, manhandling my way through the crowds, killing the minutes before the hourglass spills down into a year the Old China Hand thought would never arrive.

In the lobby of the Excelsior Hotel, a band is playing and a smoke machine is respirating vaporous clouds and young women in ersatz Annie Oakley frillery are proffering hits of José Cuervo at ten dollars (Canadian) a shot and calling it a "special promotion."

On the opposite side of the six-lane expressway that leads to the tunnel to Kowloon and, ultimately, to the border of the Middle Kingdom itself, a party tent has been set up. Next to the tent is the Noonday Gun celebrated by Noel Coward in *Mad Dogs and Englishmen* and this is to be fired at the stroke of midnight, as it has been every New Year's Eve (and daily at 12, of course) since the Japanese surrender. Already, at 10:30, guests are arriving, landward by limousine and seaward by yacht.

Jack Edwards, MBE, etc., has instructed me how to get across the highway to the gun without committing suicide in the screaming IndyCar traffic. A "secret" passage, he advises, leads from the parking garage of the Excelsior, under the motorway, and up a flight of steps to the party tent. And so it does.

Popping up on the other side, I find myself scrutinized by demobilized Gurkhas in grey berets but I brush past them as if I

belong. I huddle among the television crews for a while, then peep
out to poke around.

It is 11:30 now, the old year waning, and with it, another morsel
of Empire and the rule of the waves. Outside the fence, a sizable
crowd has gathered to watch the changing of the tide.

"Why have you come?" I ask a middle-aged man in a blue windbreaker who is pressed against the barricade.

"Last time, this," the man replies with irreducible eloquence. I
search for delight or resignation in his voice but can find neither.

It is nearly midnight. A Chinese orderly in a grey uniform with
a chevron on his sleeve steps to the gleaming gun and fits a six-
inch brass shell into the barrel. I assume it is a blank; otherwise, it
spells certain doom for Fred and Wilma Flintstone in their giant
granite chariot across the channel.

Now two younger Cantonese men, kilted, playing bagpipes,
lead a procession to the base of the gun. There are torchbearers,
and a seven-piece brass band – all Celestials – in stiff, starched
whites adorned with silver braid. It is almost a parody of colonial-
ism – a scene from a pantomime – but it is real. A burnished brass
bell is rung eight times. The night watch is over.

A socialite and patron of charitable works named Mona Leong,
Member of the Most Excellent Order of the British Empire, steps
to the howitzer and is handed a lanyard. Mrs. Leong is as Chinese
as the Song empresses, as Chinese as her incomparable city. A
distant sovereign has honoured her with an imperial title, but
soon this Elizabeth will be merely a foreign queen, her island a
tiny speck out in the sea.

I hold my ears. Favoured or doomed, knowing not which, Hong
Kong tenses as she pulls the cord. The explosion is stupendous. It
is 1997. There are six months to go. And the Chinamen in silver
braid are playing "Auld Lang Syne."

– Saturday Night

NORTH AMERICA

Previous page: Post Office, Dogpatch (Linda Abel)

As a boy, I was space-mad, starry-eyed, moonstruck – a willing Explorer, a Vanguard, a Pioneer.

Had anyone told me back in 1961 that, 40 years after the flights of Yuri Gagarin and Alan Shepard, we still wouldn't have a chance to dance in moondust, I would have thought him insane. But here we are, Earthbound, still waiting for the Space Age to begin, for purposes less lofty than Hubble telescopy or aged John Glenn's giant sleep for mankind.

As the 21st century opens, fewer than 400 men and women have been encapsulated and sent into orbit, a tiny percentage of those of us who shared their cosmic dreams.

Imprisoned on my home planet, I have been privileged to interview six of the 12 men who walked on the moon; perhaps the only men who ever will. They were transcendent moments: Gene Cernan showing me how he traced his daughter's initials in the lunar dust; Alan Bean leading me outside his home in Houston, looking up at Luna with me.

Absent from this roster of unforgettable encounters has been the most distinguished flier of all. I do not expect ever to meet the paramount hero of my generation. But I have been in the house he grew up in, and that will have to do.

Wapakoneta

·

OHIO

On Benton Street, in what should be the most famous small town in the world, a frame house the colour of wetted sand awaits its wandering boy.

A detonation of bright red flowers bloodies the corner lot, and a handmade signboard swings from a wooden post. Above it, a flagpole offers the national ensign to a white-hot, thirsty sky.

The little sign reads: "Eagle's Landing – Boyhood Home of Neil Armstrong."

Thirty years ago tonight, watched by a lunatic world, three men raced from Earth at the speed of magic. They would arrive within days at the virgin Moon, prance in the powder of the Sea of Tranquillity, then rocket home to what they, and all of us who remember that time, dreamed might be an altered, lifted Earth.

This did not happen. Eleven more moonwalkers followed Neil Armstrong of Benton Street, loping, hopping, singing, saluting with reverence and bonhomie the most marvellous material achievement in history, but within three and a half years the missions had ended and the frisson had faded, never to be revived in my lifetime, or yours.

Down on Earth, we hardened and outgrew wonder, just as an auditor's son with wings on his heart once outgrew Wapakoneta.

The old Armstrong house at 601 West Benton never has been consecrated as a national shrine, nor has the town of 9,800 gained the touristic cachet of Teddy Roosevelt's Oyster Bay on Long Island, or the LBJ Ranch in Texas, or Jimmy Carter's picayune Plains, Georgia. (This was not Neil's only childhood address. His father, a state auditor, moved his family 16 times in 15 years before settling on Benton Street.) The current owner of the home, a grammar-school principal named Karen Tullis, does not expect Neil to come home for this anniversary, or ever. She has not met him, and like most of us, probably never will.

"Sometimes you look at the moon," Ms. Tullis says, as we sit in the parlour of this Lincoln's log cabin of the Space Age, "and you think, 'Someone walked on the moon, and that same person walked through this house.' Not that I immortalize him, or anything – it's just interesting."

"Does he mean anything to the kids at your school?" I ask her.

"To kids today, it seems like a hundred years ago," she says. "It's sad – we're moving at such a fast pace, we don't take time to remember who the heroes were."

Thirty years after the first footprint, resolute in his reticence at age 69, a virtual hermit with his second wife down near Cincinnati, Neil Alden Armstrong remains a difficult man to immortalize. Few flock here to his native village – 45,000 visitors annually at an excellent space museum and planetarium; occasionally, "a gentleman from France," or "a German three or four years ago," at Karen Tullis' house on Benton Street. The uninterested millions rocket past on Interstate 75.

A new museum in Alvin, Texas, hometown of the baseball pitcher Nolan Ryan, is likely to draw thousands more pilgrims than Wapakoneta, yet all Nolan Ryan did in 1969 was win the World Series with the New York Mets.

I mention to the owner of Neil Armstrong's boyhood home that, when I was at Cape Canaveral last October for John Glenn's return to orbit, a Florida newspaper reported that not one of the high-school students it surveyed could name the crew of Apollo 11.

"I would imagine that most kids here would know Armstrong," Karen Tullis says. "But they probably wouldn't know who else was on the ship with him."

"Do you know who else was on the ship with him?" I tease her.

"I'm sitting here trying to think," she replies. "I just saw something on them last night . . ."

The other man on the moon that July evening is marking the date by appearing on a television shopping channel.

"The air is abuzz anticipating the convergence of cosmos, color and commerce when QVC offers Peter Max's interpretative artwork celebrating the 30th anniversary of the historic moon landing and walk by Apollo 11 astronaut Buzz Aldrin," the network's Web site shouts.

"PRINCESS CRUISES ROLLS OUT THE 'BLUE CARPET' FOR ASTRONAUT BUZZ ALDRIN," blares another blurb.

"Now adorning the entranceway to the Aldrin's home in Los Angeles, the carpet first caught the Aldrin's [sic] attention last fall when they were guests aboard the world's largest cruise ship, Grand Princess, where the design is featured in the dramatic Skywalkers Disco."

In his office at the Neil Armstrong Air and Space Museum, curator John Zwez reflects on the disparate paths of the crew of Lunar Module Eagle.

"Much has been made of Mr. Armstrong's being quiet and aloof," says Mr. Zwez, whose father's cousin's wife was a cousin of Armstrong's mother, Viola. "Sure, I would like him to come up here once in a while and walk through the crowd.

"But I have to respect his privacy, as opposed to Buzz Aldrin, who will literally sell you the shirt off his back for money."

At the Neil Armstrong Air and Space Museum, the hero's high-school yearbook and Navy flight suit speak to the ordinariness of his origins and the fearlessness of his ambition. Rightful respect is paid to the Soviets who went into space before him – even before Ohio's sainted John Glenn – and there is a glittery chunk of vesicular basalt fetched home from the moon's dark *mare*. To someone who grew up in space, as I did, the displays are meaningful and humbling; to most other folks, they are a runic bore.

"I got a phone call from a young man who said his teacher had told him to do a project about Apollo," says John Zwez. "When I answered the phone, he asked me, 'Is this Apollo?' He had no idea what Apollo was.

"'What did they do?' he asked me. I told him, 'Apollo was the first time that human beings set foot on another celestial body.'

"He said, 'Is that all they did?'"

A daughter of Auglaize County named Trish Murphy, currently performing on the "B Stage" of the Lilith Fair concert tour, was asked about her hometown by the *Wapakoneta Daily News* and she answered, "It's flat and hot and there's a lot of cows and nothing to do."

"I hate that stuff – 'There's nothing to do,'" Dave Christiansen is telling me now. "I once heard my kids say that and I sat them down and made them write out a list of all the things there are to do."

Mr. Christiansen is the president of the Flags of Freedom Foundation, Inc., which is trying to raise money to build a 30-acre park and museum just off I-75 to honour the star-spangled banner. We're at lunch in a town where the speciality at the local inn is deep-fried sour pickles.

Mr. Christiansen and his partners believe that their exhibit, featuring a 30-by-50-foot American flag, would put Wapakoneta on the map, which it isn't, he admits, despite the otherworldly achievements of its famously introverted son.

"You can thank Neil Armstrong for that," Mr. Christiansen sniffs when I wonder aloud why Wapak, as the townsfolk call it, isn't as prominent as Washington's Mount Vernon or even our dear old Shawinigan, despite its many unique attributes. (Wapakoneta is also one of the last places on this planet where a local telephone call still costs five cents.) "I talked to Neil on the phone one day, and I thought I had him convinced to come on board with us. Then he turned 180 degrees in the same conversation and turned us down flat."

"The people here have no vision," adds Larry McLean, a Vietnam veteran who is vice-president of the Flags of Freedom Foundation, Inc. "We're going to help Wapakoneta in spite of itself."

In the spotless, lifeless core of the town sits the law office of Edward Stroebel.

Thirty years ago this weekend, Ed Stroebel, the hero's family friend and attorney, stood on the lawn with Viola Armstrong and they looked up at the moon. And Mrs. Armstrong said, "I was worried that the moon might be too soft and that he would sink in too deeply."

Barrister Stroebel is 83, and still holds his private pilot's licence. Now he sits in his trifocals and his bright yellow suit jacket and says of his moon-skipping client, "He has been a loner. He has not capitalized on his achievement. He has preferred to remain a private person. And I protect him."

Pilot Stroebel says that he is amazed, as he flies around the United States, how many people have never heard of Wapakoneta, Ohio. "We can't accept that people don't accept what Neil did as being as important as we do," he says.

"Do you still look up at the moon?" I ask him.

"Always, always, always," he replies. "And I think of Neil up there . . ."

He begins to cry.

I leave the old man and wander into the steaming summer day, past the post office and the Apollo Travel Agency and a long, peeling mural of the true Episode One of our starry destinies, Neil Armstrong at Tranquillity Base. There is no one else on the sidewalks of what should be the most famous small town in the world.

Down by the railway station, a single rusted boxcar sits on a siding. As I come closer, a cottontail rabbit hops out from beneath it. He looks at me and exits in slow, measured bounds – just like a man on the moon.

– National Post

Too Old to Change Now

•

As a full moon the colour of melted butter jumps from the Georgia pines, 14 race cars growl their way around a loop of crimson soil. A smear of chalk dust marks the starting line; a concussion of noise evokes war. When the green flag is out and the pack goes by, you can feel the earth shake.

This is Cordele Motor Speedway on October 27, the last day of the 1996 Sportsman division racing season. A few hundred women and men are in the bare cement grandstand, sprawled on patio chairs, watching the racers as they hurtle, shudder, and career through the packed-clay turns. The cotton field beyond the north rim of the oval gleams ripe and white in the moonlight. It's harvest time in Crisp County.

The vehicles on the track are so battered that the races ought to be picketed by the Society for the Prevention of Cruelty to Automobiles. The tow truck turns more laps than the pole sitter; the yellow (caution) light shines just about as often as the green.

Tomorrow, the men who steer these cars will once again be small-town mechanics, labourers, and farmers. In their off-hours they will tinker and dream toward the new racing year that begins in March 1997. They will pass the winter in hamlets such as

Fitzgerald and Coolidge and Arabi, adding up the modest gains and bank-breaking debits of another year on the dirt. None will get rich driving one of these whining, wounded wrecks, yet the emotional poverty caused by giving up racing would be too much for any of them to endure.

Among this fraternity – yet simultaneously removed from it by the distance of generations – is 73-year-old Harvey Jones. Once long and lean and fiery, now thicker, quieter, deliberate in movement, Jones may be the most remarkable active sportsman in the U.S. Forty-seven years after he drove (and won) the first heat he ever entered, 34 years after he pulled his dying brother from a race car in Valdosta, Georgia, Jones remains as competitive and skilled as rivals one-third his age. He will be back in 1997, God willing, and many years after that.

Asked about retirement, he says he will quit if and when he can no longer win races. He says, "I ain't gonna sit there and watch the races from a race car."

At Cordele (pronounced core-DEEL) in 1996, Harvey Jones finished the season sixth in points in the Sportsman division – and might have finished higher had he not missed four weeks while doctors fitted his left eye with a lens implant. (Rubbing his eye, he had torn a retinal blood vessel, flooding the vitreous cavity with blood and making it seem, he says, "like I was lookin' through a stained-glass window with water runnin' down it.") This year his plans for the off-season include installing a new engine in his blue Oldsmobile racer and having the cataract in his left eye removed. Eight years ago he had heart bypass surgery. An Aspirin a day and undiluted pride keep him ticking.

Jones never attained the pinnacle of his profession – a rich man recruited him to drive the Indianapolis 500 in 1960, but Jones turned the offer down, fearful of abandoning his full-time job with the telephone company in Tallahassee. He has reigned, instead, at Lake City and Dothan, Alabama, Wewahitchka, Florida, and Valdosta, amassing countless trophies, regional celebrity, and so little prize money that, even after half a century, $50 plus or minus at Cordele makes a measurable difference in his mood.

What matters to Jones is how his car performs and where he finishes. (The biggest payday of his career was $2,500 for second place in a 100-lap special.)

"Do you feel," I ask him, "as if the Lord must be on your side?"

"I don't know," he replies. "Sometimes I see all these wrecks on the racetrack, and I think he must be off someplace else, and he's let the devil take over round here."

In 1943, Jones tried to join the army but he was told by the enlistment officer that he was considered unfit to go to war. As a toddler he had clambered up a rocking chair, trying to reach some treat on the mantel, and had tumbled into a bed of hot ashes, burning his left hand. The hand remains strong, but the middle fingers are slightly misshapen.

He was born in 1923 on a Florida panhandle farm, the son of a wanderer who had moved east from Alabama with only a mule and a wagon. Harvey was born in a barn – the house his father was building had burned to the ground. The Joneses had 33 acres of nuts, corn, and cotton. On the side, they made booze. Their bucolic distillery, as described by a state treasury agent named W. George McMullen in his self-published memoir, *Twenty-Eight Years a T-Man*, maintained a production capacity of 400 gallons of corn liquor. Moonshining, Harvey admits, brought in easy money.

On July 12, 1950, McMullen and his men raided the still. They chased, tackled, and arrested Harvey's younger brother Hulon and reached the house where the rest of the family was holed up, intending to impound the Jones family auto.

"I thought I was about to win out," McMullen wrote, "when suddenly Harvey Jones stepped to the driver's side of the car (a late-model Mercury), reached in, pulled the keys from the switch, ran behind the car to a side gate, through the gate and began to call for someone to bring him a shotgun.

"He went into the house by a back door, still calling for a shotgun.... I figured if Harvey came out with a shotgun, he would never live to use it."

As it turned out, Harvey came out unarmed. McMullen holstered the .45 he had drawn. A few months later Harvey, who never was much of a drinker even of his own products, gave up on the distilling industry and concentrated on his full-time job. On the weekends he drove a souped-up 1940 Ford for prize money.

At Cordele, the final Sportsman division feature race of the 1996 season is to be 25 laps, three-eighths of a mile to the circuit. Jones has qualified fifth of the 14 entrants, claiming the inside position on the third row. It takes about 18 seconds to go around once.

The racers here start two abreast, although Turn 1 is wide enough for only 1½ vehicles. Jones's strategy is simple: Stay back, stay cool, let no one pass you, and wait for the front-runners to get silly and crash. Jones hates accidents: He fumes that his blue number-6 Oldsmobile Cutlass suffered $1,200 worth of damage a couple of weeks earlier when, as he cruised along in the fifth or sixth spot, he came around Turn 3 and ran smack into a pileup caused when everybody else was blinded by the setting sun.

"To win the race," Jones reasons, "you got to be there at the end of the race. These guys who tear up their cars at the start of a race – well, it's a lot of hooey."

Most men his age couldn't climb into a race car through the glassless window, let alone drive one. But Jones is in his crash helmet and his royal-blue racing suit for the feature. Asked if his suit is fireproof, he replies, "I had me one that they said was fireproof, and they told me it was custom-made, but it was so big, a whole family must've moved out of it before I climbed in. When I put my hands in the pockets, I never did touch bottom."

He has driven 2½ hours from Tallahassee, towing number 6 behind a 1981 Chevy Silverado with 146,000 miles on the odometer. When the racing is finished tonight, he'll drive the 2½ hours home.

When he was still living on the farm, Harvey attended high school in Tallahassee, and when he was 26 he began racing. In 1951, after two divorces, he met his current wife, Hazel. Her father drove the wrecker at the Tallahassee track, so he was acquainted with Jones and she was acquainted with stock car racing.

Harvey and Hazel were married on Christmas Eve, 1952, and have lived on the same street in Tallahassee since 1953. Theirs is a circumscribed world: Harvey has never been to New York City or anywhere west of Texas. He has never flown in a commercial airplane. Hazel has worked for the Florida state government since 1949. Harvey's '34 Chevy two-door sedan is still in the garage. He and Hazel have four children, his complete pit crew at Cordele. He also has a daughter by his first wife.

"Those other two wives are dead," Harvey says. "But I had nothin' to do with none of it."

Hazel doesn't work in the pit crew with her two sons and two daughters. This evening she sits in a lawn chair in the top row of Cordele's grandstand, absorbed in a Harlequin romance titled *Lady of the Upper Kingdom*. The moon is up higher now, helping to illuminate the back straightaway, where darker-coloured cars such as Harvey's tend to disappear.

The first few laps are uneventful – one caution flag, no serious wrecks. Jones slips back to sixth position. The leaders, including Randy Ellenberg in red number 28, pull steadily away. Number 6 doesn't seem to have the engine power to catch them. Or Jones might just be playing his waiting game.

Ellenberg, 34, a jocular giant from Valdosta, takes pride in having outpaced a 73-year-old man. "I beat him twice," he says. "I wanted to do that before he died."

Jones estimates that dirt-track racing is "60-per-cent dishonest."

He says, "I try to build a car that's legal." Among drivers, accusations of cheating – for building too powerful an engine for the class or using an aluminum flywheel or some such novelty – are common, if costly. Jones boasts that no protest against him has been successful. "Down in Valdosta," he says, "I won the feature six or seven weeks in a row. Well, we were pushin' the car backwards onto the track all the time, instead of driving it in reverse. After one race, these guys come over and they say they're protesting that I'm not carrying a full gear box. It cost them $125 to do that, you know.

"They say, 'We want to see you drive it in reverse.' So I put it in gear and backed it up. I told 'em, 'It'll go forwards and it'll go backwards. It'll go anywhere but straight up.' They were so mad! They said, 'Then how come you've been pushin' it backwards all the time?' And I said, 'To give damn fools like you somethin' to be angry about.'"

On June 2, 1962, Hulon Jones was in the centre of a pack of three cars heading into Turn 1 at Valdosta. Harvey Jones, four years older, was a few hundred feet behind his brother as the cars all went down the front straightaway. Then Hulon's car got sandwiched, and he rode up the side of one of the other cars.

Harvey saw it happen. It was all right in front of him. "He bounced three times, every time right on the top of the car," Harvey says of Hulon. "It caved the roll-bar system in. It was just a black iron pipe back then – that's all we had. It couldn't stand punishment like the stuff we use now." Hulon was unconscious when his brother and others pulled him from his car. The ambulance arrived quickly. Within ten minutes the race was restarted.

Harvey won, as he almost always did back then. Then he was told that his brother was dead.

The next week Harvey went back to Valdosta and won again. Two weeks after that there was a special memorial race, and Harvey won that one too.

"Why didn't you quit?" I ask him. "Had you and Hulon ever talked about what you'd do if this happened?"

"Nothin' never really was said," Harvey answers. We're alone in the cab of the Silverado. "I liked racing. What happened to him didn't mean it couldn't happen to me. I don't think he would have wanted me to quit."

He is quiet for a while and then says, "I don't want to die before my time. The good Lord's got a place for you, and I hope mine's 20 years off. I don't want to die like my daddy died. My father died in 1947 in a barracks they were makin' into a hospital, but they didn't have anything in there yet. He had a heart attack. I was in the room when he had another one. They didn't have no sedatives. He just lay there and hurt. That was a bad death to have to watch somebody die, particularly when it's your daddy."

"Was Hulon's a good death?" I ask, as respectfully as I can.

"He had a good life to that time," Harvey replies. "He didn't never know it happened. He was unconscious when we pulled him out. He never woke up."

Eight laps into the Sportsman feature, a white car, number 51, head-butts Jones's number 6 from behind as they are going down the front straightaway at 100 miles an hour. There's no consequence to the collision – the racers hold their positions, and the race resembles bumper cars at Coney Island.

Hazel is shouting, "Come on, Harvey! Come on, Harvey!" But he has slipped back to eighth place.

A couple of caution flags allow the field to bunch up at the restarts. Jones is sixth at Turn 3 on the final lap when two of the front-runners spin out and vanish into the darkness. Checkered flag. Fifth place.

Twenty minutes later, down in the infield, Jones is still in his blue racing suit (he'll drive home to Tallahassee without changing). Number 6, a little scraped up but undamaged, is back on its trailer. The season is over. Forty-seven years.

Hazel comes down from the pay window, where she collected Harvey's prize. It is suddenly quiet; the roaring of the engines has been stilled.

"How much is the purse?" I ask her. Her reply is barely whispered. For five hours on the highway and 25 laps on blood-red Georgia clay – for half a century of roar and risk and ardour – the bonanza is two hundred bucks.

– Sports Illusrated

Inuvik Taxi Drivers

•

NORTHWEST TERRITORIES

Way up north, where the midnight sky is painted pink and gold, the first resident a lonesome traveller meets is a brown man from the Blue Nile.

Ebaid Emam drives car number 24, a well-worn Crown Victoria, for the United Taxi Co. in a town that may have more cabs per capita than any other metropolis this side of Manhattan. He has spent the past eight years north of the Arctic Circle, motoring up and down and up and down and up and down and up and down Mackenzie Road, supporting a bride and a baby son, and utterly befuddling his Sudanese kinfolk back in frost-free Khartoum.

"When you phone home, what do you tell them about Inuvik?" I ask Mr. Emam as he imports me from the air terminal, along the only 10 kilometres of paved highway in the entire northwest Northwest Territories.

"I don't tell them anything," he replies. "They don't believe the midnight sun. They don't believe the driving on the river in winter. They don't believe the two months of darkness. They don't believe the 45 below zero. So I stopped telling them."

At the United Taxi Co., the fleet has known cleaner and sounder days, and there isn't much point in hosing the cars down or tuning them up. Just getting the vehicles here from civilization requires four or five days of jittering, jolting, gravel and dust on the Dempster and Alaska highways. But there is no doubting the need for public transportation, even in July, when the wind comes bellowing unblocked from Tuktoyaktuk and the weak-kneed little trees duck for cover.

We're not halfway in from the airport when Mr. Emam invites me to join him and his friends for sundown prayers, even though I am not an adherent of Islam.

"How can you have sundown prayers if the sun doesn't go down?" I wonder.

"We looked to the Holy Koran for guidance on this matter," Ebaid Emam says. "We are going by Edmonton time."

"Welcome to United Nations headquarters," says the Filipina behind the desk at the Swiss-owned Finto Inn. It is dawning on me that Inuvik is not the tripartite society I envisioned this far north – Inuvialuit, Gwich'in, and Anglo-Canuck.

(I don't remember seeing any Sudanese in Povungnituk or Davis Inlet on previous trips to the tundra. But it works both ways – the night clerk at the Finto is an Inuvialuit woman who previously ran a vegetarian restaurant in Vietnam.)

"We have been here only two months from Ontario," says the Bangladeshi woman serving chop suey, pizza, falafel, and caribou burgers at the Blue Moon Bistro. "Every day my little son is crying, 'I want to go to Swiss Chalet.' But I must tell him that there is no Swiss Chalet."

I wander into the kitchen of the Blue Moon, which is tenanted, aptly enough, by an axe-wielding chef from Hong Kong named Moón, though the man's mood is anything but cerulean.

"Why did you move all the way up here?" I ask him, after he has put his cleaver down.

"In Edmonton, make money, go to casino, money go goodbye, Charlie," he answers, doubling up with laughter. "Inuvik, no casino. Money stay in pocket."

"What about the winter time?" I persist.

"Winter time, stay in kitchen," beams Moon. "Kitchen always hot."

Mohamed Mohamed was working in a Palestinian convenience store on Mackenzie Road, early in his first January in the Far North, when he heard the unmistakable sound of explosions coming from somewhere in the town.

"I didn't know what it was," he says. "Then a native woman came running into the store, very excited. She was shouting, 'The sun is back! The sun is back!'

"Now I know what the explosions were – every year, they have fireworks and a big celebration of the first sunrise after the weeks of darkness. I think it means a lot spiritually to them."

We are in the living room of Mohamed Mohamed's little green house and, despite the brilliant sky outside at 11 p.m., it is sundown, Edmonton time. Ebaid Emam is here, and an Egyptian cabby named Wa-Il, and a Lebanese teamster named Hassan El-Khalid, plus the symmetrically named homeowner and United Taxi Co. driver, who is explaining how he happened to end up, like all the others, at the top end of life's winding highway.

"When I left Sudan, I went to New York, to the Bronx," he says. "I lasted there only one week! I went up to Canada as a refugee. They believed my story, so here I am.

"Inuvik is a very interesting place. Basically, you find every nationality: Egyptian, Yugoslavian, Turk, Lebanese, Syrian, Czech, Greek, Albanian, Hungarian, Tunisian . . ."

"And everybody gets along?" I ask.

"Not really," Mohamed Mohamed says.

"I think you find discrimination everywhere you go," Mr. Emam notes.

"You find that everywhere, but here it's clear," Mr. Mohamed says.

"You know everybody," Mr. Emam adds. "But he doesn't show his feelings to you until he gets mad."

The United Taxi Co. of Inuvik, Northwest Territories, is owned by a Sudanese named Abdul Mohamed, a distant cousin of Mohamed squared. Its radio dispatch desk is in a corner of a small grocery shop, which he also owns, midtown on Mackenzie Road. Abdul Mohamed says that his three children "fight every day to go back to Africa," but he has found success in the North, and success is not an easy thing from which to walk away.

"In the South," the businessman says, "when they see a new immigrant coming to a job, they look at you and they say, 'You do not know the system.' And they use the system, whatever it is, to keep you at the bottom.

"Here, I am struggling and working to be the system."

The owner suggests that I speak with another of his drivers, universally known as Crazy John. Crazy John drives car number 2, which under all the dust turns out to be a 20-year-old, powder-blue Cadillac Brougham as long as a 12-dog sled team.

Zivojin Jovanovic, the driver's true name, is a Serb from south of Belgrade who has been in the Arctic for 30 years. He allows that this is "much too long," but our interview proceeds no further.

"They call me Crazy John, the bastards," he says, as I step out of the Caddy. "If they think I'm crazy, let them come get tested with me."

While the Muslim men attend to their prayers, I flip through the Holy Koran. One thousand, seven hundred, and eight pages in, I notice Sura LXXXIV:

Like the sunset Glow or the shades of Night,
Or the Moon's ever-changing light, man's life

Never rests here below, but travels ever onwards,
Stage by stage.

"How long do you think you will stay up here?" I ask the men,
when their obeisance concludes and we are sharing tea and fruit.

"I feel that I could leave at any time," says Ebaid Emam, who
has a diploma in electronic maintenance, and could certainly find
work farther south. "But I have said that for eight years."

"It is a fascinating place," Mohamed Mohamed says.

"You have the Northern Lights. You think of the Eskimos and
how they lived."

"What did they eat?" Mr. Emam wonders. "There is nothing
green."

"In Grade 4 or 5, we learned about them in Sudan," Mr.
Mohamed says. "They were small people who rode on the dogs
and they don't have farms."

Now they were living in the same vast land of sunset Glow and
shades of Night.

"What do you miss the most?" I ask.

"To sleep in the desert, by the river," Mr. Emam says.

"You try that here, the mosquitoes pick you up and carry you
away," interjects Hassan, the Lebanese, who has been here for five
and a half years.

"Last winter, it was minus 45 for six weeks straight," Mohamed
Mohamed says. "It's good for business, but you get depressed. Like
now – I'm tired of this daylight."

"Put garbage bags on your windows," counsels the Upper
Egyptian, Wa-Il.

"How did you figure out which way was Mecca?" I inquire. (It
is a requirement that praying Muslims face their Holy City.)

"In Toronto, there is no problem – just face East," Mr. Emam
says. "But here, we're almost halfway."

I look out the window where the dipping sun has set the clouds
on fire.

"We used to face the other direction," smiles the world's most northerly Sudanese. "But it is not a question of the compass. Your heart tells you where to pray."

– *National Post*

Herschel Island

———————— • ————————

YUKON

A little fear is healthy. It will focus your mind.
— Yukon Parks handbook

We are standing calf-deep in cold brown water, staring at white men's graves. Behind us, across a narrow channel, lies the continental mass of Canada. Northward extends a small, threadbare, bear-happy island of chamomile, chickweed, and lousewort, and beyond it, three thousand miles of heaving pack ice, followed by Russia.

At noon in July, it is two above freezing, with billows of vanilla fog.

Our trekking party consists of a young woman named Cindy from Manitoba, a birder from Ontario named Dave, two backpackers from Grenoble, France, and the great Nimrod himself, armed with a guidebook and a Mr. Big bar, in case we miss lunch. A Yukon Park Ranger named Frank Elanik has wisely stayed back at his command post, which is a winter-beaten blubber shed, relic of an age when beautiful whales were boiled here to light the lamps of San Francisco.

We have flown in from Inuvik in a single-engine Cessna and landed on pontoons in the whalers' cove. Now we have only a few hours to hike the dark brown beach, visit the old graves and haunted warehouses, and watch the caribou nuzzle patches of last winter's dying snow. Then we will fly away home again, unless one of the Yukon's 6,300 grizzlies gets us first.

"I had to shoot one a few weeks ago," Ranger Frank informs us on arrival. "I had to. It entered the rangers' cabin. While the rangers were sleeping."

"What do we do if a grizzly charges?" I ask as we depart on our hike.

"Climb the nearest tree," he advises, "which in this case is three hundred miles away."

Far above the treeline, just off the Yukon's only salt-water coast, the tundra of Herschel Island is broken by the tumbling shacks of the 19th century, and the tombstones of a lonely place to die. A dozen of the markers pose off-kilter before us, still faintly hand-painted, softly sinking into the squishing bog, the last repose of men and boys who died of typhoid fever, or drowned in the uncaring sea. Five men froze to death, my pamphlet says, when a sudden blizzard caught them playing baseball on Ptarmigan Bay.

Around the graves, tufts of wild rye and tiny blue forget-me-nots tremble in the breeze. A rough-legged hawk screams out a eulogy as we roust her from a driftwood aerie.

Only a few hundred visitors ascend each year to this ultimate sliver of the great Northwest. Fewer still hike or raft or canoe the rivers of Ivvavik National Park at the top of the Yukon mainland, just across the inlet. Up here, this day, we are outnumbered by musk ox and moose and the blinding purity of snowy owls.

Not to mention the grizzly, against which we are equipped with a whistle around the neck of the woman from Grenoble, very little common sense, and my Yukon Parks handbook.

"If you are looking for a surefire method of getting out of a bear encounter," it says helpfully, "you won't find it here."

Two weeks ago, the *Weekly World News*, which is published in
Florida, reported the following item, which I quote in its entirety:

INUVIK, CANADA – A Haitian voodoo priest visiting the wilds
of the Inuvik Region reportedly saved the lives of 15 fellow
tourists when their campsite was attacked by a giant grizzly bear.

Witnesses say quick-thinking Jean-Louis Buisson, 45, borrowed a child's teddy bear and a woman's sewing needle and
used them to dispatch the rampaging predator. "The moment
he plunged that needle into the stuffed teddy's chest, the bear
stopped trying to bite people and keeled over," said Australian
visitor Tom Brickertee, who was camping with his wife and
two small children. Wildlife officials attribute the grizzly's
death to a sudden heart attack.

Ranger Frank's birth name is Avingakpuk; he is a son of these
sunless shores. As a Parks Branch employee of the territorial government, he works two weeks at Herschel Island, followed by two
weeks in the tiny community of Aklavik, or in a coastal fishing
camp, or alone on the land. He says, "Wherever I lay my head,
that's home," and smiles at his own sagacity.

Avingakpuk walks us through the old wooden buildings, now
the roosting places of jet-black guillemots and fluttery snow
buntings. He shows us crates of penny nails, gap-toothed sawblades,
whale skulls, caribou shanks, moose antlers, a shelf of rusted pot-
bellied stoves. In the factory where the whales' fat was rendered
into profit in great reeking vats, he tells of the hanging here in 1924
of two men who had shot to death a constable named Doak.

"There is a danger of the natives concluding that crime is a
thing to be rewarded by the White man," the Commissioner
declared at the time.

"Kindness has failed in the past," said an attorney in the case,
condemning Alikomiak and Tatamigana to the rope.

Outside the execution chamber, our guide points out the

mounds that mark where sod-roofed huts once stood. Once, fifteen hundred whalers wintered here, overwhelming the Inuvialuit who, for centuries, had survived in their fashion, on the bounty of the Beaufort Sea.

"When the tourists leave and you are here alone," I ask him, "what comes to you?"

"I meditate, I contemplate, I try to go back to that time," he answers. "I see the kayaks lined up in the cove. I hear the dip of the paddles. Pre-contact, I would consider this place pretty much heaven. The marine mammals are here. The sea animals are here. The heat's not here. The bugs aren't here. The dust's not here. I can throw a rock and hit an Arctic char."

He looks around at the wind-bleached wood, bends down to touch a flower.

"This is where drums beat. This is where ladies learned to sew their stitch. This is where men sat in their councils. Listen – this is where legends were told."

The Senior Warden of Ivvavik National Park dares to dispute the veracity of the *Weekly World News*. Steve Travis acknowledges that a healthy population of barren-ground grizzlies does exist both east and west of the Mackenzie River Delta, an area that would encompass Herschel Island and correspond roughly to the Floridians' appraisal of "the wilds of the Inuvik Region."

"But to the best of my knowledge," he assures me, the day before we fly to the Yukon, standing in line for the Chinese buffet at an Inuvik hotel, "there have been no Haitian priests registered in any of the national parks of the Western Arctic."

"In theory," I ask him, "what would you do to prepare yourself in case of an attack?"

"Usually, the bear would flee," Ranger Steve replies. "There have been no reports of contact. But from now on, I am going to carry a small teddy bear, just to be safe."

Back on Herschel Island – named by Sir John Franklin in 1826 for the great British chemist and astronomer – the French have gone off on a separate trail and Dave the birder has returned to park headquarters, having added the long-tailed jaeger to his life list, plus the Lapland longspur, the glaucous gull, and the red-throated loon. This leaves Cindy and me.

"Too much fear can be crippling," my guidebook counsels us as we travel on. "It can take the joy out of your wilderness experience. . . . And there's no reason for that."

Then we see the bear.

It is a superb female grizzly, as golden as summer grain, her shoulders rippling as she runs down a muddied slope at the centre of the island. There is a cub loping behind her, adding to the danger, and the thrill.

Now I am shouting at Cindy and she is fumbling for her camera and this magnificent beast is running, running, and I am trying to recall what the guidebook said – "If contact appears unavoidable, protect your vital organs and keep still" – but there is no shelter here, not a tree or a bush or a rock – and I am thinking, Well, *you wanted to see a grizzly bear . . .*

I reach for my Mr. Big. Thank goodness we're seeing it from the plane!

– National Post

The Century of Al Capone

CHICAGO

Al Capone turns 100 on Monday and there ain't gonna be no parade, see? The birthday boy did not live to toast his own centennial with bootleg beer or his poisonous "Old Log Cabin" whiskey, though the bullets of his rivals never found him. He survived the gang wars of the Roaring Twenties and the comforts of Alcatraz only to expire, too young but still unperforated, in January 1947, numbed by neurosyphilitic complications, a defunct warlord on a Florida islet, unmourned by the Midwestern metropolis he once ruled.

Publicly, Chicago still shuns the man who became the bloated emblem of his city and his age. The civic wounds of carnage and corruption are too fresh – even after 70 years – for Chicago to establish what jocularly might be called "Scarface Days," to recognize a notorious killer and syndicate chieftain in the way that more ancient villains like Jesse James and Billy the Kid have been rendered the stuff of folklore.

"We kind of shy away from that," says a publicist named Rachel Crippin from the Convention and Tourism Bureau, when I mention the gangster's name.

"Al Capone turns 100 and Chicago is silent," observes Crain's Chicago Business.

"Warner Brothers created the legend," the honoured author Studs Terkel tells me at the Chicago Historical Society. "Jimmy Cagney and Edward G. Robinson made him immortal. And that's all I know."

But there is more to know. Remaining accessible on the anniversary of Capone's birth (in Brooklyn, New York, which likewise disavows him) are a soft-spoken nephew in Nebraska, a hokey but profitable tourist attraction on Chicago's South Side, a very few authentic landmarks, and a 93-year-old federal judge named Abraham Lincoln Marovitz who, as a young and honest lawyer, served as defence attorney for a hoodlum called Winkler who had (allegedly, of course) stood at the safe end of a Tommy gun in a certain Clark Street garage on St. Valentine's Day, 1929.

"Al Capone was like a god to a lot of people," Judge Marovitz reflects in his chambers, which are decorated with hundreds of busts and portraits of another Mr. Lincoln (no relation) and the autographs of celebrities spanning the spectrum from Sinatra to Oprah to Pope John Paul II ("To my favorite judge").

"He controlled mayors and important politicians and he really ran the town," Judge Marovitz continues. "Most decent people saw him as evil, but he also did a lot for people. Especially in poor neighbourhoods, people didn't care who helped them. They just needed help. I attended affairs where some Master of Ceremonies would introduce Capone and he would be applauded. I guess that decent people who were sitting next to a mob guy were afraid that if they didn't cheer, they'd get a punch in the nose."

Next month, it will be exactly seven decades since a group of gunmen disguised as police officers, possibly including Gus Winkler, working on behalf of "Machine Gun" Jack McGurn on behalf of Alphonse Capone, mowed down seven members of the "Bugs" Moran gang in the most flamboyant savagery of a savage time. No one was ever convicted, though one man, "Killer" Burke, went to prison for life for a separate killing. On the morning of the St. Valentine's Day Massacre, Al Capone was in Miami Beach, Florida.

"I represented many of the Capone guys," Judge Marovitz admits. There is no dishonour in the confession; even the basest thugs deserved counsel. "That Winkler, he was a Jekyll and Hyde – a generous guy, but a tough guy.

"I know it's hard for people to understand how a professional, decent guy could represent people who had people killed. Many times, they asked me to fix a case, to get somebody to talk to a judge. This sounds corny, but I was a very lucky guy, in that I was able to retain their respect even though I wouldn't do everything that they wanted me to."

Judge Marovitz's decency has never been impugned. He was the first Jew elected to the Illinois State Senate. Appointed by John Kennedy a month before the president's death, he served with distinction on the federal bench. During the Second World War, though colour-blind, he finessed his way into the Marine Corps.

"I used as much influence to get in as Quayle and Clinton used to stay out," the jurist testifies.

A multimedia museum and gift shop called Capone's Chicago closed its doors two years ago and is now the Rainforest Café. The bricks from the S.M.C. Cartage Company, where the St. Valentine's Day Massacre took place, are in the possession of a Vancouver collector.

In 1986, Geraldo Rivera cracked a "secret vault" in the old Lexington Hotel, Al Capone's former headquarters, and found nothing whatsoever. The hotel has been demolished and the site is now a vacant lot at 22nd Street and Michigan Avenue.

Around the corner on State Street ("that great street," in the words of the famous song), and a few blocks closer to the downtown Loop, a former target range and firearms shop has been converted into a dinner theatre called Tommy Gun's Garage, one of the few businesses still thriving on the sanguinary aura of the gangster age. A 1928 Model A Ford and photographs of Scarface and his murderous kind ornament a recreated speakeasy. On weekends, tourists, many of them from crime-free Europe, enjoy a meal and a stage show with dialogue that includes:

> Thugs: (Enter with Bugsy, put him in chair, tie him up)
> Tommy Gun: (Brings in huge bag of cement)
> Norma: Here, Bugsy, here's a Lake Michigan Special. I sure do hope you like water, 'cause where yer goin', there's gonna be a lot of it!

A young Toronto actor named Bryce Bermingham has just completed a season singing, dancing, and waiting tables at Tommy Gun's Garage. When I meet him at the saloon – he has come to pick up his final paycheque before heading off to try to crack Broadway – he says that the appeal of the era is "the class. You've lost the class nowadays – the suits, the Flapper dresses. The gangsters were so high-profile back then. It's like, people would forgive them because that was their job – to go out and kill."

The theatre's owner, Sandy Mangen, is unhappy with the lack of civic festivities to honour – or at least acknowledge – the Capone centennial.

"The City of Chicago and the State of Illinois think that the tourists think that it's still like that. But the people who come here from France and Germany and Austria know that Chicago's not full of gangsters any more. I think it's kind of stupid for the city to ignore its history because that's what people really like."

Against its wishes, certainly, Chicago has achieved one distinction in time for the anniversary: it has become Murder City, U.S.A. In 1998, the city's 698 homicides, although the fewest killings here in a decade, surpassed New York City's total (629, down from 2,262 in 1990) for the first time. Per capita, Chicago's murder rate is now double that of New York.

"It is upsetting and very disturbing that we have now passed New York City in the number of murders," Arthur Lurigio, chairman of the criminal justice department at Loyola University, told the Associated Press. "I am at a loss as to why Chicago's reductions are not commensurate to other large cities."

"There is no country that does itself such harm as America," Professor Norval Morris of the University of Chicago tells me, when we speak of then and now, Capone and cocaine, "Machine Gun" McGurn, and today's adolescent assassins of the drug industry. (Professor Morris, born in Australia, has lived in the United States for 33 years.)

"I think there is an analogy between what happened during Prohibition and the crack cocaine epidemic today," Professor Morris says. "In the same way that Prohibition made killers out of young gangsters, the cocaine trade fuels the killing of young dealers."

Yet even at the height of the "Beer Wars," the casualty figures were, by current standards, trifling: 36 "gangland-style" killings in 1922, 52 in 1923, 54 in 1924, barely a body a week.

Judge Abraham Lincoln Marovitz sees a distinction between the current bloodshed and the mayhem perpetrated by the men he knew and sometimes defended. "The big difference as I see it is the age of the people involved," he says. "In the 1920s, breaking the law was rampant. Money had a lot to do with it – they had liquor laws that made a lot of guys rich by breaking them. Then they spent that money protecting their interests. But by and large, the people breaking the law were adults.

"Now, these are just kids selling dope. They just can't control their thinking. They take a chance on being penalized, but they just can't resist what they're doing."

Whatever Al Capone was in his prime, he was not a common pusher or thief. Certainly, he had murdered men personally with his own weapons. (He was 18 and still living in Brooklyn when he shot a man named Perotta who had welshed on a gambling debt to Capone's boss.) At the Lexington Hotel, he perceived – and advertised – himself as a chief executive officer who laboured to maintain an orderly supply of popular, though unsanctioned, pleasures. Liquor supply, horse races, and municipal elections all were enterprises that needed to be regulated. If men were killed in the course of this commerce, they were mugs who had tampered with the rightful order of things.

"His involvement with the massacre endowed him with a certain grisly glamour," wrote Laurence Bergreen in his monumental biography, *Capone – The Man and the Era* in 1994. "There had never been an outlaw quite like Al Capone. He was elegant, high-class, the berries. . . . No one was indifferent to Capone. . . ."

"Probably no private citizen in American life has ever had so much publicity in so short a period," said *The New York Times*, three months after St. Valentine's Day.

"Three million people are being held up by six hundred gangsters," John Gunther charged in *Harper's Monthly*.

"Capone has become almost a mythical being in Chicago," Judge John H. Lyle thundered, trying to bring the kingpin down. "He is not a myth but a reptile."

"120,000 MEALS ARE SERVED BY CAPONE FREE SOUP KITCHEN," reported the *Chicago Tribune* in 1930.

"Chicago's bad reputation is bad for my business. It keeps the tourists out of town," said Al Capone.

"You have reached Harry Hart, son of Richard 'Two Gun' Hart," says the gentle voice on the answering machine. I call back. And back again, to Homer, Nebraska.

Seventy-two-year-old Harry Hart, a retired wallpaper hanger and house painter in a tiny prairie village, is Al Capone's nephew. His father, Vincenzo Capone, born in Italy just before the clan's emigration, left Brooklyn as a teenager. As Two Gun Hart, his true identity unknown and unsuspected, he roamed the Great Plains on the side of the law, smashing stills and duelling with bootleggers engaged in his baby brother's trade. Only much, much later was he exposed.

"It doesn't bother me that Al Capone was my uncle. Not one bit," Mr. Hart says when I finally reach him. "It bothers some of the other family members – they don't like it one bit. But it doesn't bother me. I'm very proud to be the son of Two Gun Hart."

Harry Hart is an honoured man in Homer, Nebraska. He has been presented the Silver Beaver for his work with the Boy Scouts and the Lamb Award by his Lutheran Church. He knew his father as a hero-lawman and his uncle (and the rest of the infamous clan) only marginally. He spent the summer of 1944 with his uncle Ralph Capone at their hideout in Wisconsin, and two weeks with his paternal grandmother at 7244 South Prairie Avenue in Chicago, a house that still stands.

"I was in Chicago only that one time," he tells me. "And I have no desire to go back there."

That Scarface Capone had a law-abiding – in fact, law-defending – brother is one of the most amazing aspects of his fascinating life. The dichotomy continues: Harry Hart's son Jeffrey works for the Nebraska State Crime Commission in Lincoln; Harry's granddaughter works for the Nebraska State Patrol and her husband is a deputy sheriff.

"I always wanted to be a state trooper, but I was too short at five-foot-nine," Harry Hart says. "My family is into crime, one way or the other."

Al Capone is buried under six feet of earth and three feet of snow at Mount Carmel Cemetery in Hillside, Illinois. The management of the graveyard has done its best to keep the kingpin's remains from being venerated, or disinterred. A hedge has been planted in front of the name CAPONE, which is inscribed at the base of a small stone monument, a slender crucifix decorated with carved grapevines. The individual markers of Al and his parents and some of his siblings are invisible in winter, flat against the sleeping soil.

I am with a University of Illinois professor named John Binder, leader of a scholarly group that calls itself the Merry Gangsters

Literary Society, a man who knows his way around the tombs of the Tommy-gun age. He points out the resting places of Dion O'Banion and the Genna brothers and other men, once so dangerous and confident, who came to Mount Carmel through the tender offices of Al Capone.

We tramp from the car to the Capone memorial, knee-deep in powder. There are no other footprints nearby. In Chicago, the most feared and famous criminal who ever lived sleeps alone into his second century.

– National Post

Once They Were Rookies

•

TEXAS

In the late 1970s, they played a sport that was, to them, their grace, their goal, their everything. They were minor-league-baseball rookies. Outfielders. Competitors. Roommates. They were still teenagers, yet already consecrated to a lifetime of glory or a legacy of failure in our continent's Grand Old Game.

An instant earlier, back home in Texas and California, they had been heroes. Moves essayed by every child had come fluently to them. The pitches were fatter, the fences closer, the bases a mere stride apart. Now, in the summer of 1978, they were Medicine Hat Blue Jays, lowliest chattels of a parent club that was the last-place laughing stock of its own league, far away.

In right field was Vincent Williams, a slim young man from a tough Houston neighbourhood. In the city's Babe Ruth League for young teenagers, Williams had batted .633 – nearly two hits for every three tries, an almost impossibly high average – and his talent had been cited in a book that lauded the best young ball-players in the world. At Sam Houston High School, he had pitched no-hitters and slammed home runs and the scouts had clustered around him with their stopwatches and notepads and their expert eagle eyes. The Blue Jays took him with their 12th pick in the June 1978 draft.

Not yet 19, Williams had already known inestimable tragedy – an older brother, knifed through the throat, had died in his arms at a family outing when Vinnie was 13. Four of his mother's other offspring had perished at birth. But he was walking, he said, in the pathways of the Lord – and running in the base paths of his idol, the great Hank Aaron.

In left field was a youth from innermost Oakland, California, one of eight children of Bird Otis Moseby, a missionary Christian originally from the cotton fields of Portland, Arkansas. A few years earlier, Lloyd Moseby had been cut from his little-league team as too weak and puny, but he had gone on to be a high-school all-American in baseball, and in basketball as well, and the Blue Jays chose him with their first pick in the June draft. The scouts and front-office men burdened him with baseball's heaviest handle: "can't-miss."

When he flew to Alberta, Moseby landed in Calgary to find that he had missed his connecting flight to the Hat. He phoned the team's manager, John McLaren, and pleaded for aid. But before McLaren could act, there was Moseby at his door, all smiles.

"How'd you get here, flap your own wings?"

"Helicopter," the Oaklander replied. The team's owner had sent his private chopper. Moseby's feet would not touch the ground again all season. Goofy with confidence, he would stand on street corners in Medicine Hat and hand out Zodiac cards on which he had written "come to the game tonight, and watch me play."

The centre fielder was Allen Ray Montgomery, fresh from Reagan High School in Houston, where he had been a star, as well as Vinnie Williams's cross-town rival. He was accompanied north by his father, Lieutenant Ken Montgomery of the Houston Police Department, who, 25 years earlier, had traded his own dream of professional baseball for a shot at college and a career. Allen's position was the most glamorous in the sport, the domain of show-boats and stalwarts – Mays, Mantle, DiMaggio. At Medicine Hat all the players were as raw and green as he was. But Montgomery was the only deaf-mute on the team.

This did not seem to be a detriment; after all, you didn't serenade the ball, you *whacked* it. Other men with disabilities had played in the major leagues: One-Arm Gray, Three-Finger Brown, Dummy Taylor, Dummy Hoy. "I want to be a professional one day," Allen had told a *Houston Post* reporter, as his father watched him mouth the words. "Because I want to make a lotta money."

By the time the Montgomerys got to Medicine Hat, the Pioneer Rookie League season had already begun. Arriving at Athletic Park with the evening's game in progress, Allen was hastily outfitted in a uniform several sizes too big, and inserted as a pinch-runner. Over at third, McLaren flashed signals that were not in the standard American Sign Language vocabulary. Montgomery, freelancing, just took off and ran. He was rounding second when his pants came loose and he fell flat on his face.

The next night, Ken Montgomery, who was himself a Blue Jay "bird dog" – a part-time scout who poked around sandlot games for prospects – was being entertained by the Medicine Hat management. Time passed, toasts were raised, and everyone forgot about the ballgame. When he finally got to the stadium, the bases were loaded and Allen Ray was coming to the plate.

Impossibly, wonderfully, just as his father found his seat, Allen hit a grand-slam home run. Circling the bases, unheeding the crowd's roar, he looked up and found his father, weeping.

In their first hours of adulthood, the three young men – along with two dozen other dreamers – rode a bright yellow bus a thousand miles a week, climbing the Rockies at midnight, crossing the ripe Alberta grainfields. I rode with them for a time, a young newspaperman engrossed in their stories.

The Baby Jays were a motley and engaging lot. There were a half-dozen Canadians on the team. More than half of the others were Dominicans and Venezuelans, some as young as 15, air-dropped into an alien, anglophone environment for the first time. Often these children would squander their daily meal money of $6.50 (Canadian) on video games and jewellery. Once, when the team found itself mysteriously short of bats and balls, it was discovered that some of the Latinos were stockpiling the equipment in their rooms at the Assiniboia Inn, scheming to take it back home in the winter.

My sojourn with the club began with a double-header in Idaho Falls, Idaho, in which the Jays prevailed in the first game, 19-7, and were trailing 13-2 in the finale when the umpires waved a halt. By that time there were 23 people in the stands.

The return trip was a 640-mile, overnight, 14-hour marathon. Exhausted players coiled in the narrow seats, sharing a single pillow, or collapsed on the floor in the narrow aisle, end to end. There was a stop in Montana to let the diabetic catcher grab a quick hot meal and a pass-the-hat assessment of $120 to help the driver pay a fine for not having a proper licence. The music of Lynyrd Skynyrd blasted from the eight-track tape deck.

Then the bus crashed. We were a couple of minutes outside Medicine Hat when a car in front of us started a left turn and our driver, heedless, pulled out to pass. The car was demolished. The front of the bus caved in. No one was hurt.

The bus empties, I wrote at the time. *Half the players jabber excitedly in Spanish; all but one of the others discuss the accident in English. Al Montgomery walks to a grassy knoll and sits down, alone. . . .*

Al Montgomery points to his left knee and writes on a piece of paper. "Football. Defensive halfback. Operation. No more football. . . . Maybe no baseball next year. Don't know."

He is shepherded by a kind young man named Vincent Williams, a fellow outfielder and Texan who cares. Three years ago, when Vincent Williams was pitching for one Houston high school and Al Montgomery was hitting for another, Williams threw a one-hitter and Montgomery got the only hit and Williams didn't mind.

Two years ago, I began to search out these men who had so captivated me a half-lifetime ago. I knew, of course, that the prospect labelled "can't miss" didn't. This spring, I visited Lloyd Moseby, a multimillionaire with more than a dozen years of big-league ball in Canada, the United States, and Japan behind him, at his rural California estate. He is a collector of rare coins, a Bob Dole Republican, and an enthusiastic member of the Sacramento Bonsai Club. Yet his days, he says, are aimless to the point of desperation.

Allen Montgomery lives in Sugar Land, Houston's sweetest suburb. He does computer-aided drafting for an engineering firm and is married to his high-school sweetheart, a vivacious and profoundly deaf woman who, against all the doctors' predictions and assurances, delivered their son, Ryan, deaf as well.

In December 1995, having heard that I was looking for him, the right fielder, the Reverend Vincent Lamar Williams, sent me a Christmas card from his mother's address in Houston. "God Bless You & Yours Always!" he wrote across the envelope, and a letter folded into the card said, "Looking forward into hearing from you soon. You can reach me at my mother's." And so, for months afterwards, Mrs. Myrtle Williams would accept my calls from Toronto and then, when I would ask where I might contact Vincent, she would reply that "he's travelling" or "he says he'll be here for Easter" or, simply, "I don't know." Then, this spring, she let on that he had told her he was living in the city of Port Arthur, Texas, an oil-refining town on the Sabine River that separates the Lone Star State from Louisiana. But she would not, or could not, tell me his address. Even when I flew to Houston and brought her roses.

This much I knew: Vincent Williams, the Babe Ruth League slugger, hit an egregious .137 in Medicine Hat, came back the next year to try again at Utica, another Jays farm club in the New York–Pennsylvania League, and managed no better than .199. He tried again with a farm team of the Houston Astros, was released, and it was over.

His life after baseball was a confusing alternation of work at a small publishing company, preaching at Pentecostal churches, and a downward spiral of despair and anger that imploded when his brother Gerald was shot to death in a Houston city park in 1980. On October 24, 1983, Williams was convicted of armed robbery in Bulloch County, Georgia, and sentenced to ten years in the state penitentiary.

He was, by all accounts, a good prisoner. He wrote often to Lloyd Moseby, who mailed his ex-teammate cassette tapes of sermons for inspiration. In 1990, Williams was transferred to Texas and paroled to his mother's care. He talked of getting back in shape and, at 31, resuming his baseball career. He returned to publishing work and his ministry, which took him across the South, and he soon married a deputy sheriff in Georgia named Rochelle Biggins. In 1992, they had a son, Brandon. Back in Houston again, he played the outfield in a semi-pro league where one of his opponents was the deaf-mute, Allen Montgomery. The president of the league was Allen's father, Ken.

"He loved baseball," Ken Montgomery remembers. "He played every chance he got." But by then, in his early thirties, the speed was gone, and the hitting stroke.

The circle of friendship closed protectively around him. Moseby, who was pulling down, at the peak of his career, $1.8 million per season, offered financial assistance. Vincent started a small business telemarketing watches, T-shirts, and caps from a two-storey building just south of Houston's downtown. Within a year, he had expanded to three offices and had several employees working under him. When the Blue Jays would come to Texas to face the Rangers, Williams would drive five hours to Arlington to see Moseby and his Medicine Hat manager John McLaren, who had risen to become a Toronto coach. They were impressed.

A former running back for the Minnesota Vikings football club, Allen Rice, had begun preaching at a white-frame church christened God's Holy Place on a side street in black North Houston. Williams joined him and was ordained a minister by a Pentecostal organization called the Rock of Salvation. He began sending tapes of his own impassioned sermons back to Moseby.

"My man Vincent," Moseby told me on the phone one day last year, "has turned his life *around*."

Early this past April, I went to Port Arthur – the town Vincent's mother had mentioned. I phoned or visited every black Pentecostal church in the city, and in neighbouring Beaumont, but I couldn't find him. I contacted the managers of the city's adult baseball teams. I scoured the city, stopped postmen in the street, haunted barbecue pits, taxi stands, and garages. Complaisant city clerks scrolled through the water and hydro rolls, to no avail. Finally, hoping *not* to find him, I called the Texas Department of Criminal Justice. The Reverend Vincent Lamar Williams was in Port Arthur, all right – in the Larry Gist State Jail.

The Larry Gist State Jail, named for a white-bearded judge whose portrait hangs in the main lobby, is an exemplar of one of America's fastest-growing industries – incarceration. It stands on the otherwise featureless plain between Beaumont and Port Arthur, in company with another state prison and a sprawling juvenile "training school," all brand-new, spotless, and gleaming in the Texas glare. "Dedicated to improving lives," reads a plaque at the entrance.

Vincent Williams, prisoner number 744195, is halfway through serving a five-year stretch for burglary, robbery, forgery, and possession of a deadly weapon. I have been told by the warden's assistant that he has agreed "reluctantly" to be interviewed and that no physical contact will be permitted. We shall speak by telephone through a pane of glass. I may bring a notebook and a pen. No cameras, no gifts, no handshakes.

But when Vincent Williams, now 37, gold toothed, broad shouldered, wearing a pure-white prison jump suit, is led to a steel stool before me, there is no hint of reluctance in his eyes. "You run from God, eventually you're gonna have to give in," he smiles, by way of greeting. We are the only parties present in a room with 46 such booths. Against the wall a grey-shirted guard is sitting at a folding table, gobbling a cinnamon roll.

For our allotted 90 minutes, we talk of baseball, families, and God. When I ask about his current imprisonment, Williams says, "I didn't do what they charged me with. A lady claimed I robbed her, but she never would change her story. I spent $26,000 fighting this thing." I let this sail past me like a high fly ball. Asked about his Georgia history, he admits his offences there, talks of his brothers' murders, and says, "I developed a lot of hurt and hate on the inside. I stopped going to church. I got involved with some people – I guess you could say it was organized crime.

"I think about what I've done in life," the outfielder says. "I guess you reap what you sow."

I tell Williams that I will be seeing Lloyd Moseby in California, and Allen Montgomery in Sugar Land. "I could read Allen's lips," he remembers, of his Medicine Hat roommate. "I was the only one who could communicate with him. They would tease him behind his back and it hurt me. We'd go back to the room and I could see the hurt in his eyes."

He says he now devotes himself full time to studying his Bible and part time to body-building, but when I had called the warden's office to request the interview, I was told that Williams was out on a manual-labour detail, working on the "hoe squad." There are outdoor basketball courts at the Larry Gist State Jail, but no baseball fields. In this prison, nobody slides home.

Williams expects to be eligible for parole in mid-October. He intends to return to the telemarketing business in Houston, and Pastor Rice has invited him to resume his preaching at God's Holy Place. Williams vows that he is "really going to do what God wants me to do this time," and once, of course, he believed with all his heart that the Lord meant for him to play the outfield.

"When I was eight years old," he says, "I *knew* I was going to be a professional baseball player. I *knew* that I had talent. When I was

13, I was playing against grown men. Sometimes, I'd play on three or four teams at the same time in different leagues. You see, the ballfield was one place where I had no fear. Baseball was my *God* when I was a kid."

For Vincent Williams, the season at Medicine Hat, filtered through time, has become an epiphany – a summer when all things were possible, when the Heavenly Father, for His own reasons, held out such shining promise, then withdrew it at His whim.

"I hit a ball real good and deep one game," he tells me, "but as I was circling first base, I felt like my leg went out from under me. Something happened to my groin. John McLaren told me to try to play with it anyway. I tried, but I couldn't. I missed a month and a half.

"When I was hurt, just sitting on the bench, the team won five or six in a row, but I couldn't play, I couldn't be part of it. I *cried* one day in the dugout, and I said to John, 'I want to go home.'"

He pauses, and shakes his head. "I guess I wasn't ready to be a professional athlete. I came from a single-parent home. I wanted to help my mother. I may have signed too early."

Too early, too late, too young, too old – the rationale of failure haunts the waking hours of all the men who never made it, just as the dream of the diamond once sang them to sleep. "I was a really emotional person," Williams says. "I felt baseball had betrayed me. I felt like I put all my love and trust in baseball and baseball didn't give me a chance.

"I had almost world-class speed. I could have played professional football. I could have run in the Olympics. I used to race Lloyd Moseby, and I'd always beat him. He might have been a better hitter, but as far as speed and arm and defence, I was probably better than Lloyd. I could have played in the big leagues, *easy*."

"Vincent," I say into the telephone, "*nobody* plays in the big leagues, *easy*."

In California, Lloyd Moseby greets me with a bone-crushing hug and a 1993 Syrah whose label promises "spicy vanilla, ripe blackberry and anise aromas that follow through its long, complex finish." It's from the small winery his investment company controls, among other businesses.

We sit down to drink it in a vaulted marble living room decorated with mahogany panelling, a framed gold record of Moseby's 1986 "Shaker's Rap," a miniature knight in full body armour, dozens of autographed baseballs, and a television set the size of the SkyDome JumboTron. Moseby's childhood sweetheart and wife of 16 years, Adrienne, is off watching 14-year-old Alicia Moseby run the hurdles in a high-school track meet. Six-year-old Lydell is still at school and soon Lloyd, Sr., will be taking 12-year-old Lloyd, Jr., to practise the boy's home-run stroke in the family batting cage beyond the swimming pool at the edge of the woods where the wild turkeys are multiplying out of control.

Right on cue, a hen turkey comes strutting past the front door, bobbing its head like Steve Martin doing the King Tut dance, right down Los Lagos Circle in the guarded, gated community of Los Lagos Estates in Loomis, California, north of Sacramento.

"Worst state in the union!" Moseby gripes. "If I kill *you*, I get one or two years. If I kill that turkey, I get a *hundred* years. These stupid things are all over the place, and they wonder why we get a mountain lion down here last year *eatin'* some lady."

The mansion, as I survey it, is a two-storey villa in beige stucco with balconies front, back, and side in case Evita Perón needs to deliver a speech, a tripartite garage for the inevitable Rolls-Royce, and a guest house for Kato Kaelin. But poor Lloyd Moseby, five years out of the big leagues and one generation out of the Arkansas cotton gins, is truly miserable.

"The game was everything," he says. "It *was* everything. It shouldn't be, but baseball was my *God*. You could have twenty-billion dollars in the bank but now you're *lonely*, man. The game made me *alive*. It made my *brain* work. It kept me up at night, thinking things out.

"That first year out of baseball, I was *sick*. Comes February and you're not leaving for *spring training*? It was as if everyone in the world had *died*. My mother was already dead. My father had been diagnosed. But this was worse – watching those guys on TV, there's a void so big, *nothing* can fill it.

"You got no knowledge, no degree. You need for time to pass. You can't just say, 'It's over.' You got to *mean* it. It takes *years*. I had the car, the house, the money, but I had nowhere to go. I said, 'Why me? Why is this happening to me?' I drove my wife crazy. I'd be outside, one, two o'clock in the morning, with my plants. I tell you, man, bonsai saved my life."

We go out to look at the lifesavers – tiny, twisting evergreens and hand-pruned red maples that the outfielder avows will become a riot of colour in the fall. Unless the wild turkeys eat them.

Moseby is 37 and there's grey in his goatee, but the wine transports us nearly 20 years, back to Medicine Hat. When I tell him of my visit with Vinnie Williams, Moseby is visibly shaken to learn that his old roommate – the youth who always wanted to race him, to match his skills – has fallen once again.

"Vinnie Williams had *talent*," he declares. "He could *rake*, he could *fly*, he could *hit*. Maybe he was in the wrong place at the wrong time. It's not easy when you go into an environment where *everybody* had been 'Player of the Year.'"

"Were you surprised he went to prison?" I ask.

"Maybe I would have done the same thing," Moseby replies. "Maybe I would have taken that quick course in getting a load of cash. Who's to say I wouldn't have done that? That's why I'm not down on Vinnie."

It is the first time I have visited one of baseball's new millionaires at home, after the cheering has ceased. The distress is palpable. Moseby says, "When you quit, the phone *stops*. Then it starts up again with people wanting to borrow money. Suddenly you hear from your relatives again: 'I need ten thousand dollars.' I give them what I've got. My wife stops me. She says, 'You're not playing any more. You're going to be retired for 50 years.'"

Lost and lonely at poolside, he telephones his best friends in the game – the mercurial Rickey Henderson, the corpulent Cecil Fielder – and tries to uphold his equality, but they shut him down – "You don't know how Clemens throws *now*, man, you've been gone three years." This kills him. He's two hours in the Rolls from the Oakland Coliseum with a lifetime free pass, but he doesn't go to ballgames. He declines to join the major-league alumni association. He gave his bats and gloves to the little league.

"I talk to Cecil," he says, "and he's telling me things like, 'I just turned down seven million, 'cause I deserve *nine*.' And I tell him, Cecil, man, seven million, eight million, nine million, that's not important. Love your *kids*, man – in a couple of years, they're all you're gonna have.'"

He never courted the riches. He wanted only to make his parents comfortable, to elevate them from the bottomlands of their poverty. For years, Bird Otis Moseby, in her Christian devoutness, would attend church each Sunday in the only white dress she owned. With the $50,000 the Blue Jays paid him as a signing bonus, her son bought her 15 white dresses. And a house. But they would sit at home, he says, with $30 remaining from their social-security cheque and 20 days left in the month, and never call him for help. His father raised his own vegetables and pigs until the day he died.

Ten years after Medicine Hat, he was at spring training when his mother passed away. He cried for months, at her loss and his own failings, but the fans and the writers saw only the Shaker, the laughs. He says, "Growing up, it wasn't about sport, it was about *working*. My dad would *kill* us if we were talking about sport. My dad never watched me play until high school. My mom never came to one game. *She never came to one game.* She was always in Tennessee or someplace, spreading the gospel. If she saw the sport today, she'd say, 'I told you so.'"

On a glowing April evening the game begins. Beyond the inner quadrangle of clumped red soil and the fat white hills of the bases, the outfielder awaits the play. He is shoe-deep in the new spring grass, tensed, alert, bouncing on the balls of his feet. The setting sun is in his eyes, a light breeze in his face.

Now the ball is pitched and there it goes! – slammed to right field, high, hard, and deep. The fielder lifts his eyes, studies its flight as it arches far overhead. Then he turns, completely the wrong way, flails his arms as if this might bring the ball magically down to him, and weaves out toward the wire fence to find it.

By this time two runners have scored, the batter is rounding second, coaches are hollering instructions and imprecations – "Third! Throw it to *third*, Ryan! Home! Home! *Home!*" – and the outfielder, who is eight years old, has retrieved the ball and side-armed it feebly toward his jumping, frantic mates, much too late.

Braves 15, Reds 1.

The next inning, the outfielder comes to bat. Digging in, swinging mightily, he piddles the ball back toward the pitcher's mound and beats the throw to first. A single! But the next "man" pops the ball up second base and little Ryan Montgomery, who is wearing a protective helmet so oversized it makes him look like Rick Moranis in *Spaceballs*, freezes a few steps off first.

When the ball plops unimpeded to the ground – catching pop-ups is an acquired skill – a committee of infielders picks it up and poor Ryan gets forced out at second. He stomps back to the dugout, kicks the ground, and flings down his helmet, just as he has seen the big-leaguers do. Then he storms to the end of the bench, sits down, and starts to cry.

I'm standing with Ryan's father and mother and grandparents behind the first-base fence in Sugar Land. But when Ryan crumples into his little drama of frustration, the father, Allen Ray Montgomery, former professional outfielder, leaves us and goes to kneel before his boy to calm him down. His eyes entreat and quiet the child. His hands are busily speaking.

Allen Montgomery never made it to the major leagues. He underwent knee surgery in 1979 and missed the entire season, as he had predicted the night the team bus crashed. In 1980, he was brought back for another shot at Utica, but his knee still wasn't sound and he felt, rightly or wrongly, that his coaches were not even attempting to communicate with him. Midway through the season the Jays decided to let him go.

Just at that moment, Ken Montgomery, his wife, Doris, and Allen's fiancée, Sharon, were getting set to motor north from Houston to watch him play. Embarrassed for Sharon's sake, Ken phoned ahead and asked the Jays if they could keep his son on board until they arrived. And they said yes.

That night – August 8, 1980 – facing the Elmira Pioneer Red Sox, Allen hit a home run in the sixth inning, another home run in the seventh inning, and a grand slam to win the game in the eighth. The release was cancelled. Montgomery finished the season in Utica. Then he came home to Sharon to stay.

An hour after the game, the Montgomery boy, named for the unhittable Texan fireballer Nolan Ryan, is sitting across from me at a Mexican restaurant, dipping tortilla chips and making silent screams of anguish when he realizes how hot the salsa is. His father is to my right, laughing with his boy and remembering The Hat and draining a long-neck of cold Lite beer.

"Tell me about Vincent," I ask him, in a written note, and he signs to Sharon and she writes in my notebook:

"The coach and the players tried to communicate with him and he didn't understand what they were saying. So Vince helped him – always told him what they were saying. He was very good to him and helped him when he needed. He was a nice roommate."

"Did you think you could ever be a major-leaguer?" I scribble.

Allen Ray Montgomery picks up the pen himself.

"My dream was to earn a lot of money if I continue to play," he writes. "I wish I play as a pro baseball player forever."

We finish our dinners, embrace in the parking lot, lip-read our goodbyes, and go. For son and father, wife and husband, right field and centre and left, the dream concludes, and life begins.

Writing this now, I think of little Ryan Montgomery chasing the ball and Lloyd Moseby in his California mansion, shaking his head and saying, "Maybe it's better *not* to make it. Maybe it's better not to make it at all." But he cannot mean it. It cannot be true. The power of the dream refutes it.

"Give me three weeks of batting practice and I could still hit any pitcher in the game," Vincent Williams had boasted at the jailhouse in Texas, in his crisp white coveralls. "I can't run as good as I did, and my arm is gone, but if I had the opportunity, I think I can hit for the rest of my life." And I understood his yearning to intercept time – to stand shoe-deep in the new spring grass, with the setting sun in his eyes.

In early June, Lloyd Moseby will leave Los Lagos Estates and his bonsai and return to baseball's lowest rung, rejoining the organization that first brought him to Canada. He is going to help coach the St. Catharines Blue Jays of the New York-Pennsylvania League, as older men once coached him on his coltish teenage ramble across the Rockies and the big-sky plains.

The rewards will be scanty, the comforts few. This does not matter. "I *have* to do it," he says, and I know why. The game still is everything. The game still is God.

– Saturday Night

HOME AGAIN

Previous page: The Abels, 1961, on Flatbush Avenue (Celia Cesler)

When my book Flatbush Odyssey *was published in 1995, I told the few stragglers who showed up at my public readings that the avenue for which the book was named had been the scene of four of America's most historic tragedies:*

• the Battle of Brooklyn in 1776, in which George Washington's newly formed rebel army was surrounded and shredded by the British;

• the first jet airliner crash in U.S. history, which saw a United DC-8 *from Chicago roar in flames, in December 1960, into a church called the Pillar of Fire;*

• the nation's worst rail disaster, a subway wreck in 1918 that claimed more than a hundred lives;

• and my bar mitzvah.

I should have added that Flatbush Avenue – Brooklyn's Great Central Road, arching eleven miles from Manhattan to the sea – also could claim one of America's most enduring landmarks.
My mother, Hennie.

The Junction

BROOKLYN, NEW YORK

My mother met Doris at Brooklyn College at a night-school course called Philosophy of Everyday Living. After class, they went out for coffee and Doris said, "I don't know if I can be your friend, because you'll hurt me."

"I'll never hurt you," my mother vowed. Doris, who was employed as a court stenographer in Downtown Brooklyn, gave my mother her business card. It was 1951.

Together, through the years, the typist and the Bride of Flatbush studied square dancing and oil painting, folk music and entry-level ceramics. One semester, my mother created and brought home a clay head of the young Allen Abel that she later had to discard because the dampness of a Brooklyn winter got into it and it became infested with small white bugs. But she did keep her calipers, using them at home to judge the thickness of her husband's hamburgers to a tolerance of millimetres, lest he take a pencil to her recipe book and mark it "BEN DON'T LIKE."

Doris, meanwhile, continued to live alone, served many decades in the halls of justice, played Scrabble with the intensity of a Boris Spassky, travelled all over the world, and purchased the first colour television set I ever saw – and very little else. This made her famous with her friend Hennie, who was the last of the big-time spenders by comparison, at least until it was time to take the stuff back to Abraham and Straus.

"Her purse was snatched," my mother told me one evening when I asked about security near the apartment building where Doris lived. "They only got her change purse, with *forty-five cents* in it. She even found the purse! They threw it away at the corner. She was mad because the strap was broken."

Doris's windows overlooked the corner of Aurelia Court where I had seen the dead red dog. It was rumoured that the victims of five separate homicides had been dumped on the Flatbush Avenue pavement right outside the building in recent months, but I could not verify this statistic with eyewitness testimony. Still, since my mother estimated Doris's accumulated worth to be in the hundreds of millions of dollars (minus forty-five cents), it was something of a surprise that she, like Bill and like Hennie, had stuck it out around here.

Most days, Doris took her lunch at a seniors' social that was held in the B'nai Jacob synagogue on Glenwood Road at the north end of the Junction. When this club announced its gala Spring Party, my mother and I were invited to attend as Doris's guests – as long as we paid for our own lunches. So, on the special day, we set out, me in my Dockers, my mother in black slacks and a blue floral-print blouse studded with faux pearls, three rings, several gold chains, beaten-silver earrings shaped like tiny owls and studded with turquoise, a slick black slicker, and the sunglasses she always wore when it rained.

Slowly, we walked the long block, past Lord's unchanging bakery and the new 99-cent stores, toward the old *shul*, fighting a tide of prancing youngsters with Jansport backpacks and Charlotte Hornet caps, two bleach-faced tourists just off the cruise ship for a day in Montego Bay. When we reached Glenwood Road, my mother paused and breathed concertedly, several times, accumulating the oxygen she would need when she made her grand entrance at B'nai Jacob.

But the front doors of the synagogue were locked, and a side entrance brought us unexpectedly to a classroom where Lilliputian chairs awaited preschoolers named Andrena, Develyn, Jakaiah, Kaila, and Suede. It was recess, and these new Sons of Jacob were outside in a narrow alley, riding tricycles, playing Ring Around the Rosy, and pounding each other with fists.

My mother found the elevator and headed up to the banquet room to find Doris, while I went prowling, for this was the synagogue where I had recited my bar-mitzvah prayers and screeched my *haftorah* on the ninth day of February, 5723. The party at the Flatbush Terrace, now Bus Stop Discount, had been held the next afternoon.

I made my way to the entrance to the prayer hall, but it, too, was locked. Through a small window, I could see the red dot of the (electric) eternal flame above the ark of the Torah, and daylight illuminating the stained-glass panels in the eastern wall. Behind me, in the main lobby, some of the coloured windows had been smashed and broken, and the whole place gave off an eerie aroma of abandonment and age.

I hadn't been in this building since the last Monday of November 1963 – nine months after my bar mitzvah – when I attended a memorial service for John F. Kennedy, shot dead the Friday before. Above the doorway, "A Tree of Life" had been endowed by the parents of my peers and successors, each gilded leaf marking a donation in the name of some 13-year-old boy or girl. I looked for an Abel, but golden tokens had been beyond our means.

The old names remained, but the benefactors had long since fled to Long Island or Florida. On Glenwood Road, there had been a sea change in tribes and traditions. In a room rented to a Haitian kindergarten on the mezzanine of a Jewish house of prayer, a poster said, "Happy Easter." I wondered how long it would be before B'nai Jacob was sold off and converted to an Église de Dieu.

Upstairs was the classroom where I had "studied" Hebrew, and, much more avidly, listened to World Series games on a transistor radio concealed in my book bag, with a cable to a tiny earphone running up inside my shirt. The room was derelict, and chairs were piled up. Covered in dust were histories of the Chosen People and biographies of Ben-Gurion and Herzl.

Wandering down long-forgotten hallways, I found the small side chapel where they would bait us boys with bagels and lox to come on Sunday mornings and bind the prayer-filled leather cubes called *tefillin* around our heads and arms. I came upon a pile of prayer books and indexed *haftorahs*, which were the portions of the Holy Scriptures a boy would have to memorize, then chant for the congregation on the Sabbath of his coming of age. I had learned mine by mimicking a rabbi's recording, and now, for the first time, I opened a bilingual reference book that told me what those dimly remembered cadences had meant, so long ago. My chapter had been from the Book of Judges: "THEN sang Deborah and Barak the son of Abinoam on that day, saying, / When men let grow their hair in Israel, / When the people offer themselves willingly, / Bless ye the LORD. / Hear, O ye kings; give ear, O ye princes; I, unto the / LORD will I sing; I will sing *praise* to the LORD, the / God of Israel . . ."

The gala Spring Party was about to begin in the auditorium. I walked in and was amazed. About a hundred and fifty senior citizens had made their way past the roti palaces and the check-cashing fronts, the incense sellers and dollar-cab touts, and now they were taking their seats at long tables set with purple cloths and bright pink napkins and bowls of peanuts and chocolate non-pareils. Most of the gents wore suits and ties. A couple of the ladies sported jewellery it would take two men to lift.

We sat down to bean-and-barley soup, my favourite. I was at the end of one table, and my mother was to my right. My soup tasted burnt, and there was a chicken neck floating in it like an overturned canoe. Then came a breast of chicken stuffed with sawdust, some de-flavoured rice, and broccoli reduced to the consistency of tapioca. All this for only $3.50.

Celebrities were introduced. A woman named Jacobs, our state assemblymember – this was the politically correct term – stood at a dead microphone, hollering about funding for in-home nursing care. She was followed by a plump state senator named Markowitz, who, aping Little Debbie's accent, told us how delighted he was to be hee-yuh this yea-yuh. I liked Markowitz immediately. He had the chutzpah to get up there and praise the meal upon which his audience was choking.

A woman named Weiss, director of the Junction Senior Citizens, had been told that I was writing a book. (*Hennie*: "This is my son. He's writing a book.") She came over and started to regale me with tales of Erasmus Hall High.

"I remember walking up and down Flatbush Avenue," she said.

"You still can walk it," I told her. "I've been walking it every day."

"I know," said Mrs. Weiss. "I'm not afraid."

She paused.

"I lied," she said. "I *am* afraid. It's *good* to be afraid."

She pointed to Markowitz, who was encouraging everyone to get out and vote in elections to the local school bo-wawd.

"They shot at him," said Mrs. Weiss. "Right outside his office." I did not see how they could have missed.

It was time for entertainment. Eight choristers, two of them men, moved to the front of the auditorium and, squinting at song-sheets, made enthusiastic attempts at "Edelweiss" and "The Battle Hymn of the Republic." These were followed by a rousing approximation of "When the Saints Go Marching In."

The audience loved it. Some sang along. Those who still could, clapped.

A man in a leisure suit the colour of peas stood up and appealed for everyone to join a bus trip to the 25-cent slot machines of Atlantic City. He said, "Think of those who *can't* get out of the house and how much they *wish* they could go." But there were few takers.

The President of the Borough of Brooklyn, Howard Golden, was called on to say a few words. Mr. Golden, a tall, lean man, who looked like the horrific actor Vincent Price, had held his office for 16 years and had become, of necessity, a pragmatist. He talked about Brooklyn being "always the land of the immigrant."

"It would be wonderful if everyone could love one another," he said. "But it's not true that we do."

The culinary segment of the affair having concluded – sing *praise* to the LORD – the featured performers set up their equipment. These were professional musicians named Bien and Gellers, the latter on Yamaha keyboard and the former on tambourine and maracas, and in a succession of silly hats.

Bien and Gellers launched into "Bye, Bye, Blackbird" and the joint started rocking like the Brooklyn Paramount.

Women grabbed women and began to fox-trot like fiends on Benzedrine. Someone started a conga line.

Then they played "When You're Smiling," and all hell broke loose.

I went over to talk to Doris. I had not seen her in a long time. Recently, she and my mother had suffered one of their occasional fallings-out, but, like most of the others, this had not lasted longer than six or seven years. She was wearing glasses and a paisley blouse. She smiled, and the first thing she said to me was, "Am I shrinking?"

She had never been a big woman. I remembered her in my bar-mitzvah year at the controls of her brand-new '63 Valiant with its incredible push-button transmission, trying to stretch herself to see over the steering wheel. She had held on to the Plymouth longer than most car-owners; actually, about 20 years longer. When she finally sold it in 1988 and donated the proceeds to charity – in exchange for a tax receipt – she had put only 51,000 miles on it in a quarter of a century.

At the auditorium on the upper floor of Congregation B'nai Jacob, my mother had gone off to a far corner to smoke, and the two-man orchestra was trying to get everyone to do the merengue, with success.

I motioned toward the gyrating, geriatric mass and said to Doris, "People my age don't know whether to be cheered or terrified by this."

"I know," my mother's classmate replied. "But it encourages *me*. I see these people and I think, 'I still have 20 years.'"

My mother came back and sat down. Organized merriment was not her style. She danced with no women.

Bien and Gellers played an old Yiddish standard called "Tum Balalaika." It was hypnotic and mournful. I didn't know the words. I looked over at my mother, who was crying behind her sunglasses and singing along.

It was time to go. We said goodbye to Doris and Mrs. Weiss. Outside, the sun had come shining through. We made our way down a side street where, in 5723, Catholic kids had thrown pebbles at us and chanted "Christ killers! Christ killers!" as we passed their yards on our way to B'nai Jacob. Now these Papists were grown and gone to the suburbs, educating children of their own.

Back home, my mother began her daily round of phone calls to friends. A man named Rudy had been at the dance, she reported. Rudy was 68. He had gestured toward the fox-trotters and disdainfully told my mother, "Look at them – they're so *old*."

"No, Rudy," she had replied as the blackbirds fluttered and flew. "Don't you understand? They're *us*, and we're *they*."

– excerpted from Flatbush Odyssey

The Fairgrounds

It is a grey day in late November, and I have stolen a few hours from another assignment to wander the grounds of Flushing Meadow, alone, to ponder the passage of time and the end of my century. Flushing Meadow is a municipal park in the New York City borough of Queens. It is mostly brown lawn, dry fountains, and soccer fields now, dotted by a few trees wearing name tags: Red Maple, Pin Oak. But once in my lifetime – and twice in the past 60 years – it was the site of a great World's Fair.

I was 14 when my fair began in 1964. Everything about the time and the place are as virtual to me today as if I were still that fidgety, underweight, sports-mad, sarcastic, straight-A, bedazzled mother's boy, striding out of dreamland just after the nightly fireworks at the Fountain of the Planets, to be driven home to Brooklyn in my friend Brucie's father's Ford Falcon, or my Uncle Jack's two-tone Bel-Air. Then, to come back to the fair again and again and again and again, never tiring of the promises it made.

The vows were of a world of boundless wonder, and all of them have been kept.

A few actual monuments endure. The emblem of the fair, a magnificent, soaring, stainless-steel globe called the Unisphere, has been cleansed of the graffiti that fouled it in the 1970s and now stands gleaming in its big blue basin, more than a hundred feet high.

"Dedicated to man's aspirations toward Peace through mutual understanding and symbolizing his achievements in an expanding universe," reads the inscription at its base.

Behind it is a long avenue ("Eisenhower Promenade") of drained fountains ("The Court of the Universe"), some of them under reconstruction, that leads to a large reflecting pond ("The Pool of Industry") filled, on this autumn day, with flat, black water and 200 Canada geese.

Just off this boulevard, orphaned by history, is an ancient Roman stone column that once adorned the pavilion of the Hashemite Kingdom of Jordan. A keystone explains that this is one of the famous "Whispering Columns of Jerash," erected circa AD 120, presented 1,844 years later by King Hussein himself to the Babylon of the New World. Some ghetto Tintoretto has sprayed his name on the relic in, appropriately, royal blue. Everything else has been ploughed under.

On the west side of the Grand Central Parkway – a screaming ten-lane freeway that carves the meadow in two – the Hall of Science is still in use as a museum. Next to it are three rockets. One is the bottom slice of a Saturn V, the thruster that would be used, four years after the fair closed in 1965, to achieve the Apollo moon landings.

The other two launch vehicles – capped with the primitive Mercury and Gemini capsules that had been orbited up to that time – are as derelict as the Whispering Column, shedding their paint, betraying the poverty of America's national memory, and mocking the heroism of the Shepards and Armstrongs who dared to ride these rattletraps into space.

Yet these missiles, however miserable, are majestic compared to the ruins of the New York State pavilion, which consisted of two tall observation towers reached by a glass-enclosed "Sky Streak" elevator that travelled up the outside (!) of the supporting columns, and an area for exhibits and performances covered by a colourful, plastic "Tent of Tomorrow," billed at the time as the largest suspended roof in the world.

The towers still stand, rusted and abandoned, as does the big, round roof, though all the panels have been popped out of it, leaving a lattice of bare cables above a cracked, overgrown floor. A small hall ("The Theaterama") has been rescued from the vandals and is used for concerts and dance recitals.

Nothing beside remains. (The poet might say of the scene.)
Round the decay
Of that colossal wreck, boundless and bare
The lone and level sands stretch far away.

A few yards to the south, a granite monument marks the trench where, in 1939 and 1965, World's Fair time capsules were interred in the Flushing soil, filled with the ejecta of the day. These are to be dug up 5,000 years hence, the inscription says, should anyone be interested, and should Queens not yet be swallowed by a rising sea.

Such is the physical world I find as I walk around Flushing Meadow. Only here, there are not lone and level sands, but basketball courts, and asphalted pathways sloppy with dying pink worms.

"There's a great big, beautiful tomorrow, shining at the end of every day," the General Electric "Carousel of Progress" promised us in 1964.

"It's a small world, after all," sang the doll-faced robots at the Pepsi pavilion.

"As the action unfolds, a surprising fact becomes clear. Computers are really not mysterious. They help solve the most complex problems with simple principles of logic – the kind you use daily," IBM's "Information Machine" soothingly explained.

"Here before you, is man roaming the moon, exploring Antarctica, working and playing beneath the sea, stretching a

highway of progress and prosperity through the jungle and over
the mountains, farming the desert and creating a functional,
beautiful new city. . . . Here is man's abiding determination to
make a better life for all," said the voice in the walls at the General
Motors "Futurama" ride.

"We of the Twentieth Century bequeath to the Seventieth
Century proof that man not only endures, but he also prevails,"
intoned the Westinghouse Corporation, manufacturers of that
time capsule of indestructible "Kromarc" steel. (Among its many
treasures, it contains a Beatles record, a credit card, an electric
toothbrush, and a bikini.)

There was none of that philosophical "Man the Creator" pap
that they would feed us at Expo '67 in Montreal (my first foreign
trip, my first airplane flight), or any monumental, inscrutable
"Tower of the Sun" such as the one that would rise, unblinking,
arms outstretched, over Expo '70 in Osaka (I spent my life savings,
$800, to get there) or the greenish tinge of Expo '74 in Spokane,
Washington ("Celebrating tomorrow's fresh new environment.")
Not in New York. Not in 1964.

Instead, we had the hard truths of the Hall of Free Enterprise
and its Pillars of Economic Wisdom:

"Government is never a source of goods . . . everything that government gives to the people, it must first take from the people. . . ."

We were in thrall to (and enthralled by) Du Pont, General Tire,
7UP, Equitable Life Assurance, Sinclair Oil, Walt Disney's Magic
Skyway, Ford Motor's Wonder Rotunda, The Bell System, Formica
Corp., RCA, Kodak, Johnson Wax, Scott Paper, the Festival of Gas.

"All out for the supermodern, the spectacular, the never-done-
before," said a guidebook I still treasure.

But we were not without culture. In the Vatican pavilion, we had
Michelangelo's Pietà, but I do not remember being affected by the
grief of the Sorrowful Mother, merely impressed that a powered
rampway ("The Moving Speed-Walk") sped you past the piece.

We had Belgian waffles and African dancers and an 800-year-
old fresco called the *Sudan Madonna*, rescued from the rising

waters of the Aswan Dam. We had the Swiss Sky Ride, a Log Flume, les Poupées de Paris, and Dancing Waters. We had won ton soup, tempura shrimps, and beef curry. We had the Protestant Center, the People to People Fiesta, the Russian Orthodox pavilion (though no Russians), Christian Science, and the Mormon Church. We had the world in Flushing Meadow.

Yes, there were picturephones and a monorail and other dead-end devices. There was an astonishing IBM computer that could read handwritten numerals – you scribbled your birth date and it spat out a punch card with the news of the world of that day:

January 31, 1950: "Sinkiang Delegation in Moscow to Join Soviet-Chinese Communist Negotiations."

There was the first touch-tone telephone; we dialled our apartment in Brooklyn (even though we were not home) just to hear the melody of the keys.

There was a tiny and not very gripping exhibit by the Swedish ball-bearing manufacturer, SKF Industries. One day, with my classmates Lutz, Melov, and Klaif, we noted (humorously, we thought) in a guest register at another pavilion that "SKF is great!" A matron thought we had written "SEX is great," and called the World's Fair Police and threw us out.

Well, I wouldn't learn about that for nine more years, as it turned out.

As it turned out, I went from the New York World's Fair to university upstate, "earned" a degree in Physics and Astronomy that I never even tried to use, managed the school hockey team, went to work selling bowling shoes, married the first girl I ever kissed, and spent (with her) every cent and every hour of 20 great years flying around the Unisphere to see the world my World's Fair had thrown open.

At Flushing Meadow, on a raw fall day, I sit on the ledge of the Fountain of the Continents and try to catch the shadow of the boy who shared this space, so long ago.

I have brought his map of the grounds, his guidebook, an unused admission ticket, and a coupon valid for a 15-cent discount for a ride on the Monorail. But there is no one to take it, only a young Chinese woman selling snacks from a wagon, bundled against the cold.

The book has not been opened, nor the map unfolded, since the boy last ran in ecstasy from these gates. But I need not study them. Everything the boy inhaled here, the man remembers.

For these 35 years, I have tried to sustain the faith in the future and the passion for exploration that I – and millions of other children – carried from these grounds. Now, with the turning of the calendar so achingly close, the feeling has never been stronger, the yearning more intense. To live in two centuries. Perhaps, if it is possible to dream such dreams, to live 50 years in each.

A few steps away from the Fountain of the Continents is one of the original World's Fair pavilions, the only exhibit, other than the destitute rockets and the Unisphere itself, still intact from 1964. It is a meticulously accurate scale model of New York City – hundreds of thousands of tiny models of buildings and bridges – viewed from a gondola that swoops around the hall as if one were flying over the metropolis, which, at 14, I had never done in a real plane. To see it again would crown the homecoming, and bring the man and the boy together.

I hurry to the door, but it is locked. The building opens at noon, a sign announces.

It is almost eleven, but I cannot stay. I have a plane to catch. Story of my life.

– National Post

Millennium Eve

•

New York City

We were casting out the century of Auschwitz and Apollo in the self-appointed Centre of the World.

Irradiated by the brightest arc lights of our human invention – and by a glowing inner fire of completion and anticipation – we came to Times Square in our hundreds of thousands. We pressed against the barricades, screamed out the seconds, swarmed the side streets, gawked at the marquees, painted our faces, held our breath for bombshells, watched a dozen foreign midnights pass across the ever-turning Earth, and waited for our time.

We were on Broadway for a one-night run, drawn, like millions before us, to "the Big Apple, the Main Stem, the goal of all ambition, the pot of gold at the end of a drab and somewhat colourless rainbow," as the columnist Walter Winchell called it in 1927.

A glistening sphere of pure Irish glass hung over us, but what heroes, and what horrors, this new century would bring, no crystal ball could foretell. For tonight, united in our tribal revelry, it was enough that we were here.

The world had already spun two-thirds of its climatic rotation when it came our turn to shriek away the old. "ALL NUCLEAR PLANTS ROLL OVER TO Y2K SAFELY," said the ticker from Moscow.

329

All the hype was evaporating, leaving only the happiness behind.

At midnight, the howl rose from our throats like a volcano, the loudest human sound ever made. The 20th Christian century surrendered and withdrew, bequeathing us its gadgets and its graves.

There were no bombs, no cultish suicides, no agent of SMERSH or SPECTRE spraying anthrax in the air. We were as obedient and mannered as a mob of a million could be.

I had been awakened at 2:50 in the morning by a police siren a block or more away, and a man's voice commanding, "Put down the gun! Put down the gun!"

This was Brooklyn, the very room I had grown up in, the misty pre-dawn of New Year's Eve.

My mother shuffled from her fitful slumber on the sofa and came in to where I was lying and said, "I just realized that I have lived three-quarters of this century . . .

"Holy shit."

At 6 o'clock, we went into the living room to watch the broadcast from Auckland, New Zealand. There were Maoris dancing and fireworks over the harbour and lights flashing "2000" and I felt my eyes getting wet and my mother said, "I hate to say this, but I'm choking up, too."

And I thought, she has made it to this great turning of the Western calendar, the last survivor of four children – born in 1923, the same year as the neon light – and so has my father, in his 89th winter, down in Florida, the last man still living of five healthy sons of an immigrant carpenter.

I drove a rented car to pick up my sister at the far end of the borough for the trip to Manhattan. The streets were oddly empty, the Brooklyn Bridge strange and dark and void. We parked on the East Side, by the United Nations, well-sited for our getaway, should hell break loose to close the American Century, and walked across town, through Grand Central Station, and along 42nd Street.

A very few had preceded us, perhaps five thousand by Friday's grey dawn, squatting on sodden sheets of cardboard on the pavement of the fabled plaza. It would be Times Square's 92nd such extravaganza, not counting the coal shortage of 1917–18, when the city went dark for want of fuel and a writer named Henry Collins Brown complained, "For a while it almost seemed as if we were doomed to live in Philadelphia."

Now the lights were back on, brighter than ever.

I would crown it all at midnight, I sighed, by kissing my sister.

Each hour of the slow-creeping day, at a stage facing northward toward the television risers and Central Park, a procession of costumed musicians and performers marked the millennium of some benighted foreign land.

We arrived a moment too late for Vanuatu – dancers dressed as jellyfish and hammerhead sharks and manta rays were just making their exit, to reappear, in less than an hour, as kangaroos.

The day cleared and turned warmer than the season deserved. The sun landed blood-red on New Jersey; night fell, but not here. The halo of capitalism triumphant suffused us. The Earth illuminated the sky.

Minelli Virgin Fridays Hard Rock Cup Noodles Gottex Suntory Stella Artois Perry Ellis Fosse Maxell Sealy Saab.

"END OF DAYS," read the marquee at Loew's Theater, but it lied. Friends had warned me of chaos, begged me to abandon the idea of Times Square on millennium eve. My mother had stayed in Brooklyn and made me pledge to phone her every hour. But I never felt safer.

Eight thousand police officers, padded in bulletproof Kevlar above their ample waists, turned the avenue blue. Apprehension dissolved into celebration. We counted down again. HAPPY NEW YEAR, Uzbekistan.

In a reverie of lights and dreams, my feet tangled in streamers, I worked the crowd. People spoke of telling their grandchildren about this night, about progress, technology, the Jetsons.

"I thought we'd all have rocket belts by now," a woman from Houston said.

"We do have them," I told her. "Tonight, we fly across centuries."

– National Post